This book is a compelling and powerful portrayal of the inner workings of OCD. Shala paints a vivid portrait of life with this debilitating disorder as well as a candid depiction of what it takes to overcome it and thrive. *Is Fred in the Refrigerator?* is a masterfully written memoir-meets-educational-meets-inspirational tale that I couldn't put down.

> —**Ashley Smith, PhD**, coauthor of *Childhood Anxiety Disorders*

Shala is a good friend and one of my heroes. In this memoir she bares her soul and the result is an inspirational story of hope for those with OCD. My patients are often concerned about their ability to do the hard work of overcoming OCD; it often seems to them that perhaps those who succeed in treatment are somehow better. Shala's recovery is not a sugarcoated fairytale. Her pain and suffering are real and her story riveting. Everyone with OCD will be able to see themselves in her struggles, and her journey will provide them with the hope that the road to recovery is one that they, like her, can travel.

> —**Jonathan Grayson, PhD**, author of *Freedom from Obsessive-Compulsive Disorder: A Personalized Recovery Program for Living with Uncertainty*

An amazing story of terror and resilience. *Fred* is at once a gripping portrayal of an unrelenting disorder and a guide for doing battle with it. It is one of the clearest descriptions of the experience of OCD and how one can learn to defeat it. A fascinating read filled with hope and inspiration. You'll cry, you'll cheer, and you'll put your *shoulders back* with Shala as she conquers the OCD demon.

> —**Randy O. Frost, PhD**, Harold and Elsa Siipola Israel Professor of Psychology at Smith College and coauthor of the *New York Times* bestseller *Stuff: Compulsive Hoarding and the Meaning of Things*

Is Fred in the Refrigerator? is a true story that reads like a novel. Shala's rocky journey to recovery will act as a guide to navigate people toward recovery and away from the pitfalls that face those lost in their own minds. Although Shala's story is sadly one that many people with OCD face due to the lack of understanding of OCD both in the generic public but also among healthcare professionals, her story is a testament to her spirit and determination to find a way in spite of this.

> —**Stuart Ralph**, The OCD Stories

In this book, Shala Nicely, a consummate storyteller, takes the reader on a journey inside the mind of someone who struggles with OCD. You are immediately transported into her life, which is crippled by OCD, ultimately finding yourself cheering her on as she learns of the appropriate treatment for her disorder. You are with her as she does battle with her internal demons and emerges empowered and victorious, having faced down her OCD and having learned that she is, and always has been, the stronger force on this battlefield. It is a story of inspiration and hope, providing insight for therapists and encouragement for those with firsthand experience of the disorder. It will serve as a great introduction to those just learning about OCD, or as a treasured addition to those building their OCD libraries.

> —**Allen H. Weg, EdD**, founder and director of Stress and Anxiety Services of New Jersey and author of *OCD Treatment Through Storytelling: A Strategy for Successful Therapy*

Shala's very articulate descriptions are fine examples of aspects of body obsessions, known as body dysmorphic disorder. Her own struggles illustrate so well how completely these types of insidious ideas can intrude on a person's consciousness and take over their actions. Her delightful prose will be a great help to many who seek to understand their own experiences through reading about those of a fellow sufferer.

> —**Gail Steketee, PhD, MSW**, Professor, Boston University School of Social Work and coauthor of the *New York Times* bestseller *Stuff: Compulsive Hoarding and the Meaning of Things*

With exquisite candor, Shala reveals how her inner BDD demon, "the salesman," cunningly manipulates and distorts her self-perception. Having walked hundreds of miles to raise awareness about BDD, I am awed that Shala covers the same distance metaphorically with elegant prose and in much less time. Since I have lived in the arena of this cruel disorder with my son Nathaniel, I know that Shala's insights about how she fights back will give courage and hope to sufferers and caregivers.

—**Denis Asselin,** Founder of Walking
    With Nathaniel

Is Fred in the Refrigerator? Taming OCD and Reclaiming My Life is a true depiction of the turmoil and disruption caused by OCD followed by the hope one can get when they finally receive the help that they need to manage their illness. As you hear the intimate details of Shala's life story, you will be educated, inspired, and moved. This book illustrates the incredible results of ERP therapy for OCD and the life-changing benefits of moving into advocacy and sharing our OCD story.

—**Elizabeth McIngvale, PhD,** Assistant Professor,
    Baylor College of Medicine and founder, the Peace
    of Mind Foundation

What starts as a gripping horror story turns into a book filled with stellar advice and inspiring action for those who suffer from obsessive-compulsive disorder and other mental illnesses. *Is Fred in the Refrigerator?* is a stunning story of growth, perseverance and hope. Shala beautifully details how mental illness shaped her life, taking us with her on her brave journey through perfectionism, shame and fear. This book is the perfect combination of entertainment, education and validation for those who are on their journey to recovery from OCD, but also for any human being who wants to live courageously and joyfully. Bravo, Shala!

> —**Kimberley Quinlan, LMFT** and founder of CBTschool.com

Shala has crafted a masterpiece detailing the suffering and pain associated with OCD, while providing hope and inspiration to those affected. Her writing style —which is a perfect combination of educational and inspirational—is certain to make this book a must-read for those embarking on their journey in beating OCD as well as for those closest to them.

> —**Eric Storch, PhD**, McIngvale Presidential Endowed Chair & Professor, Vice Chair & Head of Psychology at the Menninger Department of Psychiatry & Behavioral Sciences, Baylor College of Medicine

Is Fred in the Refrigerator? is one of the best books ever written about obsessive-compulsive disorder. It reads like a page-turning novel. Shala brings the reader into her world, and she helps the reader truly understand how OCD operates in one's mind as well as how to lean into it, externalize it, and develop the skills to live a fulfilling life. This book provides the reader with key elements that would greatly benefit everyone with OCD as well as their friends and family who are trying to understand this debilitating disorder. It's so helpful to have a book that tells the story of OCD from the person experiencing it who has also become an expert in treating it. Ultimately, the book instills hope, compassion, and the motivation to thrive in the face of OCD.

—**Becky Beaton, PhD**, founder & clinical director of The Anxiety & Stress Management Institute and cofounder, OCD Georgia

I have known Shala for many years. I have learned her story of OCD and her growth into an OCD therapist. After this book, I really know Shala and have an even better understanding of the day-to-day difficulties and struggles a person with OCD must overcome to just get out of bed, go to work, or be social. If you have had trouble understanding just how interfering OCD can be in one's life, you won't after reading this book. Thanks Shala.

—**Patrick McGrath, PhD**, author of *The OCD Answer Book: Professional Answers to More Than 250 Top Questions about Obsessive-Compulsive Disorder*

Shala Nicely has a story worth telling and she tells it brilliantly! Shala bravely shares some of her most intimate struggles with OCD and BDD and brings us into her world of unrelenting and often terrifying intrusive thoughts. Her writing cuts to the quick when describing the suffering that lies beneath the exterior that others see. If you struggle with similar problems or want to better understand them, you'll appreciate Shala's candor. But she also goes steps further, sharing what she learned from some of the best teachers in our field about how to accept and even welcome uncertainty and imperfection. Her wealth of knowledge, humor, and gift of storytelling shine a much-needed light on how to successfully pursue and embrace the treatment you need. Bravo Shala!

> —Joan Davidson, PhD, codirector of the San Francisco Bay Area Center for Cognitive Therapy, and author of *Daring to Challenge OCD: Overcome Your Fear of Treatment and Take Control of Your Life Using Exposure and Response Prevention*

Shala brilliantly captures the relationship between the mind of a person with OCD and the OCD itself. She shows the reader why calling the OCD's bluff is worth it, and her defiance against this disorder is, for lack of a better word, infectious. For a memoir, it is refreshingly not just about her, but about all of us with this kind of mind.

> —Jon Hershfield, MFT, director of The OCD and Anxiety Center of Greater Baltimore and author of *Overcoming Harm OCD*

Many excellent books have been written about OCD. Some promote compassion by articulating the challenges of a life tormented by this condition. Others inspire as they chronicle the struggle to recover. Some educate about treatments that can change lives and others bridge resources to those in need. *Is Fred in the Refrigerator?* does it all. Shala Nicely's story is at once compelling and enlightening.

—**C. Alec Pollard, PhD,** founding director, Center for OCD & Anxiety-Related Disorders and Professor Emeritus, Saint Louis University School of Medicine

Is Fred in the
Refrigerator?

TAMING OCD AND RECLAIMING MY LIFE

Shala Nicely

Is Fred in the Refrigerator?
Taming OCD and Reclaiming My Life

Excerpt of the blog post "Ring Ching Ching" used with permission of Jennifer Kahling Czupek.

Publisher's Note
This book portrays the author's experience with mental illness, and the publisher's intent is not to provide psychological services with the material presented. If you are in need of treatment for OCD and/or related disorders, please seek therapy from an experienced mental health professional. The Resources and References section at the end of this book provides a variety of self-help resources as well as links to treatment provider databases.

Author's Note
The identities of some people in my story have been disguised or composited to protect their privacy. Any clients mentioned in this book are composites of multiple people with whom I have worked and do not reflect the experiences of any one individual. Any errors in recollection of the events of my life portrayed in this book are strictly my own.

Published by:
Nicely Done, LLC
2993 Sandy Plains Road, Suite 110, Box 4
Marietta, GA 30066
www.shalanicely.com

Edited by Julie Miller, The Editorial Department
Cover design by BespokeBookCovers.com
Layout by Stephanie Anderson, Jera Publishing

ISBN   978-1-7321770-0-0 (print)
        978-1-7321770-1-7 (eBook)

Library of Congress Control Number: 2018905672

For Mom and Dad

Contents

Foreword

Full Disclosure.

I can't imagine two more fitting words with which to begin this brief introduction to *Is Fred in the Refrigerator?* and the truly remarkable woman behind it.

As someone living with obsessive-compulsive disorder (OCD), I've long battled compulsive urges to disclose what might not otherwise be apparent. My natural inclination is to delineate here the myriad reasons why I simply cannot be impartial in extolling the importance of Shala Nicely's story. She is, after all, both my longtime advocacy partner and my best friend.

But because I no longer allow my OCD to dictate what I can and cannot do, I've humbly accepted Shala's invitation to write a few words about the story you're about to read. I'll also further tweak my "Doubt Bully" and declare with great confidence that Shala's recovery journey is the most inspiring I've witnessed in more than a decade of doing OCD advocacy. What makes it so are again those two words: *full disclosure.*

For Shala, full disclosure is the very antithesis of what OCD demanded of her for so much of her life. As you'll read, her unforgiving "Rule #1" long kept Shala from breathing a word about her inner challenges, even to those she trusted most. That she has chosen to disclose in these pages the most intimate details of those trials, with unflinching courage and candor, speaks volumes about both how far she has come and how committed she is to using her story to help others.

In our shared advocacy work, Shala and I aim to help individuals impacted by OCD reap the benefits of what we call "Greater Good" motivation. We're big believers in the notion that "we help ourselves by helping others," and, more specifically, that *purpose* and *service* are far more powerful motivators than *fear* and *doubt*. Throughout our workshops and online course, we offer up day-to-day examples of our own applications of these principles, but time and again, I find myself pointing to Shala's personal and professional transformation as the ultimate demonstration.

In 2010, at the age of 39, Shala made two Greater Good decisions that would forever change her life (and the lives of countless others, I'd argue). First, she decided she'd put her story down on paper so others could learn from it. After years of going undiagnosed and then stumbling her way through the mental health system, she'd found proper treatment, and she knew she could be of great *service* to so many other tortured souls by recounting her journey. Doing so, of course, would require her to push through full disclosure fears of a magnitude few of us can even fathom.

And yet, Shala chose *service* over *fear*.

She committed herself to write this book, and she began the long, tedious process of making that happen.

Sensing almost immediately how powerful that decision was, Shala soon made an even bolder one: after years of building a highly successful, secure career in marketing and business, she decided she'd go back to school and reinvent herself as an OCD therapist so she could teach others what she'd learned about treatment. I still shake my head when I think about that commitment, because I know just what Shala had to sacrifice to make it: namely, every semblance of security and comfort she'd attempted to find for herself up to that point. She willfully stepped into a profession all but defined by its uncertainty and lack of traditional control.

And yet, Shala chose *purpose* over *doubt*.

She threw herself into her studies and worked tirelessly for years to build a successful practice that, day after day, requires her to fight her OCD's demands for outcome certainty, a luxury that simply doesn't exist in the treatment world.

As Shala will share with you, another of our common beliefs is that there's great power in choosing to believe the universe is friendly. No, of course we can't prove that to be the case. But that's not the point. By choosing to live our lives *as though* this is true, we turn the tables on our OCD Doubt Bullies, who would have us believe that the universe is out to get us.

Shala's story, I believe, is a testament to the incredible value of this attitudinal approach to confronting OCD recovery, and for that matter, for navigating life. I want to encourage you to keep this in mind as Shala, through her beautiful writing and skillful narrating, takes you deep into her decision-making evolution over the course of her journey. I'm certain you will see for yourself just how much the "friendly universe" concept has transformed Shala's life.

Finally, I'm compelled to leave you with one last full disclosure—some fine print that Shala and I have committed to attaching to all of our work—not for OCD reasons, but rather because we believe it's one of the most important pieces of our stories.

We, as we're fond of saying, are works in progress, *recovering*, not recovered, individuals with OCD. We cringe at the word "cured," and we go out of our way to gently correct any references to us that include that word. If we're held up as OCD success stories, we want that flattering label to reflect our having learned to successfully live with OCD, not any erroneous notion that we have put this debilitating disorder behind us.

This reality, I'm convinced, makes the memoir you're about to read that much more powerful. It's not some historical record of triumph, but rather the backstory to a truly inspiring, still-unfolding tale of phenomenal success that Shala continues to write day after day. And the hard-earned wisdom she has committed to share here and in all her work can and will change your life.

I know it did mine.

Jeff Bell
Sausalito, California

Jeff Bell is an author, mental health advocate, and radio news anchor. His two books, *Rewind, Replay, Repeat* and *When in Doubt, Make Belief*, have established Jeff as a leading voice for mental health awareness and "Greater Good" motivation. He served for eight years as a national spokesperson and board member for the International OCD Foundation, and he co-founded the nonprofit A2A Alliance to showcase and foster the power of turning adversity into advocacy. He and Shala co-founded Beyond the Doubt, an initiative dedicated to helping people learn to thrive through uncertainty. Jeff currently co-anchors the KCBS Afternoon News in San Francisco.

Prologue

I stood back, aghast. The jagged hole in the kitchen wall shouldn't have surprised me, considering the force that had created it. Stunned, I watched as eddying wisps of plaster dust pooled gently on the floor.

It was a gaping maw, lightless and foreboding. Appropriate, really, as I felt a similar darkness growing inside me, engulfing me.

What was happening? What was I turning into?

I slid down the opposite wall, tears obscuring the destruction in front of me. Stifling a sob, I grabbed the phone and dialed the number I knew by heart.

"Sydney, it's me," I choked. "I think I need help."

PART 1

CHAPTER 1

The Accident

I'm four years old, in a room that's pale blue all over. Everyone in it is pale blue, too. What I see is dreamlike in quality, hazy and indistinct. People milling around on the edge of my vision. Machines chirping and whirring. I notice that I'm pale blue, too, lying down, unable to move. Yet strangely, I'm also hovering above myself. Watching. Waiting.

The mask is the first thing I see that's razor sharp in focus. Not a Halloween mask, but a black mask that looks a little bit spongy, attached to a funny tube. With the mask and its taillike tube hovering over me, I think of the long pieces of tire rubber I see on the sides of the highway, the ones that always remind me of fat snakes. The tube looks like a road snake, I think, and I try to smile, but I don't seem to have control of my face.

The mask is hissing softly, rhythmically, and it's coming toward me in slow motion. I am mesmerized by the mask. What is it doing? Who is the woman pushing it toward me? She has a mask on, too, but hers matches my surroundings, ghostly and pale blue. She is saying something that sounds like kids trying to talk under water. I don't understand her garbled words. I just keep staring at the mask.

In the way of dreams, it takes forever for the mask to reach my face, and yet it takes no time at all. Once the mask makes contact, I watch the "me" suspended above my body slowly disappear, and everything goes black.

I know something like this happened. I just don't know if it happened like that. Honestly, everything I remember about Sunday, August 17, 1975 and the weeks and months that followed is suspect, because, first and foremost, I was four years old. How much does anyone remember accurately about being four?

Of course, that's not the only reason my memory is fuzzy. There was the trauma. The Accident. How much would I really be expected to remember about an event so sweeping in its consequences that it would change the course of my entire life?

"Are we going to go feed the ducks at Warriors' Path?" I asked. I looked up at my mom, shading my eyes from the sun with my fingers.

"I'm sure your dad will be back from the lab by the time we get home, so you can ask him what he's got planned," she replied.

"Hooray!" I yelled, excited to spend an afternoon at the local park with my dad.

Mom and I started off across the church parking lot. Dad didn't often go to church with us. He preferred his chemistry lab on Sundays. I imagined him pouring glistening, brightly colored liquids into funny-shaped vials, like I'd seen cartoon characters do. It made sense why he'd want to do that, instead of sitting in a big room at church listening to someone talk.

"Did you have fun in Sunday school today?" Mom asked.

"Yeah, we read stories and colored," I answered, still squinting at the noonday sun. "What did you do?"

Mom stopped and pulled from her purse a pair of orange sunglasses with ducks on the rims. "Here, put these on," she said, handing them to me. "Well, today we had someone famous speak to us. A man named John Palmer. He's on the news program your dad watches on TV. And he's from Kingsport, just like you."

"Kingsport, Tennessee?"

"That's right, Kingsport, Tennessee."

Now that was big. Someone from my hometown on TV.

Looking back, I wonder what my life would have been like if my parents had chosen another town. It wasn't as though I was destined to live in Kingsport. We could just as easily have ended up in Rochester, New York, the headquarters location of the company where my dad worked, Eastman Kodak. We could have lived there in a different life, with a different end to this day.

Mom turned and waved back at her friend Carol, who stood at the other end of the parking lot. Brushing the curly brown hair out of my eyes, I spied Carol's daughter Anne standing near her and gave her a big wave. Anne and I were in Sunday school and Montessori together.

Mom and I turned again and started walking toward the road. As we drew closer, bossy bursts of wind gusted behind the cars, as if they were trying to pull me along in their wake. Spying our Crayola-green Plymouth Duster parked on the other side of the two-lane road, Mom and I stepped down off the curb between parked cars to wait for traffic to clear. With my duck-themed sunglasses, I stared up at the Appalachian Mountains, their blue haze haloed in the sun, and thought about the fun I'd have that afternoon.

But it would be more than a year before I was able to feed the ducks again.

Another memory I might have made up:

I'm lying down, and everything is black, although I know it's sunny. Why can't I see the sun? It's as if someone has flipped a switch and turned off all my senses, except for hearing. I hear people screaming. I hear Anne screaming. I know it's her because I recognize her voice, as we spend so much time together at school. Lots of footsteps pound the pavement. Someone is breathing hard, like he's just run a race. I hear words without sentences: *ambulance, blood, leg,* and one I don't understand that sounds like "turn a cat." There must be a cat nearby. That's good. I like cats. We have a cat at home named Katie.

The sirens start then. Lots of them. Lots of people shouting. No one needs to shout. Don't you know I can hear you? The sounds, mixed up, senseless, become an unlikely lullaby that plays me to sleep.

The Kingsport Courier
August 18, 1975

Mother, child injured in accident outside of church

Kingsport—Two Kingsport residents were seriously injured in an automobile accident Sunday afternoon. A southbound automobile struck a car parked on the shoulder of Highway 23, which then struck Heather Nicely and her young daughter, Shala. Both Mrs. Nicely and her daughter sustained multiple fractures and contusions. Mrs. Nicely, of Foothill Road, was listed in "fair" condition at Henderson Memorial Hospital on Monday morning. Four-year-old Shala is listed in "poor" condition.

August 20, 1975

Mildred Henry
Henderson Memorial Hospital

Hattie Hauser
Tampa, FL

Dear Hattie,

I wanted to give you an update on Heather and Shala. We arrived from North Carolina the night of the 17th. I'm so glad we came as Vince really needed the support. He's been staying with Shala, and we're on another floor of the hospital with Heather. As Heather's parents, we get updates around the clock.

Heather has a badly broken leg, but she's conscious. She doesn't remember much of what happened, thank goodness. Shala is in worse shape: her pelvis and both legs are broken. They put her in a body cast up to her armpits. I have no idea what she remembers of the accident—I hope nothing.

Vince told us, somewhat dazed, that Shala's leg looked like a piece of beefsteak rolled in gravel before she went into emergency surgery. What a devastating thing for a parent to witness.

Did I tell you on the phone about John Palmer, the reporter for NBC? He was speaking at the church that day. Heather's friend Carol told me he put a tourniquet around Shala's leg before the ambulance came. And thank goodness—who knows how much blood she'd already lost.

I will give you a call later with more information about how they're doing.

Love,
Mother

To: All Nursing Staff
From: Henderson Memorial Orthopedic Staff
Re: Shala Nicely
Date: August 24, 1975

Please be advised that Shala is having hallucinations; she seems to be seeing things on the ceiling and walls. These are likely normal based on the trauma she experienced, but please note anything out of the ordinary on her chart.

Her father is quite upset by the hallucinations as they seem to cause Shala a great deal of distress. We have assured him this is something she will go through and there is nothing we can do to prevent them from occurring.

Please continue to check vitals on a regular basis and give Tylenol as needed for pain.

September 4, 1975

Mildred Henry
Henderson Memorial Hospital

Hattie Hauser
Tampa, FL

Dear Hattie,

Thanks much for the stuffed animal you sent for Shala and the flowers you sent to your sister. The flowers brightened up Heather's room, and Shala loves the bear.

As you know, we've been staying with your sister in the hospital so Vince can stay with Shala. He's been staying in her hospital room around the clock. Even though it's been a few weeks since the accident, it looks like they will both be here a while longer. I heard the doctor say another couple of weeks for Heather and even longer for Shala.

Thank goodness Vince is with Shala, although I can't imagine how hard it must be for her to be away from her mother for so long at age four. I'm sure she doesn't understand.

I should go—a nurse is coming in to run some tests. Take care of yourself.

Love,
Mother

To: All Nursing Staff
From: Henderson Memorial Orthopedic Staff
Re: Shala Nicely
Date: September 12, 1975

Please note that Shala's father has requested that the temperature in Shala's room be set no higher than 70 degrees. He mentioned several times that hospital staff are turning up the heat thinking the patient must be cold. Shala is complaining of intense itchiness under her body cast, which is exacerbated by heat.

Shala's father bought a small TV for her room. If he is not there you can turn it on for her, as it distracts her from the discomfort of the cast.

Please continue to check vitals on a regular basis and give Tylenol as needed for pain.

September 18, 1975

Mildred Henry
Henderson Memorial Hospital

Hattie Hauser
Tampa, FL

Dear Hattie,

Your sister is now home from the hospital after almost a month. She has to use a walker, but they expect her to regain full use of her leg.

Shala will be in the hospital for several more weeks. She has been moved to a room with another little girl named Jennifer. When I was visiting with her the other day, she asked me why Jennifer has bacon wrapped around her head. I asked her what she meant by "bacon" and she said they take the "white hat" off Jennifer's head and then they unwrap bacon from underneath the hat. Finally, I understood. Jennifer has a head injury, and they change her bloody bandages each day. I've asked the nursing staff to close the curtains from now on when they change Jennifer's dressings. Shala has seen enough.

Fortunately, Jennifer and Shala get along. Jennifer has a Cootie game that she and Shala play. I think you know the game, the one where you put together big, plastic bugs? Shala has always liked bugs, so she and Jennifer are entertained for hours.

I've heard Vince call Shala his "mighty tough tyke" several times. After what she's gone through and survived at four years old, "tough" is an understatement.

Love,
Mother

October 16, 1975

Mildred Henry
Henderson Memorial Hospital

Hattie Hauser
Tampa, FL

Dear Hattie,

Finally—they released Shala from the hospital. But before doing so, they had to take off her cast. They used this little electric saw, but it must have looked to Shala like a chain saw. She screamed as they cut the cast off. Vince was none too happy with the doctors.

She had her first water therapy in a whirlpool today. She's going to have to relearn how to walk. She'll need to have physical therapy several times a week for a few months. Vince took her to A&W for her favorite orange soda afterward—he's doing a good job of trying to make all this bearable for her.

Love,
Mother

November 4, 1975

Heather Nicely
Kingsport, TN

Mildred Henry
Zirconia, NC

Hi Mother and Dad,

Some good news: Shala saw Dr. Cox on Monday and he gave her permission to begin walking again. She pitched a fit at therapy, but her physical therapist and Vince just let her scream it out until she was ready to try. When she and Vince got home, she showed me how she could take some steps with crutches. Her legs and soles of her feet get tired and sore, which is understandable after two and a half months of disuse. She'll get over her reluctance to walk in time—she hollered about the whirlpool bath at first, too!

Let us know how you're doing!

Love,
Heather

February 16, 1976

Heather Nicely
Kingsport, TN

Mildred Henry
Zirconia, NC

Dear Mother,

Thank you for the lovely gifts you sent for Shala's birthday. She's getting much better every day—from a body cast, to a walker, to crutches, to finally being able to walk on her own.

Yesterday we took her to the orthopedic surgeon's office for the first of what will be annual checkups. It's likely that her right leg will be somewhat shorter than the left. We'll see how much as she grows.

You and Dad have been so supportive throughout this whole process. I can't tell you how much it's meant to Vince and me, as well as to Shala. She loves her Poppop and Nana!

Love,
Heather

February 25, 1976

Mildred Henry
Zirconia, NC

Hattie Hauser
Tampa, FL

Dear Hattie,

Can you believe it's been six months since The Accident? It seems like that's become what we call what happened on August 17. It's a time marker for our family. When we talk about events involving Heather, Vince, and Shala, we refer to them in relation to The Accident. Everything was either "before The Accident" or "after The Accident." At least there is an after.

I recently talked with Heather, and she said Shala will have some pretty big scars on her legs. They look like caterpillars where the surgeons sewed her skin back together. On her left shin there's one that's at least four inches long. Vince rubs cocoa butter into the scars every day. The doctors said that will make them less visible, but according to your sister it's not working too well.

But more concerning to me are the scars we can't see: the scars buried deep in her mind. I can't even imagine what she's seen, how scared she must've been over the past six months. If I catalog the horrors she's witnessed, I could include The Accident itself, her hallucinations, being separated from her mother for two months, that awful body cast (and the trauma of being sawed out of it!) and seeing all the sick and injured people at the hospital. A few weeks after The Accident, she kept asking me questions about a mask. She said she was dreaming about a blue room where they put a black mask on her face. I think these were memories from immediately before her surgery. How she could remember anything after being hit by a car I don't know, but she remembers having the anesthesia mask put on before her operation.

Shala has learned the world can be a very dangerous place. She's safe now, but I wonder, will she believe that?

Love,
Mother

CHAPTER 2

Rule #1

"**G**oodnight, Mom!"

"Goodnight, La," Mom said, as she turned off the light and closed my bedroom door.

I turned over on my side and hugged my stuffed dog, one of twenty or so stuffed animals given to me after The Accident that resided on my bed. Closing my eyes, I thought about tomorrow.

Field Day. I loved Field Day. I was going to win the 100-yard dash, I just knew it. Well, if I could keep Priscilla from beating me. She was fast, but I was faster. I thought about what it would be like at the starting line, with all the third graders cheering. How proud I'd be to win, especially since my right leg was shorter than my left, corrected by an extra half-inch layer of foam visible in the sole of my right sneaker. Kids sometimes teased me about my shoes, but they wouldn't make fun of me when I had a blue ribbon in my hand.

I smiled and rolled over again in my nest of stuffed toys.

As I snuggled under the covers, the scene in my mind abruptly changed. Third graders disappeared, replaced by a crowd of raucous adults dressed in medieval attire. Hundreds of them swarmed, buzzing, agitated, all looking the same direction.

I froze, tensing beneath the quilt. I knew what was coming. I whirled around in my mind to see what had captured the mob's attention, afraid of what I'd see. What I always saw.

They were there, of course: two people lying on wooden slats. Glinting steel blades hung precariously above their necks: a guillotine. My mind mercilessly flung me forward to see the faces of the innocent people about to die. Reluctantly, I looked—and uttered a pitiful "no" as I stared once again into the eyes of the condemned.

Mom and Dad.

With a sharp intake of breath, I sat up, fumbling for the lamp on my bedside table. Clicking it on, I grabbed my head, as if I could pull these horrid thoughts out of my mind.

"No, no, no, no," I cried. "I don't want that. I don't want that."

Why did I see these things? What was wrong with me?

I thought about my friends. During sleepovers when we shared our deepest secrets, whispering quietly in our sleeping bags, no one talked about seeing their parents' heads chopped off on a nightly basis. No one.

At nine years old, I knew it wasn't normal to see these things. I knew I was somehow different, and not in a good way.

I also knew what I needed to do. How I took care of these thoughts. Still sitting up, I closed my eyes tightly and began my nightly ritual of replaying the grisly scene. I conjured a crowd of grungy people from the Middle Ages, tightly packed around a platform, chanting with raised fists. Mom and Dad came next, laid out on planks, dressed in the clothes of royalty. Their necks were bare below the quivering guillotine blades, hanging mere feet above their heads.

The blades started to fall. "No!" I screamed in my mind, as I forced the blades back up, repeatedly raising my hands, palms up, as if I were weighing invisible objects. This movement was important, I knew. I needed it to keep the blades from falling, from killing my parents.

Because there was going to be no death in the story I now played in my head.

Why didn't my mind understand that?

As I continued my new story, the executioner—my nemesis—kept releasing the rope that held the blades in the air. He wanted them to crash down and sever the heads of the people at the center of my world. The people who were my protectors.

I fervently pushed up the guillotine blades with my hands, eyes closed, willing my mind to stop, to let me recreate the story my way. After several moments of mental struggle, the executioner finally held the rope firmly in place. I had won a temporary stay of execution.

Quickly, I turned around in my mind. I spied modern bleachers, filled with a studio audience of decent-looking people, tucked just out of direct view behind the executioner's platform. I looked up. Cameras and lights hung near the ceiling of my sound stage. Glancing over at the man to my left, the cameraman, I saw his "thumbs up" signal, which said he was ready to roll.

"Action!" someone announced, and my new movie was off and running.

My parents, lying on the platform, looked brave and beautiful. Music swelled from my mind's speakers, heightening the scene's tension. Mom and Dad clasped hands. From the music, the studio audience knew the blades were about to fall, to end the lives of the courageous Sir Vince and Lady Heather Nicely.

Suddenly, a knight, resplendent in armor and chain mail, on a steed closely resembling the Black Stallion, thundered into the crowd. The stallion reared, splitting the mob. Without a word, the knight dismounted, rushed onto the platform, and pulled my parents to safety. The executioner, sensing his last chance, allowed the blades to fall, a moment too late. They missed their mark, just as they always did in my movie, splintering the wood below with a hollow clunk, signaling the start of the triumphant aria that ended my mental masterpiece.

I opened my eyes and breathed a sigh of relief. I'd saved my parents again. I saved them every night. In my twisted world, I was my parents' protector.

Sitting on the sloped pitch of my front yard in the fading dusk, Brian and I played with our Snoopy action figures. "You take Charlie Brown," he said, handing me the small plastic toy. "I'll play with Snoopy for a while."

"Okay," I said, taking the Peanuts character. "Do you want to go inside and play?"

"No, I have to go home soon. Mom told me to be home at dark," Brian said, glancing at the disappearing outline of his house across the street.

"Okay." I had to go in soon, too. But I didn't want to. I didn't want to go to bed, even as I tiredly rubbed my eyes, which were always ringed with smudgy dark circles in my school photos. I wanted to stay outside and play.

Field Day had come and gone, and I'd returned home proudly carrying my blue ribbon for the 100-yard dash. My neighborhood friends and I now basked in the warm, languid days of summer. We slept in, meeting up daily in the late mornings for hours of imaginative play.

"Are you still going to Hilton Head next week?" I asked Brian.

"Yeah, but I wish you could go, too."

"That's okay. I'll have fun at the farm," I said, knowing he and his sister Emily really would like me to go with them. I didn't want to hurt Brian's feelings by telling him I'd rather go to the farm.

What started out as a place to help my dad get away from work, the farm became our family's beloved weekend retreat. My dad craved intellectual challenge and loved his chemistry laboratory at Kodak. Loved it so much, in fact, that sometimes he had trouble leaving it. When I was in Montessori, I'd once done a worksheet where I completed a sentence starting "I wish ..." with "... I could see my Daddy more." My wish was resolved by the eventual purchase of a sixty-acre mountain farm, just far enough away from the lab to make going into work on a whim inconvenient for my trying-to-recover workaholic father.

At the farm we had no phone. No TV. No air conditioning or heat, except what our wood stove produced. During our weekend visits, if I wasn't entertaining myself by bareback riding my two paint ponies, Misty and Flicka, or helping my dad with one of his farm projects, I was lying on the porch swing, reading everything I could get my hands on. From *The Black Stallion* to *Ramona the Great* and *Encyclopedia Brown*, I craved my daring literary friends and their incredible adventures. I loved them because they reliably ended their journeys with a happily ever after.

As I lay in the swing, reading in the drowsy heat of summer weekends, I recognized I was a lucky kid. My parents made sure their only child's every need was met while they tried hard not to spoil me—an effort at which they failed miserably. How many kids had not one, but two ponies? How many children had sixty acres, half of them forested, to roam at will with a beloved dog, Mac? How many girls had a clubhouse built just for them into the loft of a barn?

And how many kids also saw, when they closed their eyes to sleep, images of those same ponies being slaughtered? The dog being tortured? The barn burning down?

I may have been a lucky kid, but I wasn't lucky enough to get out of having to go to bed, where I now employed a brand-new strategy to try to tame the ever-morphing monster in my head.

"Dear God, please bless Mommy and Daddy, Poppop and Nana, Grandma and Granddad, Mac and Cricket and Patches ..."

I stopped, aware something was off. I'd said the names of our cats out of order. It was Patches and Cricket, not Cricket and Patches. I had to start over. Again.

Kneeling on the carpet beside my bed, I craned my head to listen to the sounds coming from the den, wishing I were still outside playing with Brian. The voices from the TV were muffled by my bedroom door and the folding door separating my bedroom and bathroom from the den. That folding door was my salvation. It made a low rumbling noise any time it was opened, giving me time to scurry back into bed where I was supposed to be.

Hearing only muted laughter from *M*A*S*H* on TV, I closed my eyes, bowed my head, and started my plea to God again.

"Dear God, please bless Mommy and Daddy, Poppop and Nana, Grandma and Granddad, Mac and Patches and Cricket and Misty and Flicka and everyone on the farm. Please bless Brian and Emily and Julie and Janet and Christy and all my friends. Please make sure that nothing bad happens to anyone, ever, and that no one ever dies or gets hurt. Amen."

I opened my eyes. The light from the hallway peeped under my bedroom door. Sitting back on the floor cross-legged in the sliver of light, I looked at my knees, deeply indented with impressions of the carpet. I had been at this for ten minutes, maybe longer. I could feel in the pit of my stomach, though, that it still wasn't right. I would have to start again.

Things had changed since Field Day. My mind had become more demanding. It wasn't enough to be the director of a block-buster mental movie, saving my parents from the almost nightly horrors of the guillotine. To be absolutely certain everyone in my world would be safe, I now had to pray. Repeatedly. Or really bad things would happen. And it would be all my fault if these things did happen because I had the power to prevent them.

I held the safety of my world in my hands.

As I sat on the floor, willing myself to have the strength to kneel and begin again, I muttered, "This all started with my stupid head." And my head wouldn't stop punishing me.

I uncrossed my legs, leaned wearily against the side of my bed, and reached back into my memory.

I'd been six, maybe seven, swimming in the baby pool at the Moose Lodge. As I splashed happily in my bright green swimsuit, I thought it would be fun to dive, just like the seals I'd seen on a TV special. Standing in the shallow pool, I plunged seallike, headfirst into the water.

THUNK.

My head smacked the bottom of the pool.

I don't remember what happened next. Did I get up out of the pool crying? Did I run to my mom? Did she even see it happen? None of that mattered.

What did matter was that later, when I was eight years old, my mind randomly fished this one sopping wet, seemingly unimportant memory from the recesses of my subconscious and presented it to me, explaining that I had made a grave mistake.

That when I'd hit the bottom of that pool with my young, devel-oping head, I'd given myself a fatal disease: head cancer. That if I hadn't made that dive, I would have been fine. But I had, and it was all my fault that now I was going to die.

It was the first time my mind had turned against me.

After that day, my eight-year-old mind increasingly preoccupied itself with that fear of dying. But I hadn't known what to do with it. There hadn't seemed to be anything to do with it, so I'd lived my life—in the classroom, on the school bus, with friends, at home—terror-stricken. So much so that on the day my second-grade teacher talked about my class advancing into third grade, I thought with sickening surety that I'd be in a small coffin, lifeless, by that time. Because why would I think such thoughts about dying, if they weren't going to come true?

Then, as strangely as the thought of head cancer—my mind's first foray into terrorizing me—had emerged, it had disappeared, only to be replaced some time later with new assaults: gruesome nighttime visions of medieval executions, animal torture, and general disaster.

I pulled myself back into a kneeling position beside my bed. It really didn't matter what had happened years ago, especially because in the past I'd just accepted my mind's death-obsessed thoughts as the truth. Now, however, I had tools to try to convince it otherwise. Tools such as mental movie-making. And praying. I had no idea where these tools had come from, but I knew I had to use them. Not doing so could have consequences too overwhelming to bear.

I bowed my head and started again.

"Dear God, please bless Mommy and Daddy, Poppop and Nana, Grandma and Granddad, Mac and Patches and Cricket ..."

There was nothing wrong with praying, of course. But deep down, I knew that while what I was doing was necessary, it wasn't *normal*. So I couldn't get caught doing it. As I repeated my angst-filled appeals to God, I listened carefully for the rumbling of the folding door, my signal to abandon my heavenly petitions and retreat into bed.

I finished my prayer and opened my eyes, stroking the head of one of my stuffed animals. Then I closed them and started praying again. Most of the time, it just felt better if I did my prayers four times. I was sure to get at least one or two of the four perfect, and perfection was mandatory to ensure the earthly salvation of those I loved. Sometimes I even needed to do my prayers sixteen times, because what could be better than four times four?

Finally finishing, I stood up and flopped exhausted into bed. I squinted at the clock softly illuminated by the light under the door. Nine fifteen. I had been at this for at least twenty minutes, maybe thirty.

All of a sudden, I heard the folding door's telltale rumbling. Then my dad's heavy footsteps, pausing outside my bedroom. I froze, pretending to be asleep.

Mom and Dad could not know what I was doing. No one could. Because my mind told me no one could know. It was Rule #1:

You cannot get caught doing these things or thinking these thoughts.
Because if you do, you will have to explain yourself.
And you don't tell what you see in your mind.
Because if you do, all those bad things you see…you will make them happen.

I didn't question this rule. I lived by it. Because I could not let those bad things happen. I had to keep everyone safe. It had become my job.

My dad, satisfied I was asleep, walked away, turning off the hallway light and closing the folding door behind him. Recognizing

I'd been holding my breath, I breathed out, releasing a little of the tension I held in my upper back as I fell into a fitful, dreamless sleep.

The tension never seemed to totally go away, however. How could it, when I was trying to bravely hold the weight of the world on my nine-year-old shoulders?

CHAPTER 3

Pas de Deux

Dropping my backpack onto the den floor, I hurried past my mom as she watched afternoon soap operas. I rudely answered her "How was your day?" with a muttered "Fine," then flew past the couch and headed downstairs to the basement.

As a seventh grader, I wasn't interested in talking to my mom after school. I was only interested in talking on the phone with my best friend, Sydney McCarson, so we could deconstruct the day's interactions with boys. It was our favorite topic.

"Did you see James today?" Sydney asked as soon as she answered the phone.

"Yeah, he walked past me on his way to band. He smiled at me." James was two years older than I was. A trumpet player with the confidence of a rock star. I was in love.

"That's a good sign," she reassured me. We were always looking for minute indications that the boys we liked actually liked us back.

"Did you talk to Patrick in English class?" I asked. Patrick was Syd's latest crush.

"A little. Today we had a test so no one could talk much," she said, sounding disappointed.

I lay down on our orange-carpeted basement floor with my feet straight up, leaning against one of our gigantic black metal bookshelves. I was not the only bookworm in the family. My parents had hundreds, maybe even thousands, of books. They were all over the place, covering shelves and tables in every room. I never lacked for things to read. At this moment, however, I lacked a boyfriend.

"Maybe you can find a way to snag a seat near Patrick on the way to the next band competition," I suggested. Syd played flute in band, and I played saxophone. Patrick played drums. Drummers were the bad boys, and Syd was always in love with bad boys.

"Maybe ..." she replied, her voice trailing off.

I knew what she was thinking. Both Patrick and James were out of our league. Even my childhood friend Brian, a year older and now part of the popular crowd, was out of reach, though he always waved at me at school. Syd and I were—sadly—not popular. Not in the club of girls who were always "going with" a guy, as we called having a boyfriend. We were part of the decidedly less attractive smart kids' clique. What other group would I belong to, surrounded by all these books? But that didn't mean she and I couldn't dream about these cute guys, out of our league though they might be.

"Are your parents going to let you spend Friday night with me?" Syd asked.

"I think so," I said, involuntarily tensing as she mentioned my mom and dad. Unlike interactions with boys, which Syd and I savored and shared in the dreamy way of teenage girls, my interaction with my parents this morning was one I'd rather block from my memory.

"Oh, good. Mom said we can order pizza and stay up as late as we want."

"I can't wait," I said with forced enthusiasm, this morning's events still raw. I hung up with Syd, after promising to bring my Michael Jackson *Thriller* album on Friday, and pulled myself back up. As long as I was thinking of this morning, I might as well see how my hair was doing. After all, as my parents had just discovered, soon I wouldn't have much left, a grim harbinger of things to come.

I walked to the downstairs bathroom, turned on the light, and grimaced at my reflection. I'd never had the glossy, thick, flowing locks of women on TV shows. I'd always had light, flyaway hair that looked like I'd just pulled my finger out of an electric socket. Without a curling iron and some blow-drying, my hairstyle had always been a juxtaposition of limp and ornery.

Now it just looked dead.

I flipped on the light directly over the mirror. Just as I'd thought. My hair was so thin that I could see right through the gauzy curtain of it falling past my chin. It was getting long enough that the wispy strands separated wherever hair hit my shoulders, like the parting of bead curtains in those roadside stores run by leftover hippies in the middle of nowhere. The strands of jewel-like beads in those mini-marts, however, would liquidly fall back into place to conceal what lay behind, unlike my hair, which splayed out in lifeless lengths. Unless I pulled it back into a ponytail, which now would be no thicker than my pinky finger.

I was slowly but surely losing my hair.

I hadn't noticed at first. Hadn't thought twice about the long strands of brown hair eddying around the bottom of the shower stall. Hadn't been worried about the hairs I'd found caught around the necks of my sweaters. Hadn't understood the need to wrap my ponytail holder around an extra time. Until one day when I'd looked at my hairbrush and noticed it was completely filled with hair, and it dawned on me that I'd just cleaned it out the previous morning.

At first I'd tried to console myself that people lost their hair all the time. My Aunt Hattie was a hairdresser, and I searched my memory for what she might have said about hair loss, something comforting like, "Oh, I have clients who shed like cats in summer!" But no matter how much mental reviewing I did, I hadn't been able to find anything concrete she'd said to assure me what I was experiencing was normal.

Seeking reassurance by examining friends' hair had been no more helpful. Syd had gorgeous blond hair that fell to her waist. After spending time with her, I always found pieces of it wrapped around my coat sleeves or randomly stuck in a bracelet or ring I'd been wearing, but over time her hair seemed no thinner.

In contrast, my hair just kept falling out, strand by fragile strand.

Over the days, weeks, and months that I'd been losing my hair—first slowly, then with growing rapidity—I'd felt my mind agitating, looking for some reason to explain it all. I'd seen where this was going. Or more accurately, I'd felt it in the pit of my stomach: that jolting, hollow sensation I had every time my mind stuck its toe in the freezing water of an idea that it just couldn't let go.

Head cancer. Raised from the depths of the horror show my mind seemed to favor, the ghost of "head cancer" had started, once again, to haunt me, filling the mind space previously occupied by the decapitation of people I loved and other nameless bad things. In fact, those gruesome worries and their attendant rituals of praying or replaying "movie" scenes in my mind had, over time, seemed to slip away all on their own. I had no idea why. There had been blessed times—months, even years—when I wasn't worried about anything other than whether I'd get in trouble for not practicing my piano lessons.

But from the moment my mind locked on the idea that my hair loss meant head cancer, I had become the principal dancer in a doom-themed mental ballet that played on for months, with few, if any, intermissions. As my hair continued to disappear, I'd pull on my mental tights and toe shoes and spin pirouettes around the idea that I was dying. I felt pulled back and forth across my mind's stage by my audience: hecklers outnumbering fans twenty to one, their shouts alternately filling me with hope and despair.

"You're too young to die!" one would call in a serene, lilting voice.

As I danced, frantic to find and hold onto that reassurance, loud, booming catcalls inevitably drowned it out. "Children die all the time! What makes you think you're immune?"

Another voice, soft and kind, tried to make itself heard above the echoes of doom. "There's no way you have head cancer. I don't even think head cancer exists!"

As I turned on the stage toward that voice—that relief—it would only be followed by menacing snarls. "Of course you have cancer. What else could cause your hair to fall out like this? And if you hadn't hit your head on the bottom of the pool years ago, you stupid girl, none of this would be happening! Do you hear me? It's all your fault!"

Panicked, I'd try to focus on the voices that offered reassurance, logic, reason—but they always slipped away, muffled by relentless catcalls from scythe-carrying specters of death who never left the theater. The theater where my mind and I engaged in a never-ending, exhausting pas de deux.

Now I gazed anxiously at my reflection in the bathroom mirror and raised my hand to smooth my hair, then watched as a few more strands fell gracefully to the sink. Head cancer. Head cancer. Head cancer. I'd thought I was safe, but that terrible mistake I'd made all those years before, diving into that pool, would now be my demise.

I was going to die. Soon. The thought brought a rush of fear so intense my vision blurred.

Unnerved, I let my mind go back to the pain of this morning.

———

Dad had been quietly eating his cereal, reading the Eastman newsletter. "Morning, La," he said as I walked into the kitchen, a bright collage of red, white, and blue wallpaper highlighted by the morning sun. Our house builders back in 1976 had called it "the Bicentennial House" and spared no expense making our kitchen the ultimate homage to patriotism.

"Hi, Dad," I said, going to the pantry and pulling out a box of Cracklin' Oat Bran.

"Big day at school today?"

"No. We're practicing for our band concert, but it's not until next week."

"Oh, that's right," Dad said, looking up. A puzzled expression crossed his face. "Did you brush your hair this morning, kiddo?"

My heart started to pound in my chest, sucking all the life out of my core, replacing it with that sinking, hollow sensation.

"Yes," I whispered, focusing intently on my cereal as it poured into the bowl.

"It doesn't look like you did. The back looks like a rat's nest." My parents were always kind to me, and my dad said this without a trace of malice. It was just a statement of fact: my hair did look like a rat's nest. Because I couldn't brush it anymore, because too much was coming out, because every strand wrapped in the bristles of my brush confirmed the coming end of my life.

"It's fine," I replied, my voice getting softer.

"I think you'd better go brush it again." My dad's tone was that of a suggestion, but I knew he meant for me to turn around, go to the bathroom, and brush out the tangles without another word. Because, always trying to be perfect, I always obeyed.

But fear won out over perfection as I shakily whispered, "No."

"Shala," Dad said. He hadn't said "La," what my parents always called me, ever since I'd coined the nickname as a toddler, when the only part of my name I could pronounce had been the last syllable. "Go brush your hair."

"No," I repeated, a little louder. I could not brush my hair. Could not stand to see one more piece of hair leave my head. Not even to avoid getting in trouble.

"Okay, let's go," Dad said. He got up, put his hand on my arm, and turned me toward the door. As he walked behind me the twenty or so feet to the bathroom, I didn't breathe. My legs moved me forward as if I were in a hypnotic trance. I began to feel as I had in the operating room after The Accident, as if I were in two places at once: in my body, and hovering above, watching the unfolding drama.

Dad opened the drawer and picked up my pink hairbrush—the hairbrush that would now be my undoing. I watched, mesmerized, as he pulled the brush down the length of my hair once, then again. Then a few more times, as realization dawned on his face. He looked at all the hair in the brush, which had been completely clean just a few moments earlier.

"How long has your hair been coming out like this?" he asked, confused, staring at me in the mirror.

I couldn't speak. Couldn't say, "For a while, because I have head cancer." Couldn't tell him his seventh-grade daughter had a death sentence.

I mutely stared at his reflection in the mirror as he turned toward the door, yelling, "Heather! Could you come in here, please?"

While we waited for my mom, he kept brushing, more slowly and methodically, and scrutinized with his scientist's eye what he saw. I stood immobile, transfixed by this moment I'd so hoped to avoid.

"Have you seen what's happening with Shala's hair?" Dad asked as Mom walked into my green-wallpapered bathroom. The builders had been fond of colored wallpaper.

"What do you mean?" she asked, looking from him to me.

Dad pulled the hairbrush through my hair again, then handed the brush, covered with my hair, to my mother. "All that hair, that just came out now."

"What?" Mom said, not understanding.

"Shala's hair," Dad said. "It's falling out."

Many hours later, as I gripped the edge of the sink in the downstairs bathroom, the memory of that morning felt as paralyzing as if the event had just happened. I didn't remember much of the rest of that conversation with my parents, only vague mentions of getting an appointment with the pediatrician or talking with Aunt Hattie to find out if I should switch shampoos. I did remember that I'd thought my parents looked scared. Or maybe I'd just been projecting, because I'd never been more scared in my life.

The thoughts I used every day to pretend my life was okay had become inaccessible in that moment when I stood with my parents in my bathroom, just as they were as I stared at my reflection now. Gone were thoughts of my crush on James, my upcoming sleepover with Sydney, anything good. I'd been pretending all day every day that everything was all right, while the feeling in my gut told me everything was decidedly not all right. I wanted to be a normal teenager who talked with her best friend about normal things like friends and boys and school. But the pas de deux was always there, reminding me that my pretense was just that: a final act before the curtain fell on my life.

Deep inside, however, part of me fought to hold onto a flicker of hope: that the well-wishers in my mental theater were right and the hecklers were wrong, and maybe I wasn't going to die. Yet I knew if I broke Rule #1 and told anyone about my fears, this hope would be instantly extinguished. "That's right, Shala, we just didn't want to tell you," whoever I told would say. "You are, sadly, going to die."

Now that my parents knew about my hair loss, I waited for "the conversation." Because I understood in those tense moments in the bathroom that my parents had probably come to the same conclusion I had, that their beloved daughter had head cancer. What else could it be? So I waited: for confirmation that the coffin had been ordered, that preparations would be made, that I wouldn't need to go to school anymore. After all, what was the point in attending seventh grade if I wouldn't make it to eighth?

After that fateful day in my bathroom, I did end up switching shampoos, as everyone in my family had become convinced the shampoo I'd been using "must have been too harsh" (as my mom would tell concerned friends and relatives). Not that a shampoo change could make much difference, as I'd already lost half my hair. As I lathered my hair up each morning, I wondered why everyone insisted on this charade. Why were we pretending shampoo was the root of my problem, when we knew the truth of my impending doom?

Until the day I suddenly noticed that my head was beginning to grow tiny silken hairs, like the soft down of peach fuzz.

"See, you're okay!" I heard from the balcony in my mind's theater. "It can't possibly be head cancer if your hair is growing back!"

Exhausted from months of dancing the intricate steps of my pas de deux, I grabbed onto this voice of hope. I held on, noticing that all of a sudden my theater offered an intermission every once in a while, and I bowed to the kind voices I now heard more clearly as I gratefully exited the stage.

As the peach fuzz morphed over the coming months into a halo of untamable, inch-long hair that, in the bright light, sharply contrasted the drooping strands that remained from my shoulder-length bob, I found I could stop dancing sometimes for days, even weeks.

As the new hair continued to grow out and I looked like I wore two different hairstyles merged cartoonishly onto one person, I frequented my theater less and less, a guest performer not even interesting enough now to attract the hecklers.

When the new growth became long enough for me to get my hair cut in layers, invisibly blending the old and new, I bid the orchestra farewell, hung up my toe shoes, and slammed the stage door firmly shut.

It seemed I had been set free. I was going to live.

But unbeknownst to me, I was not going to live the normal teenage life I'd hoped to have.

CHAPTER 4

The Quest

I put my pencil down, looked over at the clock, and sighed. Eight thirty p.m., time for a break. I rubbed my eyes, strained from staring at calculus problems for the last three hours, then wearily pushed myself out of my chair and walked to the kitchen. I needed a snack. Then I could keep going.

Rummaging through the many tin boxes that lined the shelves of the pantry, I found one containing brownies Mom had made last weekend. Not bad, I thought, as I took a bite of one and leaned against the patriotic red, white, and blue kitchen wall.

I had the house to myself this evening. My parents were at an Eastman Travelogue, a cinematic exploration of various countries around the world. Tonight's was Greece. No—or was it Belgium? I was too tired to remember. Grabbing another brownie, I replaced the box on the shelf and headed back to the study. I had to get back to studying. Because I had to make an A on this calculus test.

My dad had proposed the idea of "the study" a few years prior, as my homework load had increased when I'd moved into high school. He'd always had a study, where he'd work on personal projects each night after getting home from Eastman. When he noticed I was spending a lot of time poring over my own books after school and into the evenings, he'd suggested, "Why don't we move another table into the study, and that way we could work together?" Thus his study became our study, and I joined him in my family's seemingly endless quest for knowledge.

Except that my quest wasn't just for know-how. It went much deeper than that. My Quest, at the young age of sixteen, was to achieve a triumvirate of distraction, perfection, and absolution. My Quest was to soothe my savaged soul.

I'd come to recognize that once my mind came up with one of its terrifying fixations—be it head cancer, scenes of medieval torture or animal cruelty, or just a general sense of dread—I couldn't stop those thoughts from occurring. But I could distract myself from them. I could temporarily lure my mind to other places and give myself relief. Like a toddler presented with a shiny new toy, my brain seemed to momentarily drop its preoccupation with atrocities when given something stimulating to do. Such as reading fiction. Or working on challenging personal projects. Or doing homework. Without any conscious awareness, as a young person I'd managed to figure out how to use these distractions to partly tame the beast in my head. Over time, staying busy had become a habit, even when the monster wasn't there.

The monster also seemed to quiet down if I did things perfectly, so I aimed for perfection as well. Not just in my schoolwork, but in everything. In fact, I only participated in activities where I could be perfect. Art class, where I could take countless hours to make painstaking, tedious lines and dots with an inky black pen until the lifelike image of a hound dog bounded off the page and onto the walls of a youth art show, a blue ribbon pasted to its frame. Track, where having legs of different lengths didn't stop me from winning races. Band, where I could practice and practice my saxophone until every note was liquid and clear, guaranteeing I'd always be first or second chair. (I only acceded with grace to second chair periodically because I knew my arch-rival, Tony, also aspired for perfection, and I couldn't be a sore loser when I had such respect for his ambition.)

I dismissed activities where I didn't already have skills or where I could fail, even if I thought they would be fun: singing, dancing, trying out for cheerleading or soccer, interacting with kids more popular than I. But what I might have been missing didn't matter. Staying busy with things my brain found interesting, and striving to do them perfectly, earned me a lot of praise. From my parents. From relatives. From teachers. From like-minded friends. From everyone I cared about.

"Wow, Shala, you've finished another book. Good for you! You're such a good reader!"

"Another A for Shala! I wouldn't expect anything less."

"You do so well. You're going to be such a success in life."

I heard my other high-achieving friends receive these same compliments, the kind anyone would pay a hardworking, disciplined adolescent. But for me, they held much more profound meaning. They fueled my tripartite Quest, because to me, praise meant absolution. If I could garner respect, admiration, and love for what I *did*, then maybe who I *was*—a girl who sometimes had uncontrollable, visually disturbing, gruesome thoughts—wouldn't be so bad.

This Quest for distraction, perfection, and absolution, which I pursued even during those times when my mind left me alone, rapidly became an addiction.

Like a helpless tree thickly blanketed by suffocating kudzu, I was struggling. Not that anyone would know. I kept up a cheerful appearance at all times because perfection demanded being universally liked, even if I wasn't "popular." I also understood that a key part of Rule #1—*you don't tell what you see in your mind*—was its dictate not to share with anyone the terrifying worries I'd had.

I had to get an A on this calculus test. A grade of B was never enough. It couldn't make up for the disturbing thoughts my mind concocted, thoughts I concealed in part because they marked me as gravely flawed. Getting a B wouldn't balance the scales enough to outweigh the damage my mind was inflicting upon my soul.

Brushing off my crumb-covered hands on my jeans, I sat back down at my desk in the study and stared at *Elements of Calculus and Analytic Geometry*. Sighing heavily, I wondered how my friends who didn't live with a calculus expert were prepping for the exam. While math wasn't easy for me, thankfully it was for my dad. Sitting in the study in a creaky, black-painted rocker with an overlarge armrest wide enough for a sheet of notebook paper, my dad had patiently explained equations, functions, and derivatives to me almost nightly during the past semester.

Still, calculus was like an inscrutable language. As the first semester of my junior year wore on, I had a gnawing feeling that I didn't like calculus. But I didn't trust my senses. They'd lied to me so often, after all, about my health and my family's safety and what was real and what was fantasy. Whether I liked it or not, however, I had to keep studying for this test. I bent over my notebook paper and started copying the next problem from the book.

I started as the phone rang, breaking my concentration. I glanced at the clock. It was nine.

"Shit," I muttered. I'd said I would call my boyfriend, Doug.

"Hey, Shala," Doug said when I answered the phone in the kitchen. I could hear the breathy saxophone from the beginning of Pink Floyd's "Us and Them" lazily playing in the background.

"Hey." I was into Doug, but not right then.

"I was wondering if you were going to call me tonight." Doug stretched out the "I" in tonight so that it was almost its own syllable.

"Yeah, I know," I said, feeling an unwelcome smile come to my lips at the coarse sound of his thick Tennessee accent. I had an accent, too, but Doug's was much heavier.

Then I remembered all I had to do that night and how precious minutes were ticking away, and my smile faded. "I'm sorry I haven't called. I've been studying for my calculus test."

"Oh, Shala." Doug sighed. "You're the smartest girl in that class. You'll do fine." "Us and Them" swelled as Doug spoke, the synthesizer-infused music echoing in the background.

I rolled my eyes. "Do you know who's in my class? Mr. Robson is grading on a curve. Tons of people are going to ace it, so I have to do well."

I heard Doug sigh again. He knew he'd never win an argument with me about school. Or grades. "Are you and Syd coming to visit us this weekend?"

"Of course. You know we are." Doug and his best friend Tom, whom Sydney was dating, had graduated from high school the year before and were now attending the University of Tennessee, where Doug was majoring in electrical engineering. I planned to major in electrical engineering, too, mostly because Doug seemed to like it.

"We thought we could watch *Texas Chainsaw Massacre*. Tom and I just got a VCR in our room."

I cringed. Doug might have been older than I was, but sometimes he didn't act like it. I really didn't want to see a horror flick, even a stupid one. I didn't need any more fodder for my already gory imagination.

"Ummm, yeah, we'll see. Maybe we can go out to lunch instead."

I hung up after promising to call Friday night to firm up our plans. Then I scurried back to the study, checking the clock over my shoulder. Ten after nine. Ten minutes had gone by that I couldn't afford to lose.

I flopped down again in my chair, grabbed my pencil, and stared at the textbook. My exhausted eyes couldn't bring the math problems into focus. Frustrated, I rubbed them again, but the problems still looked fuzzy.

It doesn't matter, I thought, squinting and moving my face closer to the book so I could see. I had thirty-seven problems to go.

"Ow!" I yelped. A tiny line of blood formed on my left hand. In my math-induced trance, I'd moved a piece of paper so quickly it had turned into a miniature knife, slicing open my finger.

As I felt around in my jeans pockets for a tissue, I noticed the sheets of notebook paper, covered in cryptic writing, strewn all over the sides of my desk, threatening to fall onto the floor. I wrapped the half-used tissue around my finger, gripped the pencil, and wrote "10." on the paper in front of me. I'd done nine problems since my call with Doug. I was barely making progress. "I can do this," I whispered. "I can, because I *have to* do this."

I'd been studying for this test for days, and I'd been working that evening since I'd arrived home from school. Further, I'd already done these problems as homework in the prior weeks, but I knew the only way to ensure an A—to be certain there were no surprises on the test—was to do them again.

As I began to write out the next problem, my hand started, ever so slightly, to shake. I steadied it and gazed at the problems I had left to do, thinking what I really needed was sleep. I didn't do well on tests without rest, no matter how much I studied.

Resting my head in my hands, the tissue still wrapped around one finger, I could smell the acrid musk of graphite as my pencil pushed against my temple. I wondered when my parents would get home from the movie about Greece. Or Belgium. Or maybe it was France. Why couldn't I remember? Hadn't my mom told me right before they'd left? I tried to remember our conversation, to see the country on a mental map, but nations and numbers and symbols coalesced into a muddled mass in my mind, and I suddenly felt exhausted.

"I can't be tired. I have more to do!" I pulled my hands from my face and slammed them painfully on the desk. Palms stinging, I looked back at the problem and willed my hand, still clutching my pencil, to copy the rest of it. But my hand just lay there, the eraser at the pencil's tip beginning once again to quiver.

I sat transfixed. For the first time in my soul-saving Quest, I felt immobilized by defeat.

A tear rolled down my cheek, splashing on the number "10" I'd written so boldly only moments before. It was a white flag of surrender in a war I knew I was just too tired to keep fighting.

"La?" my mom called from the stairs.

I'd heard my parents come in a few moments earlier. The garage door closing sounded like metal barrels slamming into each other as they rolled down a hill. No one could ever sneak into our house through the garage.

"La?" she said again, sounding concerned. I'd left all the lights blazing. I had to have total darkness to sleep, so my mom knew I was still awake.

I heard my dad's heavy footsteps coming up the stairs. "Where's Shala?"

"I don't know," said Mom. "She must still be up."

I was still awake—but I was no longer studying, or even in the study. Instead, I sat on the end of my bed, sobbing. Clasping my knees, I absentmindedly rocked back and forth like my old Weeble toys. *Weebles wobble but they don't fall down.* As I remembered the advertising jingle, I started to cry even harder—because *I* had fallen down. Despair had overtaken me, and through my sobs I chanted tonelessly, "I cannot do any more math problems."

I looked up and saw my parents framed by my doorway, frozen. I looked back down and kept rocking. And chanting. And crying.

Recognizing I wasn't going to volunteer the cause of my distress, my mom sat gently next to me on the patchwork quilt, a hint of lavender lotion recently purchased from the Avon lady following in her wake.

"Shala," she said, sounding confused. "What's wrong?"

I wasn't a big crier. Dramatic displays of emotion had never resulted in getting my way, so I'd learned acting pathetic wasn't a good strategy. Plus, when my parents had left hours earlier, I'd been fine—jovial, even. In a matter of hours, I'd transformed from contented daughter to inconsolable stranger. No wonder they seemed confused.

I raised my head to look into her concerned eyes and wept, answering her question with the only words I was able to say. "I...cannot...do...any...more...math...problems."

"What happened last night, Shala?" Dr. Prasad asked, leaning back in his chair.

I squirmed on the periwinkle-blue couch across from him, the psychiatrist with whom my parents had arranged an emergency appointment after they'd found me sobbing and chanting on my bed the prior evening.

I picked at the pattern of lines in the couch fabric with my fingernail. I'd recently tried growing out my nails but gave up when they kept breaking. I wasn't a nice-nails-kind-of-girl; it didn't fit with my farm-influenced tomboy upbringing. As I moved my thumb back and forth, thinking about how to answer Dr. Prasad, the ragged edge of my nail snagged on the raised pattern. Flushing, I stopped. I didn't want to get in trouble.

I'd always had respect for figures of authority. I assumed they knew more than I did. Why else would they be in a position of power?

But one authority figure loomed larger than all others. One that had ultimate say over me in any situation. One I'd listen to above my parents, teachers, friends' parents—anyone.

My own mind.

Anyone who looked inside my head expecting to see the mirror reflection of me—a respectful, obedient teenager—would have been taken aback, because my mind was a rebel. I had a feathered bob, but my mind's hair was short, spiked, and dyed jet black. I listened to Phil Collins and The Police; my mind preferred heavy metal. I dressed preppy, while my mind dressed in all black, wearing torn jeans and any one of a dozen concert T-shirts from its favorite "screw authority" hard-rock bands. While I still loved soft, comforting stuffed animals, my mind stockpiled hard military-standard equipment—including radar to scan for anything that might hurt me, and surveillance cameras to check and recheck for danger the radar might have missed.

Fortunately, its hardware had turned up little in the way of threats lately—ever since my hair had grown back in—and my goth-like monster of a mind had mostly left me alone.

My mind was an enigma to me, one I couldn't trust. I never forgot the damage it was capable of inflicting, no matter how it presently behaved. Its paranoia had hounded me for months when I was younger with those grisly scenes of animal torture and my parents' death, along with its menacing whispers about head cancer. Then, suddenly and unexplainably, it would go blessedly silent for months—even years—on end. I'd been in one of those silent periods for some time now, but I could read the signs. My reprieve was about to end.

As I sat on Dr. Prasad's couch, I could feel my mind stirring. I could tell it was angry. I heard it utter swear words as it readied its most deadly equipment, the weapon it brandished in emergencies. Then I heard a telltale metallic clicking and felt the cold hard barrel of a pistol pressed into my temple.

I tensed. My mind was going to hold me hostage again.

Fear coursed through my veins, rose like molten lava in my chest. I could taste its hot malevolence at the back of my throat.

Certain that it now had my undivided attention, my mind thrust forward its manifesto—words scribed in a Satanic-like font reminiscent of a heavy-metal album cover—and screamed, *READ IT!*

I knew the words by heart. I silently recited them in my head:

You cannot get caught doing these things or thinking these thoughts.
Because if you do, you will have to explain yourself.
And you don't tell what you see in your mind.
Because if you do, all those bad things you see ... you will make them happen.

I nodded assent, telegraphing to my mind that I understood. That I would not break Rule #1. Now. Or ever.

My mind relaxed a little, but it kept the gun's cool, polished barrel kissing my temple. Lest I forget, or let this nice man sweet-talk me into revealing too much.

I cleared my throat. "I'm just your ordinary, overachieving teenager. Like everyone else, I get stressed about school. Dobyns-Bennett High is really competitive. I just got a little worked up last night."

Satisfied, my mind further relaxed its grip on its weapon. It knew I understood. I would proceed to lie. To cover up. To waste my parents' money in service of saving them, saving me, saving everyone I loved.

I met with Dr. Prasad a number of times over the following months. My parents also attempted to impart wisdom that might ward off future meltdowns. One night, as I bent over my desk in the study, slumped like a wizened old woman, my dad walked in carrying a book he'd retrieved from our voluminous downstairs library. He set it atop *Elements of Calculus and Analytic Geometry*, esoteric equations replaced by a white cover, emblazoned in arresting red and black font: *Type A Behavior and Your Heart.*

"What's this?" I asked. I opened the cover and saw my mom's distinctive handwriting in the upper corner of the fly leaf, where she'd written "1974." Three years after I was born. My dad had owned this book for a while.

"I think it would be good for you to read this, La," Dad said, standing over me. I closed the book and again took in the cover, its colors those of an ambulance on a lifesaving race to the hospital.

"Why?" I asked, bemused.

"You've heard me talk about Type A behavior, right?"

My parents and I discussed all sorts of topics at our nightly dinners. Several years earlier Dad had explained— reluctantly, as though he were sharing a foregone conclusion—that I exhibited what he called Type A behavior: a focus on accomplishments, a drive for success, a yearning to win.

"Yeah, but I thought it was good that I'm Type A," I protested, at the same noticing the words in smaller type on the cover: *How and Why Type A Behavior Leads to Heart Disease*.

"Yes, there are good things about being so driven," my dad agreed, the corners of his mustache turning up as he spoke. "But there are not-so-good things as well. I think it's safe to say you're as much a Type A as I am, and I've found this book really helpful. I think you might relate to what these doctors say."

"Okay," I said. My dad nodded and walked back into the den, where the tinny *M*A*S*H* theme played on the TV. I picked up the book and impatiently flipped through the deckle-edge pages, wrinkling my nose at the slight musty odor I associated with the stacks at the library.

I closed it and placed it on a shelf above my desk. I knew I wouldn't read it. I didn't want to know if Type A behavior was bad for me because it was the only way I knew how to be, and I couldn't pursue my Quest without it.

I knew my parents were trying to help me, so I felt bad that I wasn't telling them or Dr. Prasad the truth. About why I needed to earn As at school. About the things I saw and thought. About how I knew there was something fundamentally wrong with me.

Over the course of several sessions in the coming months, Dr. Prasad taught me visualization techniques, or how to picture a successful outcome for whatever I was doing. True to form, I was a model student, practicing the exercises until I could skillfully visualize success.

But at my core, I was still a hostage, forced to act as though everything was okay while I honed my Type A behavior in service of the Quest. While I pretended I could handle all the stress and pressure. While I lied to the person who could have helped me.

Years later, I learned that Dr. Prasad had suspected I had a monster. But I hadn't given him enough to go on. Because I couldn't take the risk that my monster's gun might go off and kill me, or my parents, or someone else I loved.

So even though I'd learned how to visualize success, I was setting myself up for defeat down the road.

CHAPTER 5

Sun and Shadows

P izza. I smelled like pizza.

I dropped my backpack into a puddle of evening light on the floor of my studio apartment and went into the bathroom. Flipping on the switch and looking into the mirror, I discovered a streak of dried pizza sauce down the right side of my face. That must have been why Matt and Mike laughed at me as I left the restaurant. I grinned as I wiped off the red smear. How nice of them not to tell me I'd been advertising our food by wearing it on my cheek.

I'd been working at the Green Street location of Garcia's Pizza in a Pan for two months. It was my part-time job during my first summer semester at the University of Illinois at Urbana-Champaign, and it was just one of many things about university life that made me deliriously happy.

Enduring happiness had eluded me in high school. Moments of joy, yes. Lasting peace and happiness, no. My sessions with Dr. Prasad had come to an end. I'd aced the AP calculus exam, enough to pass out of two semesters of college calculus. I graduated top ten in my class. I always had a boyfriend and plenty of friends. Yet it seemed I could never relax and enjoy life the way many of my friends could. Success, for me, clearly didn't equal happiness. In fact, the more my accomplishments stacked up, the longer and darker the shadows they cast. Shadows that weighed on me, imploring me to do better, to work harder, to never let go of my Quest.

As I thought about colleges, I imagined that if I went far away, somewhere no one knew me, my inability to be happy might change. Maybe the shadows wouldn't survive in a new environment.

I'd toured a number of colleges the summer after my junior year in high school, but I'd known from the moment that I set foot on the squishy, rain-soaked quad of the University of Illinois, gazing out from under my umbrella at the god-like dark good looks of the campus tour guide, that this was the place for me. That I'd be happy here, shadow-free in this perfect enclave of learning, freedom, and fun.

Sydney had gone to the University of Virginia. She'd liked UVA, or at least seemed to, so I thought I had an ally in the "I cannot get enough of university life" club. But on one of our weekly phone calls during our first few months of college, as I again went through the litany of reasons I loved Illinois—from the hot guys and parties to the classes filled with smart and interesting people—I was taken aback when Sydney, clearly not as enthralled with UVA, snapped, "That's right! Everything's sunny at Illinois!"

For the first few months of college, Syd was right. Everything *was* sunny. Sunny and perfect. Until the shadows once again began to form.

Pulling off my slightly greasy clothes, the aroma of crushed tomatoes overpowering as my shirt went over my head, I braced myself to look in the mirror again. My chest tightened, and I could feel my happiness from the day spent at Garcia's start to drain away, as it always did when I prepared myself for the ritual I did any time I stood in front of a mirror. Any time no one else was looking. Any time I thought what I'd see might be different from what I'd seen before.

The bathroom mirror in my apartment only went to my waist, so I climbed up on the toilet in my underwear, watching my feet as I carefully placed each one on the long edges of the lid. I knew from experience that this part of the toilet would hold me, but if I edged my feet just an inch toward the bowl, the cheap plastic lid, already worn and yellowed with age, would start to crack. Then I'd have to lie to my roommate about why I'd been standing on the toilet. Again.

Convinced I was balanced, I raised my gaze to the mirror, ever hopeful. Today might be the day. Today I might see what I wanted.

I stared. I knew what I'd see at first glance might not be accurate. That I might need to gaze for a while. I might need to shift the angle at which I was looking. To make sure I hadn't missed a miniscule change in my favor.

But no matter how or which way I looked, the answer was the same tonight as it had been earlier that afternoon. And as it had been that morning. And the day before. And the week before. And the month before.

I sighed. My thighs, especially the part right above my knees, still didn't look thin enough.

Why couldn't they be thinner?

I jumped off the toilet and headed toward my tiny closet. My stomach gurgled plaintively. I ignored it. My inability to sculpt my legs into the shape I wanted was creating yet another thing I didn't want: a goddamned shadow, darkening otherwise sunny days at my beloved university.

But I had plans that might help ward off these shadows. Dinner would have to wait.

I stepped out of my first-floor apartment into the evening air as a car whizzed by, the soulful staccato of The Police's "Don't Stand So Close to Me" coming from a nearby frat house. I began my daily four-mile run around campus, heading south on First Street along the university's western edge. Dusk spray-painted dusty graphite over the melon-colored remains of the day, and I exhaled deeply into the evening air. I loved running.

Having dropped out of physics the previous semester, which ended my career as a budding electrical engineer, I couldn't calculate the force at which my feet hit the pavement. But I did know something magical happened when I ran, something that couldn't be explained by science. That the concrete sidewalks seemed improbably to bounce both my mood and my body upward, higher and higher with each step, as if I were running on a trampoline. That every fusion of my sole with the ground melded my soul to this place I now called home.

I was in love. With the state of Illinois and its flat, horizon-stretching cornfields. With the university and its imposing, scholarly buildings. With the other students, the majority of whom were from the Chicago metropolitan area. My fellow students were beautifully exotic creatures, with their Midwestern accents, casual good looks, and sophistication I knew they possessed from living their whole lives an hour's drive from the sparkling sky-bound buildings of the Windy City.

As I rounded the corner from First Street to Kirby Avenue, leg two of my four-mile square, I saw a woman jogging in place a few strides ahead, her short, wavy, brown hair curtaining her face as she fiddled with her watch. Marci, my running buddy.

"Hey!" she said as she saw me approach. With a final glance at her watch, she fell into place beside me, her light steps keeping rhythm with my own.

"New watch?" I asked, a little breathlessly. Realizing from my shortness of breath that my speed was too fast, I shortened my stride, slowing down.

Marci pulled ahead briefly, saying, "Yeah, got it yesterday in town," then slowed her stride. Turning to look at me, she grinned, the dimpled corners of her mouth seeming to reach all the way to her eyes. "You were really busting a move down First. Thanks for slowing down for us old folks."

I punched her in the arm. "You're not so old."

I loved Marci. A farm girl from southern Illinois, she was in grad school doing a degree in social work. We'd met at the end of my second semester. I'd been running past Mount Hope Cemetery, bordering the southern edge of the campus, when I saw her jogging ahead of me. Running put me in a good mood, and as I'd caught up to her, I'd decided to strike up a conversation. "Sort of creepy, running past here," I'd said, in that "runners are all friends so I'm just going to chat with you like I know you" tone. "It is," she agreed, giving me her big Marci grin, and that was the beginning of our friendship. We'd been running together almost daily ever since.

"How was class today? Which one did you have again?" she asked.

"Econ 101. It was okay. You know how these big lecture classes are."

"Yeah," she agreed. "They can be a little dry."

I had decided, after finally coming to terms with the fact that I had no passion for hard sciences and math, to drop out of engineering school at the beginning of second semester freshman year. I was now by default in Liberal Arts & Sciences, aka LAS, or what fellow students affectionately called "Lost and Searching." But even though I had no interest in physics or differential equations or any other engineering class—and in fact had no idea what an electrical engineer did day to day—giving up my slot in the engineering school had not been without its issues. After a pre-dropping-out meeting with the school's dean, I'd sobbed to my dad on a pay phone from the Illini Union.

"He said if I drop out, they won't let me back in!"

"That's okay!" My dad had laughed. "You don't want back in!"

That was true. I didn't. But I also didn't like being denied options when I had no clue what I wanted to do.

Which wasn't my fault. After all, it was hard to know what I wanted when I was a tenant in the kingdom of a cruel lord who demanded fealty in the form of complicated mental gyrations, all devised to procure that most elusive form of wealth: certainty. Certainty that I'd be okay, that everyone I loved would be okay, that nothing bad would ever happen. I just didn't understand that certainty was the domain of fools.

It's not surprising that a few days after my tearful phone conversation with Dad, after I let the engineering dean know I could handle not getting back into his school, I felt I needed to decide immediately what I was going to do if I wasn't going to be an engineer. I couldn't not know, after all. *Any* decision would be better than the uncertainty of no decision.

"Business," I decided in about ten minutes. "I'll get a business degree. You can't go wrong with that."

Mistaking certainty for happiness, I took all of ten fateful minutes during my second semester of college to decide my next twenty years.

Getting into the undergrad business school would require a transfer in my junior year and meant I needed to take a bunch of business courses to catch up. Thus Econ 101.

"Do you have big plans this weekend, Marci?" I asked, changing the subject. The loamy smell of fallow earth and blackened, moss-kissed tombstones filled my nostrils as Mount Hope Cemetery slowly slid by on our left.

"Some of the other social work students are having a party off campus Saturday. You want to come?"

I looked away into the depths of the cemetery. "I'm working that night, but thanks for asking." I shuddered a little, as if I'd laid to rest a tiny part of my soul in Mount Hope with my ritual-enabling lie.

I didn't have to work Saturday night. It wasn't that I didn't want to go to the party. I did. But I also wanted thin and beautiful thighs. Well, if I was completely honest, it wasn't that I *wanted* model-like thighs. It was as though I *had* to have them. As though I were driven by some single-minded salesman who endlessly whispered that if I just worked hard enough, I could have them and finally be happy.

You're so close, Shala, so no empty calories from beer at a party—we'd just better skip it, the salesman cajoled. I listened. And obeyed.

I wasn't always so dutiful. A non-drinker and non-partier in high school, I had discovered at Illinois that beer wasn't half bad. Being a little intoxicated (and sometimes a lot intoxicated) wasn't that bad, either, as alcohol seemed to press the mute button on my mind and its obsession with catastrophe. My college friends and I did a lot of drinking that first year at U of I. Mostly beers at the campus bars Kam's and C.O. Daniels or at frat parties. My best friend Evie and I were especially fond of O'Malley's, a dark, crowded, sloppy-drunk college bar, thick with the mingled scents of beer, sweat, and Drakkar Noir, where we'd imbibe an unknown alcoholic concoction called the Blue Fucker from cheap souvenir plastic mugs on Saturday nights. We always stayed until midnight, when we could sway arm in arm with other students, intoxicated with booze and the freedom of college life, slurring as we sang along to Don McLean's classic "American Pie" as it blared from the bar's speakers.

With my copious consumption of beer, late-night pizzas, and unlimited dorm food, it was no wonder I'd gained the dreaded "Freshman 15" first semester.

Not that it had bothered me. Prior to my second semester at Illinois, I had never in my life noticed or even known how much I weighed. I also couldn't have told you how any particular part of my body looked. In fact, even after a guy friend of mine told me as we sat in the band room in high school, holding our alto saxophones, waiting for the start of class, "Your butt is sort of flabby, did you know that?" I'd never given his criticism a second thought, other than to reflect that it was rude. Who died and left him Judge of Looks? I thought I looked fine.

Until one night, that is. The night when everything changed.

It had been a weeknight just like any other. Studying in my dorm room, I'd been trying to ignore my roommate Sylvia, who was reading at the wooden desk behind me, fortunately facing the other side of the room. She and I had just never clicked. We didn't dislike each other, but we didn't like each other, either. Correcting a hairy problem for Differential Equations, a course I was committed to finishing even though I wasn't in engineering anymore, I swore under my breath and accidently flung my eraser across the room.

"Everything okay?" Sylvia asked in a way that seemed meant to simultaneously convey caring and cover annoyance, but that came out a little like a sneer.

"I'm fine," I muttered, getting up to collect my eraser.

As I sat back down, my pant leg bunched uncomfortably under me. I shifted to straighten it out, looking down as I did so, and I saw my thighs for the very first time.

They were huge.

Gigantic.

Like two beached blue whales, sides heaving, dying back to back on a deserted shore.

My heart started beating loudly and a wave of heat enveloped my face. Oh my God. I touched my thighs, swathed in my favorite navy-blue cotton pants, and noticed how they completely filled my hard wooden chair, spilling out a little over the sides. I could suddenly feel the fat as if I were a tiny creature trying to free itself from an oozing, gooey bog. It was disgusting. I shuddered and stood up suddenly, knocking my chair over into Sylvia's.

"Whoa, what's wrong?" she cried, with a surprising tone of genuine concern as she turned around to look at me.

Pivoting, realizing what I'd done, I stuttered, "What? Oh, yeah. Sorry, it felt like something stung me. I think the chair just pinched me." I was a master at lying on the fly to explain odd behavior. I righted the chair, continuing, "I'm ... I'm really hot. I think I'm going to put on shorts."

"Shorts? In March?"

"Yeah, it's kinda hot," I mumbled. I grabbed a pair of shorts from my chest of drawers, dropping my pants to around my ankles. Shame burned my eyes as I noticed for the first time the little ripples of fat right above my knees.

Without a word, I pulled on my shorts and left the room. I had to see what I looked like in a mirror. Stepping into the gloriously empty hall bathroom, I stared at my legs in the wall-size mirror over the sinks. White, pasty, lumpy. I pulled my shorts tight around my thighs, so I could see their contours. Wide, round, gross. I turned sideways, first to the left, then to the right. No better. Still disgustingly fat and out of proportion to my relatively thin torso and calves.

I stepped a little closer to the mirror, gazing more intently at the area just above my knees. Grayish, almost bruise-like markings etched their way horizontally across my skin, outlining the small rolls of congealed fat below. Mortified, I roughly grabbed the upper part of my right thigh with both hands and pulled up. My leg, while still huge, was now smooth, the markings having disappeared. I let go, and they reappeared.

I stood in front of the mirror, grabbing and pulling my thigh, letting go, grabbing, letting go, over and over again, until a sophomore from down the hall came in and I had to stop and pretend I was about to wash my hands. As the blessedly cool water poured over my fingers, I heard a whisper, one that would echo across my consciousness for years to come:

If you can fix the way your thigh looks temporarily by pulling the skin of your leg up, you could fix it permanently by losing weight.

I knew intuitively that this whisper didn't come from my monster. My appearance had never been a concern for my goth-like monster of a mind, which was only ever obsessed with danger and death. This seductive suggestion came from a part of me I'd never encountered before. A part of me that, like a slick salesman, now offered an easy solution to an urgent problem that only minutes before, I hadn't known I'd had.

I turned off the water. "That's right, this is fixable," I murmured, agreeing with the whisper, feeling relief for the first time since I'd pitched my eraser across the room. I can fix this. I can make this right. I can undo what I've done.

The next day, I ran four miles around campus. I'd been running this same four-mile loop daily ever since, as if I were trying to outrun the whisper's echo.

"Hey, I need to stop in the bookstore," Marci said as we rounded the corner to Green Street, the heart of campus. "Do you mind if I cut our run short?"

"No, not at all. Same time and place tomorrow?"

"Yup, see you then!" she said as she stopped in front of the bookstore, windows decked out with T-shirts in the school's bright orange and navy blue.

I kept running, my feet pounding the pavement. It was dark now, and summer-school students already swarmed around O'Malley's. I brushed past them, annoyed at their ability to have fun. Annoyed that I couldn't do the same.

My stomach growled. I was famished. Without Marci's presence, I noticed the gnawing feeling in my stomach. I picked up my speed to distract myself, but like a horsefly who stays with a pony on a ride through the woods, hunger kept buzzing around my ears no matter how fast I ran. This was, of course, only natural. No human could live comfortably on the diet the salesman had sold me in service of sculpting my thighs. Fat-free yogurt. Bagels. Granny Smith apples. And lots and lots of Diet Dr. Pepper.

I'd learned about Diet Dr. Pepper from Lynsey, the other student who shared my summer lodgings. She watched her weight, even though she didn't need to, and she always kept the blue-and-silver cans of the zero-calorie beverage in our fridge. Wanting something new, I'd tried one on one of my first days in our little studio apartment and was instantly hooked. Soon, one a day wasn't enough. Neither were two, three, or four. Sometimes I had six a day. Sometimes twelve. I filled myself with diet soda, hoping to plug the holes of hunger the salesman's whispered solicitations created.

The only treat I allowed myself became a sacred ritual: a scoop of chocolate cookie dough. Tucked away just off the main quad, a tiny store had opened that sold not just cookies, but servings of freshly made raw cookie dough. Each day I'd buy a scoop and walk with it the few blocks to the quad, holding the paper cup with the reverence of a priest offering Holy Communion. Sitting in the dappled shade of the trees, my eyes never leaving the glistening mound of chocolate decadence, I'd convey tiny spoonfuls to my mouth with a slow, almost pantomimed motion. I savored every sensual delight: the grittiness of the sugar, the acidic sweetness of the cocoa, the rumbling crunch of the chips between my back teeth, the warm breeze on my shoulders as I ate.

No one walking by would have known the roles I hoped that lump of glistening cookie dough would fulfill: lover, energy booster, lifeline to humanity. But it failed me miserably time and time again, like scraps thrown to a beggar that only served to make him more ravenous.

The paradoxical dichotomies in my life seemed to escape me. My love for my new friends, competing with my hatred of their freedom to eat whatever they wanted. My yearning to fulfill my Quest—to be both perfect and special—but also to fit in as one of the crowd. My hope that buying my salesman's spiel would give me my heart's desire, at war with my deepest wish that his whispers would stop reverberating through my mind. My need to control, always and forever battling my desire to be free.

Rivulets of sweat streamed down my temples in the hot Illinois evening as I pushed forward, and I could feel tendrils of flyaway hair coming loose from my ponytail and sticking to my face. My feet had lost the buoyancy of the first half of the run, and as I completed my square around campus, I felt as if my tennis shoes were anvils heavily dropping onto the street. I was so hungry at this point that I wasn't hungry. It was as if my body had been deprived for so long that it had decided to just give up on ever getting food again.

My apartment building, one of those cheap two-story boxy structures covered in dirty red bricks, loomed ahead. I pumped my arms faster, willing my legs to keep pace, until I reached the door and fell against it, my sides heaving in time to the crickets chirping in the night air. Fingers shaking as I tried once, twice, three times to jab the key into the keyhole, I noticed no lights coming from within, a signal that Lynsey was staying with her boyfriend again. Good, I thought, I don't feel like talking to anyone anyway.

Fourth time was the charm, and I stumbled into the main room as the door swung open under my weight. I made a beeline for the fridge. I wanted chocolate ice cream. Fat-free, of course, but chocolate nonetheless, and I wanted it now.

Just a few spoonfuls, I told myself, as I yanked the half-gallon tub from the freezer and pried off the lid. Even through the freezer burn, it was amazing. Cold. Creamy. Delicious.

I sat down on the dingy carpet so I could get a better grip on the tub. One bite. Another. Then another.

Okay, that's enough, said a voice in my head.

"Just one more bite," I replied, for once not listening to the salesman.

No. Stop. Now.

But with each mouthful of smooth, velvety ice cream, I seemed less and less capable of stopping. Spoonful after spoonful seemed to move from the tub to my mouth without my conscious choice, as if my right arm belonged to a marionette, controlled by a powerful but invisible puppeteer.

Time sped up as I ate. What else could possibly explain the sudden disappearance of all the ice cream? I dropped the empty tub to the floor, still ravenous, and moved to the shelves beside the sink where Lynsey had left a package of vanilla crème sandwich cookies. I ripped it open, took the five remaining cookies, and started stuffing them into my mouth.

The crunching and chewing, rhythmic, insistent, drowned out the salesman. For the first time since that fateful night in my dorm room, I not only couldn't hear him, I didn't care what he had to say. Because eating felt absolutely necessary.

Cookies finished, I looked around wildly for more food and noticed two bananas lying on the counter. I tore off the peel and downed the first one, somewhat mushy and bruised from age, in four bites.

As I peeled the second banana, the sharp tang of overripe fruit filling my nostrils, I suddenly noticed I felt a little better. Was this what full felt like? I couldn't remember. I slowed down, finishing the banana in a trance.

Leaving the peel on the counter, I dropped drunkenly onto my back on the floor and breathed long and low, exhaling deeply into the stale air of my apartment.

And then I heard it.

What have you done?!

I froze, holding my breath. It sounded as if the volume on the TV had just been turned up in the middle of a violent argument, one character mercilessly screaming at another.

Do you have any idea how many calories you just ate?!

I sat up, horrified.

If you don't do something, all your hard work will be for nothing! Pounds and pounds of fat will glue themselves to your thighs overnight! Do you want that to happen?!

No, I do not want that, I thought as I jerkily got to my feet. The salesman's uncharacteristic tirade and adept use of the FUD factor—fear, uncertainty, and doubt—had produced the desired results.

What *had* I done?

One moment's satiety transformed to gut-wrenching panic.

I had probably just eaten two thousand calories. Or more.

Oh my God.

Appeased by my response, the salesman lowered his voice, adopting a veneer of professionalism. Then he whispered the words that didn't need repeating: *You can fix this, you know.*

I stood, heart pounding, and dropped my gaze to the floor. I still had my running shoes on.

I *could* fix this.

I grabbed my key where it had fallen on the floor and headed back out into the night to do another four-mile run, the salesman smiling slyly in my wake.

"So you couldn't stop yourself from going out and running again, even though it was late at night?" Carol asked.

"No, I couldn't," I admitted.

I was, once again, sitting in a therapist's office.

"What was it like … the run?"

Carol was a social worker with a private practice in Champaign, and I had no idea how to answer her question. How could I explain the competing terrors of that run to this person I barely knew? How could I make her understand the depth of my fear as I ran, for the second time that night, through a corridor of suffocating darkness bounded by the quarter-mile long Mount Hope Cemetery on one side and endless black nothingness on the other?

I could tell her I'd felt the hair on the nape of my neck stand up as I imagined hundreds of socketless eyes peering out at me from the inky vastness of the graveyard as I ran by, breathless with fright. I could also share that I couldn't have turned around and headed back to my apartment, not even to ensure my physical safety, because an unstoppable force had propelled me like a fish on a hook reeled in by a fisherman eager for his trophy. I could also admit I understood what fueled the power behind this force: compared to the fear of binge-induced cellulite my salesman convinced me had accumulated on my thighs, how truly scary was going for a "midnight jog" in pitch black all by myself where no one knew where I was?

It wasn't scary at all.

"It was scary," I replied, simultaneously telling her nothing and everything.

I'd been seeing Carol for a few weeks now, our relationship commencing after a tearful phone call to my parents the morning after my run, when I admitted I was clearly out of control. They'd driven up that next weekend, taking me to St. Louis for a much-needed break from my madness. Over sips of my dad's beer and bites of soft, salty pretzels at a Cardinals game, and while shopping with my mom for oversized sweaters at Express, I'd spun out my tale for them, explaining everything I wasn't eating and why. That I didn't know how to stop restricting my food intake, even though I didn't think I was fat; I only thought my thighs were fat. That I couldn't seem to stop exercising compulsively in an effort to fix my thighs. That I didn't know how to escape the echoing whispers that I could fix this, and if I did, I would be happy.

My monster also favored eliminating the echoes, mostly because my salesman-provoked issues were on the verge of breaking Rule #1. My monster and my salesman had been living what was for them a peaceful coexistence, until my monster had realized that all these exercising and food-restricting compulsions would clue people in to the fact that something was wrong with me. My monster didn't care if people knew about the salesman, but there was no way my monster would let him blow its own carefully crafted cover.

After my parents' visit, I'd gone to McKinley Health Center on campus, hoping someone would tell me how to stop all this salesman-induced, self-destructive behavior. Told I hadn't lost enough weight to qualify for an anorexia nervosa diagnosis, I learned I didn't technically have an eating disorder. My salesman seemingly hadn't done a good enough job. Still hoping someone could help me, I attended a support group filled with other young women who struggled with eating challenges. The majority of them, however, seemed to be competing for who could buy the most from their own slick salespeople—as if they were trying to get better *at* their eating disorders, not *from* them. So I never went back, instead deciding to go to Carol, whom I chose because she was relatively close to campus and accepted my university insurance.

I didn't receive any official treatment during that time, because I didn't technically have an eating disorder. I certainly didn't reveal to Carol anything about the monster that was my mind. I could still feel the impression of the gun barrel that had been pressed to my temple in Dr. Prasad's office, and I didn't want to incur my mind's wrath again.

So Carol and I talked each week. And I kept running, four miles a day, every single day.

"What are you doing tonight?" Evie asked, as we sat down in the dorm cafeteria one October evening the first semester of our second year.

"I've got a meeting at the sorority house," I said, dropping my light-green tray in front of me on the table. The room, loud and cavernous, reverberated with the metallic clinking of silverware that students threw into the wash bins as they returned their trays.

Evie looked up, muttered "Oh," and started digging into her food.

My sorority was a sore subject between my roommate Evie and me. We'd been best friends all of our freshman year, and going into sophomore year we'd thought nothing would be better than living together.

Then came sorority rush. She and I had gone through rush together in August, but she'd dropped out partway because the houses she'd liked weren't the ones who asked her back. I'd ended up pledging one of those houses, and it was driving a wedge into our friendship.

I pushed my salad, swimming in low-fat Catalina dressing, around on my plate, trying to think of what to say. I could tell her I thought some of sorority life was kind of silly. That I wasn't all that happy being in a sorority. That I didn't feel like I fit in.

But I knew none of that would make her any happier.

I speared a few carrots among the vegetables that floated lazily in a sea of dressing and iceberg lettuce on my plate, watching Evie eat, eyes still cast down, in silence.

As I crunched through my rabbit food, I dwelled on the reason I was having so much trouble fitting in at my sorority.

The salesman didn't like me being around people who weren't fit and healthy. Most of my sorority sisters were, but in a sorority house with a membership of two hundred women, not everyone could look like they'd just stepped off the cover of a fitness magazine. I knew that. I understood that. But the salesman did not. He couldn't stop noticing and pointing out women in my sorority who were a few pounds overweight, then urgently whispering, *We should only be around people who are totally fit. That's how we keep from becoming overweight, too.*

He also liked to point out thin women wearing clothes emblazoned with the letters of other sororities. The University of Illinois had the country's largest Greek system, so he had plenty to work with, taunting me daily as I walked around campus. *Oooo, there's someone thin. Maybe we should have joined her sorority. Or look, there's someone thin from another one down the street. Maybe that one would have been better.*

I'd had friends who weren't perfectly skinny during my freshman year, no problem, even after that night in my dorm room when I'd discovered what my thighs looked like. But being in a sorority, which supposedly transformed mere friendships into "sisterhood," was too much for the salesman. If these women were my sisters, he deftly reasoned, then we were *all going to become exactly alike.*

It wasn't like I'd dropped into my sorority out of the Miss America pageant. According to the salesman, my knees and thighs severely lacked tone and definition, even with the miles and miles of running I did, and he didn't ever worry that anyone else was going to catch *my* looks. He stayed totally focused, in a fashion that resembled my monster's, on the potential danger to me. If he didn't like the way women in my sorority looked—thighs too big, arms too flabby, gut too large—his whispered sales pitches would become fevered. *You must keep your distance,* he'd implore, *or you'll end up looking like your "sisters"!*

Sometimes it was just too much to bear. With every cajoling, derogatory whisper from the salesman, I grew to hate the person I was becoming.

I knew my sorority was filled with mostly wonderful, kind people. That's why Evie had liked it so much. Women who lived in my sorority house didn't even lock their room doors because no one would ever dare take anything. While there were cliques and gossip, they were far less than I would have expected given the size of the sorority. It was a good group of women, something my myopic, appearance-obsessed salesman just couldn't see.

I came to dread going to the sorority house, because I hated what I heard in my head when I was there. I hated how the salesman made me cringe when I walked into the house and found women from my pledge class sitting in the TV room, watching soaps, laughing, and eating buttered popcorn. They were having fun, while I walked brusquely by, trying not to look at them as he lamented: *How can they just sit there like that, inhaling gallons of fat?*

Sometimes I'd make excuses to skip events with my house. I begged off going with the other forty-nine members of my pledge class on Walk Out, a weekend bonding trip, with the excuse that I had to work proctoring tests for the U of I Testing Center, my part-time job during the school year. I never went out to bars with members of my pledge class, instead going with Evie or other friends. I never lingered in the house, chatting with other people. I was in and out quickly, staying just long enough for the meetings I was required to attend.

A piece of silverware floated under my nose. "Shala?" said Evie, waving her spoon in front of me. "Do you want to get dessert?"

I looked up, realizing Evie had already finished her dinner and was trying to get my attention. "Oh. No. That's okay," I said, as Evie pushed her chair out, heading to the soft-serve ice cream dispenser. "You go ahead without me."

Dessert was one of the many things the salesman had skillfully coerced me not to eat. My sessions with Carol, which had stopped before the beginning of fall semester, seemed to have no effect on the salesman. My monster did have an effect, however, and the salesman understood he must help me maintain a façade of normalcy or my monster would boot him out of this most lucrative of sales territories.

He'd decided, therefore, that his new sales pitch would rest on the slogan of *It's healthy!* because healthy was normal. In one of his most compelling whispered sales presentations to date, he'd carefully detailed how I must have gained weight in my thighs because I ate too much meat, which was fattening and unhealthy, so meat had to go. And hey, since I was an animal lover, giving up meat was not only healthy but righteous.

The salesman was so skilled in the art of instantaneous mental thrust and parry, I didn't even know I had options other than what he eloquently offered. Instead of meat, I'd dutifully eat salads for both lunch and dinner. *Let's eat lots and lots of vegetables,* the salesman would say, encouraging me with *It's healthy!* He didn't offer a substitute source of protein as part of my new "healthy" diet, because the fact was, he really didn't care about health. He also didn't want me to eat anything that wasn't low-fat or fat-free. But he did finally acquiesce and let me have booze, as abstinence wouldn't have appeared "normal" for a Big Ten college student.

The salesman's sole goal was meeting a quota for thin and toned thighs. The only part of me that became thinner from his unflagging efforts, however, was my hair. Months after I started my salad diet, my hair began to fall out again, strand by fragile strand. *It's just lack of protein, not head cancer!* the salesman whispered, panicked. Knowing the potential power of my monster's death-themed marketing messages, my salesman couldn't let "head cancer" take hold again, as he knew I'd cease to care about my appearance if I thought I was dying.

So he quickly delivered a new proposal: *Put chicken back in your diet and cut your hair really short so no one will notice it's thinner.* I signed on the dotted line and once again endured months of regrowing half my head of hair.

Despite the salesman's steadfast efforts, my thighs never did get any thinner. Not during my sophomore year, as Evie and I grew further and further apart, and I managed, with effort, to make a few friends at my sorority. Not during my junior year, when I moved into my sorority house and was accepted into the U of I College of Commerce, following the decision I'd made two years earlier, after ten minutes of hurried thought. Not during my senior year, when I'd taken a semester off to work at Walt Disney World as part of their College Program, coming back for my final semester only to have another breakdown that stemmed from my Quest for distraction, perfection, and absolution. A breakdown very much like the one I'd had in high school, this one left me sobbing alone on my bed at my sorority under the suffocating weight of shadows I couldn't seem to escape.

After running four miles a day for more than three years, graduating in the top three percent of the University of Illinois class of 1993, and earning a sparkling new job at a big company in Chicago … were my thighs and knees any more to the salesman's liking?

Of course not.

It would be another two decades before I'd truly understand what happened to me during college. And before I'd fully grasp a fundamental principle of life: that sunlight doesn't exist without shadows. That shadows are always most distinct in the brightest sun. That an imperfect, gauzy smattering of gray clouds is the only thing that makes shadows disappear.

A few years ago, as I surfed Facebook, I found a link to a blog post written by one of the women in my pledge class about her time in our sorority. I started skimming the post, assuming I knew what she'd say, but by the second sentence, I realized our experiences of our sorority had been completely different:

> As I whittled down the list of potential new places to live and people to become friends with, one house stood head and shoulders among the rest. Because the girls were just so cool. And I wanted to be part of their coolness. At the last party, the president of that house offered a nugget of sage advice to me and the rest of the clueless rushees. "Pick the house where you can imagine yourselves brushing your teeth with the women around you."

And that, my friends, is one of the many reasons why I chose [our sorority]. They truly were the coolest chicks. They were laid back. Real. Sarcastic. Happy to hold your hair back for you on your 21st birthday, and also willing to call bullshit on you when necessary. They cut my bangs and loaned me their computers. They broke rules, poured me beer and listened to me when I needed it most.

I finished reading, then read it again. And again. Because for the first time, I understood what it must have been like to sit in that TV room and eat buttered popcorn with "sisters." To go on Walk Out. To bond with people who were very much like me in all the ways that really counted.

I felt a sick rush of regret and finally understood the recurring dream I'd had ever since I'd graduated and left my beloved university full of both sun and shadows:

> I'm walking on campus. I feel giddy, I'm so happy to be back. I whirl around, looking for familiar landmarks, and realize I'm lost. This is the quad, isn't it? I start running up to buildings, panicked. Is this the English building, where I took Rhetoric? Red brick looms in front of me, but there are no white stately columns, so it must not be. I whirl around again, looking for Altgeld Hall, that craggy old grandfather of a building where I labored over differential equations. Where is it? I run willy-nilly, because these landmarks are on Wright Street, and I'm trying to find Wright Street. Wright Street, I mouth silently, turning in circles. Where the bus line runs. Where the bike lanes are. Where my sorority house stands.

I know I'm at the University of Illinois. Sometimes I even know I'm in a dream. I also know instinctively, every time, that I'm supposed to go back to my sorority house and live there. But can I find it?

And if I do, will they know me?

Will I know them?

Or will I continue to be lost, lost, lost, entranced by enticing, echoing whispers, and miss the life that's right before me?

PART II

CHAPTER 6

The Gravitron

I stared at the mile marker in the distance, willing it to announce that I'd made progress in my last fifteen minutes of driving. Squinting, I tried to make out the numbers to the right of what I knew must be "Atlanta." Did it say 70 or 60? As I stared, I reached down, picked up my Diet Coke, and sipped it mindlessly.

"Thank God for caffeine," I muttered as my Honda sped along. "Otherwise I'd never be able to stay awake and I'd probably end up in a ditch alongside the road somewhere."

Maybe the crash would kill you, a voice from far away suggested. *Even at age twenty-eight, that would be a lot better end than what's in store for you.*

I cringed, my shoulders tightening against my mind's constant harangue. Would it never let up? Would I ever get a break?

"I'm fine," I said, willing my mind to be silent, just for once.

The road sign was coming closer, its unnatural green in sharp contrast to the surrounding springtime Alabama landscape.

Seventy. Damn.

Still holding my sweating tumbler, I took another swig and tried to remember how much was left of the two-liter bottle of Diet Coke I'd shoved in a cooler before leaving the house this morning. As I reached to unzip the cooler's top, my cell phone began its insistent chirping.

I sighed and cued up my best I-love-my-job-and-I'm-so-happy-right-now voice, one I'd perfected when I'd worked in attractions at Disney, trying to make "keep your hands and arms inside the ride at all times" sound something other than rote.

"Thanks for calling RR Donnelley, this is Shala."

"This is Rocky," the caller said in a singsong voice, playfully parroting my greeting.

"Rocky! Save me from this drive. I still have seventy miles to go."

Rocky, office manager for RR Donnelley's sales office in Buckhead, was to me part Girl Friday assistant, part rock-solid friend, and part kindly grandmother. A decades-long employee of the printing juggernaut that was Donnelley, Rocky helped me and the two other Atlanta-based sales representatives manage the juggling acts necessary to meet multimillion-dollar annual sales quotas.

"Oh, poor baby," she said, her gravelly voice half caring, half dismissive. "Bob from the Pontiac plant called to see how your meeting went."

I'd joined the ranks of Donnelley's sales team four and a half years earlier, as part of the Chicago-based information services group for the international printing company. Our group sold to nontraditional Donnelley customers: advertising agencies, corporations, mom-and-pop catalog companies, niche book and magazine publishers. Our job was to "fill the holes": the gaps of time when the mammoth printing presses weren't running millions of copies of newsstand magazines or the latest *New York Times* bestseller.

I was driving home from meeting with a new customer, an interior designer in Birmingham, Alabama, who had printed her design magazine with Donnelley for the first time the month before.

"You can tell Bob that Rosalind was pleased with the first printing. She wants us to do quotes for a multiyear contract. Even though I won't be her rep anymore, I think she's going to stay with us."

"Well, that will make him happy," Rocky said. "Are you coming back to the office when you get into town, or going home?"

The voice piped up again, dripping with sarcasm. *Glad you're keeping up appearances, making your coworkers happy. Although won't that make their shock all the more pronounced when they find out the truth about you?*

I'd learned a lot about happiness—or more accurately, projecting happiness—while working at Disney in their College Program during my senior year. How to appear happy whenever I was "onstage." How to make it look as if there were nothing else in the world I'd rather be doing than what I was doing right then. But while I seemed to be a champion at making other people happy, I seemed to be an expert at making myself miserable.

I looked over at the cooler, still wondering how much caffeine was left. *It doesn't matter how much soda you drink, so drink up, because the long term doesn't matter, don't you get that?* The voice, like a radio permanently turned to "on," had a comment about everything.

"Shala, are you there or did I lose you?"

"Oh, sorry… probably going home. I'm really pooped after getting up early to drive to Birmingham."

"Okay, then. See you in the morning."

"Yup, see you then." I rang off and pulled the fabric handles of the cooler toward me so I could pour the rest of the Diet Coke into my cup.

Whereas my first sales job had entailed covering various suburbs on the South Side of Chicago by car each week, my job at RR Donnelley required me to fly all over the country, and sometimes all over the world, to visit prospective customers and be with them when their jobs printed. I did have some customers within a few hours' drive of my current home base in Atlanta, but I still spent a lot more time on airplanes than I did behind the wheel.

Wish I could have flown to Birmingham, I thought. I lifted my cup, the hypnotic hissing of bubbles drowning out the highway noise.

Draining the cup, I marveled at how I'd consumed an entire two-liter bottle of Diet Coke in one day. I hadn't had that much soda since college, when I'd purchased it in bulk. During my junior year, I'd stored my stash of Diet Dr. Pepper in my drafty sorority house closet, only to have it freeze and explode during a particularly harsh Illinois winter.

Staring at the Alabama fields slowly going by outside my window, I thought about the horizon-stretching vastness of the Illinois cornfields. About how it had felt, in the years after college when I was living in Chicago, to drive on its vast network of arterial highways, pushed along by the speed and momentum of people in front of me, behind me, beside me. How my life in Chicago after college had thrummed with pulsating energy that made me feel vibrant and happy and alive.

Life after University of Illinois had seemed too good to be true. I had landed a job in Chicago as a disability sales consultant with UNUM, a disability insurance company. My office, one side of which was floor-to-ceiling windows, was on the fortieth floor of the sixty-five-story southernmost jewel of downtown Chicago's glittering tiara of a skyline. On overcast days, of which there were plenty, I'd come into my office and see only clouds outside my windows. That seemed appropriate, because at age twenty-two, I felt like I was in heaven.

Our building was in the Loop, the downtown business district, appropriately named because it was encircled by the elevated subway, known to locals as the "L." On the days I wasn't driving to my South-Side sales territory, I rode the L to and from the office. After taking the L home at night, I'd unabashedly gaze from my eighty-plus-year-old apartment—nestled on the border between the Gold Coast and the Near North Side neighborhoods, its ancient radiators hissing and popping in the background—into the windows of the high rise across the street, imagining the lives of people rich and successful enough to afford such luxury. After determining that I wasn't yet among them and couldn't manage paying for my apartment in this opulent neighborhood, I'd moved to a walk-up studio apartment in the yuppier area of Lakeview. Riding shoulder to shoulder on the L with other Lakeview Big Ten graduates, we faked being as comfortable in stiff business suits as we'd been a short time ago in our college attire of jeans and baggy sweatshirts.

I fell in love easily in those days, but not with people: with universities, cities, and public transportation. I was as infatuated with the L as I'd been with the University of Illinois. To a girl from Tennessee, riding it was a sensory symphony: the high-pitched keening as it clumsily navigated sharp turns; the rumbling thunk-thunk-thunk, thunk-thunk-thunk as the cars lumbered along the age-old, elevated tracks; the homes rushing past, lit windows giving flashes into the lives within, mere feet from the passing train. I felt at home on the L in a way I'd never felt at home in any other place. I felt a communion with the other passengers, all of us lucky enough to have been chosen to work among the rich, the powerful, the credentialed. I felt, as I rode the L, as if my life had a soundtrack, something like the song "St. Elmo's Fire," with its crescendo of guitars and horns and synthesizers so typical of the eighties anthems that had pervaded my adolescence.

With each passing day since I'd graduated from college, I'd cared less and less about what the salesman or my monster had to say. I still didn't love my knees or thighs, but they were hidden under hose and the knee-length-or-longer skirt of my Brooks Brothers suit ... out of sight, out of mind. I was captivated, not by any horrific thoughts, but by Chicago. During the week I drove around the South Side, talking to insurance brokers, fascinated by people whose identities hinged so proudly on their eastern European, Irish, or Italian cultural heritage. On the weekends, I spent hours walking or biking Chicago's neighborhoods, memorizing the orderly grid of streets, or playing softball with the Chicago Social Club in the fields by Lake Shore Drive. My only worries during that time were whether I'd make my sales quota and if my plans for the weekends were worthy of all that Chicago's glittering nightlife had to offer.

When I'd started at UNUM, I never would have guessed that after a year and a half of my fairy-tale new life, I'd get laid off from my dream job, the one that allowed me to ride the L and explore the city that had become my new home. But UNUM decided at the end of 1994 to close our entire office with the exception of a handful of reps, leaving my manager, most of my coworkers, and me out of a job.

Fortunately, I'd already started looking for another job months earlier, in between closing deals during the week and living it up on the weekends, because by then I'd seen the writing on the wall at UNUM. And I'd set my sights on RR Donnelley.

***

RR Donnelley had sales reps rumored to be like the ones who sold for IBM: the best in the business. I'd learned there might be an opportunity at Donnelley through my UNUM coworker Meredith. She'd previously worked as a Donnelley rep, and her husband, Mark, still worked there as a manager. While he didn't have an opening, he knew a vice president who did, and he'd passed along my résumé.

UNUM's hiring process had been thorough, but Donnelley's process was on another level. I interviewed with a bunch of people. I took psychological tests. I even peed in a cup. Most importantly, I met multiple times with the hiring vice president, Peter, a warhorse with more than twenty years' experience etched into the ruddy features of his face. I could tell Peter wouldn't be won over by anything other than exceptional salesmanship, and he made no pretense about the tightrope I walked in his eyes: that he thought my success might be a masterful trompe l'oeil.

"This job is not like marketing insurance," Peter said to me somewhat dismissively during one of our later interviews, his dark-green eyes boring into mine, mouth turned down, as if his words left a bitter aftertaste. "As you've probably heard from Mark, we sell multimillion-dollar printing projects to big companies. They involve multiple printing divisions. They're complex. And even after they're sold, reps, who are paid on commission, don't get paid until the customer pays the invoice, so it's up to the rep to make sure the job goes smoothly."

With a swift knock on the door, his secretary popped her head in. "Peter, sorry to interrupt. I need a signature." She walked briskly to his desk, glancing at me with a warm, "hang in there" expression. He swirled around in his chair, took a Mont Blanc pen from his cherry credenza, and signed the papers.

Turning back to me as his secretary left and silently shut the door behind her, he continued as if the interruption hadn't occurred. "No one is going to give you a list of prospects. Our reps find them. You'd have to build a sales pipeline large enough to make your quota each year, knowing some of the big deals can take years to cultivate."

I don't think I'd moved a muscle since Peter started talking. He had to be the scariest person I'd ever met. I shifted in my suit, stiffly patterned with tiny green and black checks, feeling the prickles in my foot as my right leg, tightly crossed over my left, started to go numb. I tried to imagine Peter with the kids I saw in the photos on his richly veneered credenza. He couldn't be this tough, this intimidating, with everyone in his life.

I leaned forward in my chair. "The complexity and challenge are what excite me about this opportunity," I said, ignoring the swirling anxiety in the pit of my stomach. "I made my quota in one of the hardest territories at UNUM in fewer than eleven months because I'm tenacious, hard-working, and a creative problem-solver. Getting laid off from the company was a blessing, because I want a more challenging opportunity where I can really make a difference." I presented my best interview-speak, because I wanted this job. I wanted the big sales commissions, the glamorous travel, the prestige. I'd tell Peter whatever he wanted to hear to get it.

What I didn't tell Peter directly, but I imagine he could gather through my demeanor, was that I was intense. I'd been an intense Type A overachiever since high school. My sessions with Dr. Prasad had done nothing to temper my Quest. I virtually vibrated with a mixture of energy, drive, and anxiety. I knew I was only as good as my last success, which had a shelf life. Like fruit left ripening on the vine, success had a short window in which it could be enjoyed before it—and my self-worth—started to decay. I was intense because I needed to be, because the survival of my very soul depended upon how well I did. Success was a form of absolution: tacit confirmation from others that I was okay.

My intensity turned out not to play in my favor with Peter. Toward the end of my months-long campaign to win him over, I learned I was competing with another woman for the job. Peter blithely told me during one conversation that while we were both highly qualified, I was coming across, in comparison to her, as "not as much fun."

What Peter didn't know, however, was that I approached having fun with the same zeal as I approached my job. None of my fun, however, was appropriate to share on a résumé, because the only way I seemed to be able to have fun and wind down from the fervor of work was to drink. While the salesman had kept me from parties during the summer between my freshman and sophomore years of college, it only sporadically interfered with partying thereafter, and I could think of numerous examples of how much fun I could be.

Someone was always available to go to happy hour on Friday evenings, and I'd hang out with them for an hour or two in dark-paneled Loop dive bars drinking Goose Island beer before heading home on the L to go out with friends from college or my softball team. The summer after I graduated, a bunch of friends rented a party bus for a Jimmy Buffett concert, and I distinctly remember cheering on my softball buddy, Sharon, while she drank beer out of her boyfriend's shoe as the converted school bus, filled with intoxicated yuppies, groaned and rattled its way back to the city after the concert.

When I'd worked at Disney, I'd met my boyfriend Ricardo in the party tent at Vista Way, the apartment complex where all the College Program participants lived. The party tent in the complex's parking lot had supposedly been set up in case parties held in individual apartments became too rowdy. I'd been at a seventies party and Ricardo had been at a toga party, and as the fun being had at both had outgrown the constraints of the thin-walled apartments, he and I had met for the first time late that night in the party tent.

As the salesman's whispered pitches had become quieter after college, I'd become better and better at having fun. In fact, I was probably *too good* at having fun, as sometimes the next morning I didn't quite remember exactly how much or what type of fun I'd had. One Sunday morning, as Sharon and I woke up to pounding headaches in my tiny apartment in Lakeview, my new cats Freddie and Abby climbing all over us meowing to be fed, she regaled me with the story of how, after I'd had one too many margaritas at El Jardin, a bar renowned for powerfully strong drinks and bras hanging from the ceiling, I'd told a bouncer at another bar to "Fuck off!" when he wouldn't let us in because I was too drunk.

"I did not!" I said, sitting up on my antiquated daybed, shocked at my own behavior.

"You did! It was hilarious. Just wake up Jamie and ask him!"

Jamie? I woozily leaned over the edge of my daybed to find that our friend from softball was still asleep on the floor below me. I hadn't even remembered he'd come home with us in the wee hours of the morning.

Fun was clearly not a problem. In fact, I always seemed to be at one end of the spectrum or the other: working to excess or drinking to excess.

Eventually, seeing qualities in both my competitor and me that he didn't want to lose, Peter hired us both. While she and I did well over the ensuing years, I felt both triumph and schadenfreude when Peter chose me for the 1996 Sales Rookie of the Year, commemorated with a nine-inch-high replica of Virginio Ferrari's *Continuity,* the soaring bronze sculpture that graced the lobby of the RR Donnelley Building in downtown Chicago.

I thrived on this recognition. No longer able to earn grades I could use to measure my value, I devised other proxies to assess my worth. The number of hours I worked, which I could keep extraordinarily high by ensuring on days when I was in the office that I arrived before and left after Peter. The number of notes I received from customers or important people within Donnelley telling me what a wonderful job I was doing. The opportunities I was given to "move up," all of which I took, afraid of losing my job and my value if I didn't, even though one was a transfer from my beloved Chicago to sprawling Atlanta. The amount of business I closed, which I could measure six ways to Sunday: number of new customers; percentage to quota and by what month of the year; and my favorite—how much money I was earning. As my bank account grew with the proceeds of fat commission checks, I saw every additional dollar deposited as quantifiable proof that I was okay.

After a few years, however, as the dust collected, literally and figuratively, on *Continuity*, I grew restless. I felt empty. The money, the power, the respect I received—none of it seemed to matter. After living for a few years in Atlanta, I started seeing a therapist, Dr. Cowles, to see if I could figure out why, with all that was going right in my life, I was so very miserable.

One reason was clearly my marriage. I wasn't quite sure why I'd married Todd shortly after moving to Atlanta. I'd dated him in Chicago, even though we didn't have much in common. I'd even broken up with him shortly before we got engaged because I'd had a fling, unbeknownst to Todd, with someone I'd met through work. But he asked me to get back together, and not wanting to hurt his feelings (because what kind of a person would I be if I did that?), I'd agreed.

I'd been in love once, but not with Todd. With Ricardo, my boyfriend at Disney. Ricardo was a drop-dead gorgeous Mexican from south Texas, built like the quarterback he'd been in high school. As kind as he was good-looking, Ricardo had worked in retail at the Disney-MGM Studios Theme Park while I worked as an attractions hostess at The Universe of Energy, aka "the dinosaur ride," at EPCOT. Our time together was a whirlwind, storybook romance, complete with frequent movie-like dates that included walking through Cinderella's castle in the moonlight and watching EPCOT's IllumiNations fireworks display surrounded by oohing and aahing children.

Ricardo and I had dated long distance during my last semester in college. He visited me on his spring break and I went to Texas on his. Which is where everything went wrong, because even though I loved him, I wouldn't have sex with him. I wouldn't have sex with anyone, because sex could lead to getting pregnant. My mind had been warning me about the dangers of becoming pregnant since dating Doug in high school, even though I'd never even come close to having sex. *Pregnancy could ruin your life!* my mind shrieked so loudly and so often that I started believing that pregnancy, and therefore sex, were just bad, even though I couldn't have explained exactly why. Ricardo broke up with me shortly after my visit to Texas, telling me over long distance he was getting back together with his former high-school girlfriend, whom I hated thereafter from afar.

I'd dismissed relationships ever since Ricardo left me. I told myself no one is supposed to be as happy as I was with Ricardo because Disney had created that happiness. That kind of love didn't really exist. In my all-or-nothing world, I either had blissful, delirious, intoxicating love that came from dating someone at The Most Magical Place on Earth, or I had a relationship that made me miserable.

I'd been sort of miserable with Todd from the beginning. He'd proposed to me in Chicago while we were out to dinner with my biggest customer, who'd flown in from Memphis so I could take him and his cousin to a Bulls game in Donnelley's box at United Center. I'd answered Todd's proposal with what I thought I was supposed to say: yes. That night, drinking champagne from box seats with Todd and Peter and my customers while watching Michael Jordan fly through the air, making basket after basket, it all did seem a little Disneyesque, big and glamorous. A year later, Todd and I got married at a restaurant on the banks of the Chattahoochee River in Atlanta.

That was the same night Princess Diana died in Paris. As it turned out, it was also the night I started to die, at least inside, because on that day I knew no more about who I wanted to be with or if I even wanted to get married than I'd known in college about what I wanted to do with my life.

I'd been taught from a young age that reality was warped, the world wasn't safe, and what I wanted didn't matter. The only thing that mattered was what my mind—my monster—wanted. My life was like an amusement-park Gravitron: my mind wielded a centrifugal force that pressed me back into a padded wall, motionless and without control, as I picked careers and partners and my life's entire course, the Gravitron dropping the floor out from under me every time.

The inspiring, glorious soundtrack I'd heard since my early days in Chicago had faded, leaving me with only a distant memory of the music that used to fill my life. I wasn't in love with Todd and never had been, as I learned during my sessions with Dr. Cowles, a kindly woman in her fifties with an office whose windows overlooked Buckhead in Atlanta.

Now that I'd moved to Atlanta, away from my beloved Chicago, I realized I wasn't in love with my job, either. Still in the Gravitron and true to form, however, I decided over the course of a few sessions with Dr. Cowles that quitting my job and getting an MBA might just get my life back on course.

That decision had brought me to my long, weary, well-caffeinated drive from Alabama to Atlanta. I'd been visiting my customer in Birmingham to tell her I was leaving Donnelley to attend Emory's Goizueta Business School in the fall. What I didn't share with her was that Emory seemed to be so impressed by my intense drive for "excellence," they'd awarded me one of a handful of Woodruff Fellowships. Another feather in my "worthy" cap.

I checked the odometer, bright afternoon sun glaring off the windshield. Only thirty miles to go. I exhaled, feeling the weight of my eyelids, and reached down for another drink. Empty. Damn. Knowing I wouldn't be able to stay awake enough to drive, not even for another half hour, I put on my turn signal and exited, pulled into the nearest gas station, and bought another Diet Coke.

As I started on what would be my third liter of soda that day, I thought about the irony of that Woodruff Fellowship. How if Emory *really* knew the capabilities of my mind, they'd commit me to the psychiatric ward of Emory University Hospital, not admit me to the ranks of their elite. Because not only had I become restless in the years since I'd moved to Atlanta, but my mind, my monster, had become restless, too. So restless, in fact, that a few weeks ago, for the first time in my life, someone had discovered my monster's presence and given it a name.

"So you can get through the next couple of months of your job, right, now that you know you're going to Emory on a full ride?" Dr. Cowles had asked at the beginning of our session.

"Sure. It won't be a problem. I'll just keep doing what I do. Doing proposals for customers. Checking them four times before ..." I stopped, realizing what I'd just let slip, and tried to recover. "... I mean just checking them before they go out, like normal. Same old, same old."

Dr. Cowles looked up and slid her reading glasses down the bridge of her nose so she could better focus on me. She'd heard the slip, and I could tell from the way she looked at me that she knew it was significant. "What do you mean, 'check them four times'?"

Shit. The heat rose in my face and I was transported back ten years, to when I'd sat on Dr. Prasad's knobbly fabricked couch, the cold hard barrel of a weapon pressed into my temple. Now my mind—restless no more and angry that I was about to screw up everything: *holy shit, what have you done?*—cocked its pistol, ramming it into my scalp.

My instantly dry mouth rendered me mute. My hands shook as once again, I heard Rule #1:

> *You cannot get caught doing these things or thinking these thoughts.*
> *Because if you do, you will have to explain yourself.*
> *And you don't tell what you see in your mind.*
> *Because if you do, all those bad things you see ... you will make them happen.*

Rule #1 was unbreakable. I would need to do whatever was necessary to uphold its solemn covenant.

"I—I don't know why I said that," I stammered, wringing my hands in my lap. I couldn't tell whether the deafening roar I heard came from the white-noise machine outside her door or the shrieking monster inside my head.

Dr. Cowles took off her glasses. Put down her papers. She was not convinced. "Are there lots of things you do four times?"

No one had ever directly asked me about my monster. I'd never had to blatantly lie. Ironically, outright lying, even about this, made my monster nervous. In its anxiety, it twisted the gun barrel into my temple and whispered, *You get us out of this, you understand? You don't have to lie. Be vague, be deceptive, be charming. I don't give a shit. But make sure she doesn't find out about me.*

"No, not really," I lied. I did things in fours all the time.

"Not really?"

"No. No." I swallowed hard.

She stared at me, still unconvinced, then got up, dug in a file drawer, and came back holding a few papers.

"Okay, what about any of these things. Are you worried about germs?"

Thank God I wasn't hooked up to a lie detector. "No more than anyone else."

"Are you worried about catching a disease?"

I froze. I thought back to New Year's Day, five months earlier. How I'd opened my eyes that morning and thought about how I had to pee. Thought I should get up and go to the bathroom.

The bathroom.

I'd sat up in bed and looked down at the palm of my hand, suddenly wide awake. It all came rushing back: a blur of colors, sounds, light. The New Year's Eve party. Being on the host committee. Having once again had too much to drink, spilling a glass of red wine on Todd's tuxedo shirt. Going to the restroom to get some paper towels, seeing what a mess the bathroom was, feeling as a host committee member I should clean it up. Squatting down in my black cocktail dress and grabbing a wad of discarded paper towels to throw them away, not realizing they were covering broken glass. A broken beer bottle. How I'd thrown away the towels to find a shard from the beer bottle sticking out of my palm. How my monster, ever since that night, had tormented me: telling me how stupid I was, how incredibly reckless, to have cut myself on a beer bottle that contained backwash from a person who'd had a cut in his mouth and who possibly, maybe, probably had AIDS. How my future had been foreshortened and now careened, like an out-of-control carnival ride, toward an embarrassing, ugly, unstoppable death.

"No," I whispered, barely audible, telling the biggest lie of my life.

If Dr. Cowles could have looked into my brain, she would have seen that thoughts about AIDS and HIV had become the new soundtrack of my life. I was still functioning at work, using my best Disney-taught onstage skills to project an aura of happiness and confidence. But wherever I was, I wasn't really there. Because I was really back on that old stage in the theater of my mind, where we once again engaged in our never-ending, exhausting pas de deux.

You've given yourself AIDS, you stupid girl!

No, that's not how you get AIDS! I'm fine!

That's what you think. And you can't even get tested because it takes six months for the virus to incubate.

It doesn't matter. I know that's not how HIV and AIDS are transmitted.

What you know is meaningless! You know nothing. I know everything, and you are going to die!

I could hear it constantly, endlessly berating me. I had no reprieve. Reasoning with my mind was useless and, in fact, seemed to make things worse. And nothing—not even my workaholic ways—would make the thoughts stop. From the first moment I woke up until the time I went to bed, drained and demoralized, I heard my monster's voice. Heard it taunt me about a disease that had terrified me ever since I was twelve years old and I heard Tom Brokaw talk about HIV and chimpanzees on *NBC Nightly News* as I ate my peas and carrots in the kitchen with my parents.

I didn't share any of this with Dr. Cowles. Not even when she boldly told me she thought I had a monster and she could tell me its name.

"I think you might be holding back on me a little, Shala. Just from things you've said in previous sessions and your comments today, I think you might have something called OCD, or obsessive-compulsive disorder. I'm going to send you to a psychiatrist for some medication, as I think that will make you feel better."

An authority figure had said I should go to a doctor, so off to the psychiatrist I went, telling her that Dr. Cowles said I had something called OCD.

The monster I could now name was eerily quiet during this visit, perhaps because while I agreed with the doctor that yes, my thoughts were a little bothersome at times, I shared nothing else.

Or perhaps because my OCD had some sixth sense of what was yet to come.

The psychiatrist said having OCD was like having a gate in your mind that would never shut.

"The thoughts just keep going through the gate because it won't close," she said. "I'm going to give you some medicine to help your brain shut that door."

I left her office that day with a little brown paper bag of this supposed gate-closing wonder drug called Medicine A.

That had been three weeks ago, and I'd been taking it ever since. While it seemed as though the drug had stuffed a sock in my monster's mouth, I could still make out its words. And its fear-driven vitriol.

Turning down my monster's volume was not all Medicine A did, however. My stomach now ached for no apparent reason. My mouth was constantly dry. I'd also stopped sleeping, thus the need to consume large quantities of soda. Night after night, I'd lie awake in bed beside Todd and stare at the ceiling, feeling numb and hopeless and alone.

I drained the rest of my Diet Coke as I exited in Atlanta, grateful to have made it home. Pulling into the driveway of our tiny one-story ranch house, I sighed with relief that Todd's car wasn't in the carport.

My cats Freddie and Abby met me at the door. I picked up Abby, kissing her on her soft, black head, feeling the warmth of the pads on her back paws as I supported her in my arms. She leapt down and I grabbed Fred, carrying him like an overlarge stuffed toy to the bathroom, tears falling on his orange-and-white back as I suddenly felt that everything I faced—my monster's unending AIDS threats, my bone-numbing fatigue, my unhappy marriage—had become too much to bear.

"I can't do it anymore, Freddie," I said, starting to cry in earnest. "I can't sleep. I can barely function. Yes, my thoughts are a little quieter, but I can still hear them. They still tell me I'm going to die. I just can't do this anymore."

I leaned against the bathroom wall, then slid down as Fred jumped to the floor, my sides heaving with sobs of grief: for Chicago, for Ricardo, for the life of freedom and joy and success that I just couldn't hold onto, no matter how successful I seemed in my never-ending Quest.

A chirping sound rang out from my cell phone in the kitchen. I let it go to voicemail.

"It's probably Rocky," I said between sobs to Fred and Abby, who loyally sat beside me. "If she could see me now, she'd never believe it."

Truth was, Rocky didn't know me. Todd didn't know me. No one knew me. Worse, I was coming to realize I didn't even know myself.

I did know I couldn't take the lack of sleep anymore. My monster made it hard enough for me to function, and with no sleep, I was coming apart at the seams. I'd battled my monster for twenty-seven years without medication, without knowing its name. Regardless of how long I had to left to live, I couldn't live like *this*. I grabbed the rest of the Medicine A sample pack from the bathroom counter and resolutely threw it into the trash, my decision's sound ricocheting through the silence.

CHAPTER 7

Fueling the Fire

"Look at this!" I held up a copy of *How to Win Friends and Influence People* so Alex could see the cover.

"Wow!" he said as he walked around the table toward me, hand reaching out to take the book.

"You want to get it?"

"Definitely."

Alex added Dale Carnegie's classic to the stack of books he carried against his hip as we both browsed the book-sale dollar table, looking for more treasures. Going to a book sale hadn't been on our agenda for this hot summer Sunday in Atlanta, but when we'd seen the enormous white tent in a shopping center parking lot, festooned with a colorful "USED BOOK SALE" sign, we couldn't resist.

Alex, short for Alejandro, was my fiancé and, like me, in his early thirties. My marriage to Todd had died a painful death a few years ago. Not one for spending time figuring out *why* I ended up married and divorced so quickly in order to prevent such a catastrophe from repeating itself, I'd wasted no time falling in love with one of the many eligible, attractive, successful men in my business school class. Alex had graduated with me in the Emory MBA class of 2001 and asked me to marry him the next year.

Eligible men had not been my only interest at B-school; I'd also become enamored of the internet, deciding I wanted to work in the fast-paced, Type A world of technology after graduation. After doing an internship at a local technology incubator, I'd been offered a job at XcelleNet, an Atlanta-based tech company. My main attraction to the company was not, however, its software products. It was the CEO, Joan Herbig.

Joan was a star. After a variety of jobs in the tech world, she'd risen quickly from a marketing role to become chief executive officer of XcelleNet. She was smart, savvy, and respected. She could command a room with poise and grace, communicating a sense of urgency with no trace of anxiety. I wanted her brand of intensity, which was like a beautiful horse running with measured, confident strides across a field, tossing its head with fiery authority. My intensity looked more like a gangly colt wobbling on unsteady legs, pushed by fear to run as fast as possible from the dangers of an unknown world.

I also wanted Joan's job. Not right out of business school, but eventually. Because what could be better confirmation that I was okay than being chosen to be a CEO? What could be a better Holy Grail in my Quest?

After being at XcelleNet for a year in marketing, I'd asked Joan's permission to start a Business Book Club. She'd readily agreed, so once a month employees from all over the company discussed business books and how they applied to XcelleNet. As a result, I was always on the lookout for good books to propose. Thus my attraction to the parking-lot book sale.

I continued scanning titles, looking for classics that the Business Book Club might enjoy, as Alex finished perusing the dollar section and drifted over to travel books.

Then I saw it. I put out my hand to steady myself against the nearest table as my world started to spin.

Kissing Doorknobs.

I knew instantly what this book was about. This was a book about my monster. About OCD. I knew this because I'd recently started kissing things that shouldn't be kissed. Like things I was throwing away. I'd kiss the trash four times while mumbling an incantation that kept my parents safe, then let the anointed object fall into the trash can, taking its whispered blessing into the magical underworld where the gods of my mind did its bidding.

No one had ever caught me doing this ritual, of course. I could stand in front of the trash can with my hand to my mouth, the piece of trash hidden in the teepee of my pinched fingers, looking for all the world like I was pondering a weighty problem. If anyone saw my lips move, they'd just assume I was talking to myself in service of solving whatever issue I was contemplating.

Even though I was a master illusionist, I really did have a weighty problem. Ever since the beer-bottle incident at the New Year's Eve party, my monster had been on the prowl. Gone were the days, weeks, months, or even years when it would lie dormant, like a cicada patiently feeding underground, waiting for the right time to emerge. The months and months I'd danced with my OCD to the tune of "Do I have HIV/AIDS?" had seemed somehow to nourish it, turning it into a super beast. Even learning from my doctor the negative results of my AIDS test, which shame-faced and frightened I'd requested six months into my ordeal, only seemed to whet my monster's appetite. Salivating, it now tirelessly searched for the next imminent threat.

Anything seemed to be fair game. If I didn't smile when I passed a mirror, my OCD said something would happen to ruin my reputation or land me in jail. If I thought something unkind about a coworker, my monster whispered that perhaps I'd said it out loud, exposing what a rotten person I really was. If I didn't pay perfect attention as I drove, my brain questioned how I could be sure I hadn't hit someone or caused an accident that left innocent bystanders bleeding and maimed. If I gave a presentation, my mind suggested afterward that perhaps I'd grabbed my crotch as I'd advanced a slide, and that's why that guy in the back row had looked at me askance.

It was hard to find relief. Drinking had always temporarily muted my monster, providing much needed respite, but I didn't drink much anymore. I'd continued my partying ways through my first year of business school, but trying to manage an overwhelming amount of B-school homework while hungover had made my monster nervous. What if someone noticed how much we were drinking? What if we were so hungover we couldn't get good grades? What would we be, if we weren't a superstar Woodruff Scholar: winning case competitions, earning high grades, and doing everything necessary to eventually make it to the executive suite in a Fortune 500 company?

For once, I agreed with my monster's reasoning. I knew drinking worked *too well* to shut up my monster in the time I was intoxicated—although not after—and I could see how easy it was for me to let one drink become two, then three, then a number I wouldn't remember the next day. Therefore, I started limiting myself to one. It took a lot of willpower, especially when everyone else went bottoms up. What made it even more challenging, however, was that I was already using my willpower reserves to fight the never-ending battle with my monster, one I seemed to be losing.

My life had become all OCD, all the time. Almost like a radio station I was unable to turn down, no matter what I did. *All danger, all the time. Your home for the worst-case scenario. All the bad things that could happen to you and the people you love, broadcast uninterrupted, twenty-four hours a day ... for your listening hell.* My own private radio permanently tuned to the danger station: WDNG.

So I knew exactly what *Kissing Doorknobs* was about. Letting go of the table, I snatched the book, hunching over as I hungrily speed-read the back cover, taking in the words "... recited prayers over and over ..." Just like I had when I was a kid.

I didn't need to read any more. I straightened up, the world righting itself again as I surreptitiously tucked *Kissing Doorknobs* under my arm, understanding for the first time I might not be the only person in the world whose head was controlled by a monster.

"So does this technique make sense to you? Do you think you can use it?"

How apropos, I thought as I sat across from this gentle, bearded teddy bear of a man, that he was my *fourth* therapist. And that I was thirty-one, which, when I added the three and the one together, equaled four. And that I was on my fourth job since college, if I counted my internship. And that it had been four years since I'd been diagnosed with OCD. Hopefully a set of four fours meant that this time, therapy would work.

"I think so," I said. "So basically, when I have an obsessive thought, I'm supposed to stop it by thinking of a relaxing image then replace the thought with a positive one?"

"That's right," he said, leaning back in his winged armchair. "In no time at all, you'll be feeling better."

I nodded and got up, pulling my copay check out of my wallet.

"Thank you. See you in two weeks," I said, as I left my second appointment with Dr. Kowalski for treatment of my OCD.

As I walked through the waiting room, I smiled into the mirror above the couch. I'd shared this little compulsion with Dr. Kowalski, and he'd told me it was okay, that it was harmless and I could keep it. So every time I passed a mirror, I continued to smile.

It had been surprisingly easy this time to tell Dr. Kowalski what was going on, to break Rule #1, I thought as I walked to my car. No gun barrels pressed menacingly into my temple. No Rule #1 screeched in my ear. No threats, taunts, or terrorizing of any kind from my monster.

Nothing.

I was in therapy again, yet my monster seemed to be ignoring this fact.

Had I been a more strategic thinker, I might have intuited that something was just *wrong* about my monster's lack of reaction. That when a general not only threatens to attack the enemy but does so with guns blazing, and the enemy acts as if nothing at all has happened, then something just isn't adding up. That perhaps the general should order a cease fire and ask his commanders the tough questions to identify what key piece of intelligence they're missing before they get ambushed from behind.

I was in too much of a hurry, however, to become a director, then a VP, then a CEO, to spend time thinking about my monster's strategy. I knew I had OCD. After reading *Kissing Doorknobs,* I also knew there was treatment. The book had said I needed behavior therapy. So in my mind, all I had to do was pick a psychologist and explain that I had OCD, and he or she would tell me the magic "behavior therapy" things I needed to do to get better.

As I got into my car to head the short distance home from Dr. Kowalski's office, I marveled at how easy it had been to find a therapist. I'd called XcelleNet's employee assistance program and said I needed to see someone who had evening hours, who was covered by my insurance, and whose office wasn't too far from where I lived.

After all, how hard could it possibly be to treat OCD? I didn't know exactly what kind of behavior therapy I was looking for, or even what behavior therapy was, but I figured any psychologist would know what to do if I just gave them the information they needed.

I'd gleaned all that information from *Kissing Doorknobs*. The book had taught me that the intrusive thoughts I had were called *obsessions*, and the things that I did to make myself feel better when I had obsessions were called *compulsions*. With that taxonomy, I was quickly able to dissect exactly what my monster had been doing to me, creating a list of nine different categories of my obsessions and their corresponding compulsions.

Instead of explaining everything verbally to Dr. Kowalski, I'd written it all down on five sheets of paper and handed them to him at my first session. Those five sheets contained an executive summary (good MBA that I was), a timeline of all the things my monster had done to me over the years, the list of all my obsessions and compulsions, a list of what exacerbated my OCD and what made it subside, and the hypothesis that had driven my decision to come to therapy: that I was destroying my relationship with Alex because I didn't want to have children, and I didn't want to have children because I had OCD. And that maybe if I could fix the OCD, I could fix the whole "pregnancy is bad" thing and salvage yet another relationship that was slowly falling apart.

Alex desperately wanted children. The night he asked me to marry him, he'd suggested we start trying to conceive. I'd said "yes" to his proposal but "no" to having kids right away. I'd gotten over the whole "sex is bad" thing, but I still firmly believed "pregnancy is bad," still found the thought of having kids repugnant. The concept of getting pregnant had been so frightening for so many years, it wasn't as if I could just magically decide doing so would now be okay. Because it didn't *feel* okay; it felt bad. Maybe because I knew I'd be asking for trouble if I tried to take care of someone else when my monster sometimes made it virtually impossible to take care of myself. At the top of my hypothesis page that I gave to Dr. Kowalski, I'd therefore written the following: "I don't want children because children mean lack of control, which means my OCD will become unmanageable."

What I didn't write was that I knew if I didn't commit to having children, Alex would leave me, just like Ricardo had left me. Alex was aware of my OCD, as I'd told him about it when we'd moved in together after I came back from a semester-long exchange program at London Business School. My characterization of my OCD to Alex, however, had been a complete fabrication: "I have this thing called OCD. It just means I worry a lot."

Alex had seen more than a few "worries" from my OCD over the past year. True, he couldn't actually *see* things like the ghastly images my OCD paraded nightly across my consciousness from its vast repertoire of imaginal carnage: for example, of Fred and Abby tied to train tracks, helpless as a train bore down, pulverizing them into masses of blood-soaked fur and gore. But he did glimpse what the disorder was doing to me, as I battled each night to stem the flow of gratuitous violence. My sharp intake of breath slicing into the quiet of our apartment bedroom. My instant rigidity as OCD's horror show started. Whispers of "No! No! No!" punctuating the stillness as I tried desperately to push the images away, to put it out into the universe that I did *not* want those things to happen.

He also witnessed my ever more frequent explosions of rage, seemingly out of nowhere. Like the night I'd been trying to go to sleep in our apartment during our last semester of business school. On a weeknight like any other, some younger coeds had decided to take a rather noisy dip in the pool—which our apartment bordered—at one in the morning. I'd listened to them splash around, every whoop and holler fueling a fire inside my chest. Did they not know people were trying to sleep? That I was a student in a rigorous MBA program that seemed to require sixteen-hour days of work? That I had OCD I could barely control? That if I didn't get sleep it would be virtually impossible to think the next day, much less deal with financial statements and case studies and interviews and my goddamn disorder that never gave me a moment's peace?

"WILL YOU SHUT UP?" I'd yelled across the pool from our balcony, where I stood in a tattered green robe and baseball cap, Alex aghast behind me. The water undulated lazily around the stunned swimmers, who were spotlighted by the pool's ghostly underwater lighting. "Do you have any idea what time it is? If you don't get out now, I'm calling the cops!"

Alex had been amazingly patient with me, my bizarre rituals, and my all too frequent temper tantrums, which always ended, once the adrenaline subsided, with me lying face down on the floor, sobbing into the carpet with shame and humiliation at the wrathful person inside me who seemed to become more powerful with every passing day.

While Alex seemingly could handle all my craziness, I knew he couldn't handle being denied children. I knew deep down that if I couldn't get my OCD under enough control that we could have kids, I would lose him.

In spite of my OCD, being with Alex made me happy. He was as laid back and gentle as I was uptight and obsessed. He was fun, loving salsa and merengue. He was smart, reading books on business and neuroscience. He was passionate, calling me "baby" and always having his hand somewhere on me. I loved him like I'd loved Ricardo at Disney, and felt that with Alex, I had a chance at that storybook romance that I'd previously dismissed as only possible if you both worked at The Most Magical Place on Earth.

I didn't want to lose him, to have yet another failed relationship on the scorecard I kept in my head: the one where I was doing phenomenally well professionally and disappointingly poorly personally.

So I bared my secrets for Dr. Kowalski, exposing my monster for the hellish devil it was. And all the while, my monster said nothing.

If I'd stopped for just one minute and paid attention to the present moment, instead of self-importantly rushing around with images of myself in a CEO's chair, I would have noticed something more telling than my monster's silence.

That my OCD was watching me. It was leaning back in its own chair, hands behind its head, feet up on its desk, in the ultimate power pose. It had a B-school-infused aura of confidence—smugness, even. A little smirk played on its lips, as it watched me spill my guts to Dr. Kowalski, do my little therapy exercises, and play myself right into its hands.

***

"So let's go over your mood log, Shala, and see how well it's working." Dr. Kowalski's invitations to share what I'd done between sessions always contained what we'd called in sales "the presumptive close."

"Okay," I said, and cleared my throat. It was my ninth session, and I was keeping a record of my obsessive thoughts and working on replacing them with positive thoughts. "The upsetting event was that I wanted to check to make sure my mail had gone down into the post-office mailbox, so I stuck my hand down into it, but after I pulled my hand out I thought I could get a disease."

"Okay, well, how did that thought make you feel?"

A fly buzzed somewhere in the room then went silent. I looked down at the worksheet, hastily photocopied at work when no one else had been in the fluorescent-lit break room. "Scared, anxious, guilty, ashamed, and tense."

These words, copied dutifully from a list of "feeling words" Dr. Kowalski had given me, did nothing to capture the emotions I'd really had upon pulling my hand out of that public mailbox, feeling my palm scrape against the ragged bottom lip of the metal slot, hearing my monster scream that some contaminant had just entered my bloodstream. I'd been engulfed by paralyzing waves of fear and shame: fear that I'd once again put myself in jeopardy of catching some sort of dread disease because I'd done a stupid ritual—pushing my hand down into the mailbox to make sure the mail had indeed gone down—and shame that *I couldn't stop doing compulsions.*

"Good, that sounds accurate. Now what were the negative thoughts that came up for you and what positive thoughts did you use to replace them?"

I heard the fly buzzing again, closer and more insistent. Looking up at Dr. Kowalski, I wanted to interrupt his methodical homework review process with, "But when will 'scared, anxious, guilty, ashamed, and tense' *stop* being accurate? When will I *stop* feeling like this?" That would have been questioning authority, however, something I didn't do.

Instead I said in a monotone, "I thought that I would get a deadly disease from contact with something on the mailbox. I believed that thought one hundred percent at first. But then I substituted the more positive thought that mailmen probably do this all the time to get stuck mail out, and it's perfectly safe."

"And how much do you believe the original negative thought now?"

"About fifty percent."

But if I have molten lava pouring over me, does it really matter if I've reduced the lava flow by half? Or does it still burn the same, searing off flesh at a rate that, while slower, is no less painful or deadly?

"Excellent, Shala!" Dr. Kowalski beamed at me. I could see the individual gray-flecked auburn whiskers in his beard as he spoke.

I envisioned how slowly they must be growing. As slowly as my therapy was progressing.

I just wasn't getting better. In the four months over which I'd had my nine sessions, my OCD hadn't really abated at all. In the past day alone, I'd spent hours obsessing over a conversation I'd had with a colleague whom I was sure I'd offended; reread an email to Joan, the CEO, more than ten times before hitting "Send" to ensure I hadn't accidentally inserted "fuck" into the verbiage; gunned my car through a yellow light because my mind told me something bad would happen if I saw it turn red; and thrown away an entire package of strawberries I'd sliced for a dessert I was making for my seventy-year-old neighbors, because I couldn't be sure I hadn't somehow contaminated it in a way that would overpower their surely compromised immune systems.

I didn't tell Dr. Kowalski any of this. It made me anxious to think of hurting his feelings, as he seemed to be trying so hard to help me, giving me typed-up treatment plans with lofty-sounding goals like "resolve key life conflicts and emotional stressors that fueled compulsive rituals."

With an aim toward reducing these "key life conflicts," several weeks ago Dr. Kowalski had set me the task of writing a letter to my four-year-old self. He'd explained to me that if I clarified my feelings about The Accident, it would help me overcome "death anxiety" and "fears of abandonment," constructs he said were solidified in my mind because I was in an "MVA," or motor vehicle accident, at such a young age. I dutifully wrote a letter to a child who didn't feel like anyone I knew, telling her, "I look at you and I feel really sorry for you. You're this cute little kid who doesn't deserve this."

I also, on Dr. Kowalski's instructions, wrote a letter to my "obsessive-compulsive behaviors," explaining to them that I just didn't need them anymore. I told my behaviors all about the new skills Dr. Kowalski had taught me, and how they could now take a permanent vacation and go off and sip margaritas on a cruise. How I could already see them sitting in a lounge chair with a good book, completely relaxed now that I didn't have any use for them.

It was true Dr. Kowalski had taught me new skills. I could talk to my OCD a little differently, pointing out how distorted its thinking was. I could breathe deeply to relax while I tried to think of whales swimming in the ocean, instead of whatever nightmarish thought my OCD preferred. I could try to replace its twisted worldview with what Dr. Kowalski called "reality-based messages."

None of this seemed to make my OCD any less of a monster, unfortunately.

"You're doing well, Shala. I think we're on track to have you come back in a few months to touch base on how everything is going," Dr. Kowalski said, leaning toward me.

I looked up from my mood log, glassy-eyed, trying to focus on him instead of the despair rising uncontrollably in my chest, and finally saw the fly walking on the window behind Dr. Kowalski's head. It buzzed again and rammed itself against the glass, seeing freedom yet unable to figure out how to actually get there.

I wasn't doing well. In fact, I seemed to be getting worse. Why wasn't this therapy working?

"Shala?" he said again, looking concerned.

I thought back to the image of my obsessive-compulsive behaviors relaxing in a lounge chair on a cruise, reading a good book. My OCD was certainly relaxed about my therapy with Dr. Kowalski, but it would be years before I'd understand why. Years before I'd realize I'd missed a key piece of intelligence I needed to make my attacks on my OCD work. A key piece of intelligence I would have gained had I been less in a hurry to "get through" therapy, to have someone tell me how to magically flip the switch that would turn off my OCD. A key piece of intelligence I would have gleaned had I just taken the time to carefully read the afterword of *Kissing Doorknobs,* where a doctor from none other than the University of Illinois had explained exactly what type of behavior therapy I needed.

"Yes," I said mechanically to Dr. Kowalski, reaching toward my wallet. "Coming back in a few months sounds fine."

Without that key intelligence, I was pouring buckets of liquid on a blazing fire and wondering why it wouldn't go out. In fact, the liquid seemed to fuel the flames more, as they encircled me, licking greedily around my ankles and trapping me in their fiery hell.

Unbeknownst to me, therapy had not filled my buckets with water.

Instead, it had filled them with gasoline.

CHAPTER 8

The Letter

I opened the door from the carport, hearing the muffled "tha-thunk" as one of the cats jumped down off a chair somewhere close by. I dropped my briefcase beside the pool table and knelt down to pat Abby as she sauntered into the room, Fred slinking in behind her. Freddie, even after living with me for almost ten years, still had the tendency to tread with the hesitancy of the alley cat he used to be, sidling his long orange-and-white feline body along walls until he could assess the safety of the situation and risk coming out into the open.

Standing up, I shrugged off my coat and leaned against the pool table, feeling the green felt of the playing surface under my fingers. "What I am going to do with you, pool table?" I asked for the hundredth time, glancing back as I walked into the kitchen at the cues gathering dust in the billiard-stick rack on the wall.

I certainly didn't need a pool table anymore. Not with Alex gone.

As I grabbed a bag of cat food, I grimaced at the garish strawberry-themed wallpaper to the right of the pantry door. Sydney had visited recently, and as we'd sat with her chubby one-year-old baby Josie on my living room's ancient grass-colored carpet, I'd told her it didn't matter to me that my house wasn't up to date. "It's fine," I'd stated with all the confidence I could muster, watching Josie squeal with glee as she patted her hands on the beaten-down carpet. "It's pretty much just like the house I grew up in."

When Alex and I had picked this house a few years earlier, I'd liked the fact that it reminded me of my parents' house. They liked their house, so why shouldn't I like this one?

But the truth was, I didn't like it. Not now. Not after Alex. Still, though the house and yard were way too big for just the two cats and me—and required many more projects than I had interest in or energy for—I wouldn't consider selling it because selling it seemed too scary. I was convinced I'd lose money on the deal (which would be irresponsible, something my OCD told me was *not* acceptable), and how in the world would I figure out what else to buy and where to live?

Too many decisions. Too many unknowns. As someone who dedicated her life to making daily, sometimes hourly, complex sacrificial offerings to the gods of certainty to prevent the death, doom, and destruction of everything she loved, to *invite* uncertainty seemed at best a lark, and at worst grave folly.

As cat kibbles clinked into Fred's and Abby's bowls, I thought about all the uninteresting administrivia I had to do at work the next day, and how much I wasn't looking forward to it. Because for once, I did have something I wanted to do instead of work. I wanted to spend time with my horse.

I'd purchased Lee, an Arabian gelding on whom I'd been taking riding lessons, a little less than a year ago, right after Alex and I broke it off. I figured if I was incapable of having a long-term relationship with a person, I would have one with a horse instead.

Buying Lee had pushed the boundaries of my OCD's comfort zone. *What if he kicks someone and hurts them?* my OCD whined. I purchased equine liability insurance—problem solved. *But what if he has a major health problem that costs thousands of dollars to fix?* I had the vet do a thorough pre-purchase check and learned Lee was healthy with only a little arthritis in one foot. *But, but… what if we can't afford having a horse?* my OCD, now fully throwing a fit, sobbed into my ear. I made a spreadsheet, asking my riding instructor for all the potential costs of owning an equine. I figured I could swing it, and much to my OCD's dismay, I plunked down a check and became the proud new owner of an Arabian horse.

Riding Lee was an entirely different experience from riding my ponies as a kid. Hot-blooded, much taller than a pony, and possessing a spirited temperament under saddle, Lee had run away with me and bucked me off numerous times during lessons. But I didn't care. Riding Lee challenged me, requiring enough of my attention to make it harder for me to hear the incessant voice in my head.

The voice that had driven Alex away. Unable to overcome my OCD, I'd waffled back and forth for more than a year after my sessions with Dr. Kowalski ended, trying to determine whether I wanted to have children. Alex and I had even seen a social worker, Marilyn, to try to work through our relationship issues. Marilyn had told us I seemed to fit the characteristics of bipolar II disorder as well as those of OCD. She'd described bipolar II's diagnostic criteria, but I knew that wasn't what was wrong with me. OCD was what was wrong with me, but I could see how it looked like bipolar II at times: frenetic workaholism that might seem like low-grade mania, interspersed with more and more frequent bouts of serious and increasingly debilitating depression.

In the end, I knew I couldn't deal with a real child when I already had an intractable child—my monster—residing permanently in my head. So Alex and I eventually gave up trying to fix our relationship. It was just too broken to mend.

With all that was wrong with me, was I, like my romantic relationships, also too broken to mend?

As I crawled into bed that night, thinking of all I had lost, the veil of depression slid over my face, slowly, seductively, as it had every night for the past several months. I welcomed its soft caresses as one by one its layers draped languidly from above: the gauzy chiffon of disbelief, the itchy burlap of loss, the suffocating velvet of grief. Piled together on top of me, they formed a shroud of hopelessness from which I couldn't emerge.

From which I didn't want to emerge.

Because the heaviness weighing me down was a kind of safety. A reason I couldn't move. A reason I couldn't care, or do, or be. Its smothering embrace held me, keeping me sheltered from the world, and its cruelty, and any more pain.

I had become comfortable under my pall of darkness, having convinced myself it was something I needed, something I wanted.

Because the dead, for whom palls are made, can't feel. And I didn't want to feel anymore.

I'm walking on the campus of the University of Illinois, on the quad, trees dappled in the orange, red, and yellow hues of autumn. I'm spinning in circles, trying to get my bearings. My sorority house is just across Wright Street from the English Building. But where is the English Building?

I pivot haphazardly, looking for answers, looking for someone who can show me the way.

And then I hear it. A bell, ringing solidly. Wait, did I hear it? Yes, there it is again! A phone! The phone is ringing! It's ringing at my sorority house, it must be for me, I just need to run toward ...

I opened my eyes, seeing nothing but darkness. I'd been on campus again. I was a frequent nighttime visitor to Champaign-Urbana, where I found equal parts peace and panic in my never-ending nocturnal search for my sorority house.

Then I heard it.

The phone.

It was ringing.

I turned on the bedside lamp, looking at the clock. 10:49. Who the hell was calling me at almost eleven o'clock at night?

I lay in bed, willing the phone to stop ringing. Most nights, I turned the ringer off to make sure I didn't get disturbed by wrong numbers. Sleep had never been easy for me. Recently, I'd entertained myself by reading a few old diaries of mine my parents had found, and I'd marveled at how many of the sparse entries referenced sleep, such as: "Saturday, January 10, 1981: I was very tired and I couldn't sleep in black dark."

Which amused me, because now I couldn't sleep in anything *but* "black dark" and total silence.

Total silence, currently obliterated by a ringing phone.

As I lay in bed, it just kept ringing. Volcanic anger started to bubble, hot and molten, just below the surface of my chest.

At this point in my life, I had clear anger issues. My rage rarely, if ever, showed itself at work. Work was where I kept it together, because work was who I was. After all, better an overeager, workaholic software marketer headed for the executive suite (my goal) than an ostracized, murdering madwoman headed for the federal pen (my OCD's worst nightmare). If I could become good enough at the one, I might keep myself from becoming the other.

When I got home from work, however, a different Shala emerged: one filled with outrage and indignation. Because it took every ounce of my strength to manage and hide my monster. From the time I woke up until the time I went to bed, then sometimes even in my dreams, I heard the radio station WDNG, my home for "all danger, all the time." It berated me, criticizing everything I'd ever done wrong or *might* do wrong. It threatened me, chiding me that this time I'd done it (whatever "it" was) and I was surely headed for jail. It beat me down continuously, and, like a sad-eyed hound kicked one too many times, I'd lash out, snarling, teeth bared, at whatever threatened to kick me again.

My loosely lidded temper had launched one of its most embarrassing outbursts one day when Alex and I were living together and my parents were visiting. I'd run outside to grab the mail before we sat down to dinner. On my way back up the driveway, I tore open the gas bill. *Four hundred dollars.* By the time I came through the carport door, I was seething at how much we owed. Not because I couldn't afford it, but because it was one more aspect of my life that seemed completely out of my control.

So I verbally thrashed the customer service representative who had the sorry luck to pick up my call—the call I just *had* to make before dinner. "What do you mean, it costs more to ship gas from overseas than it used to?" I said, mimicking my OCD's caustic tone. "You can't ship gas in a boat for God's sake! That's ridiculous!"

Alex and my parents sat at the table and stared at their plates as they listened to me rant and rave. When I joined them at the table, having pulled the stopper from my sink of adrenaline, I took one look at them—at what I perceived as disappointment and embarrassment in their faces—and I crumpled into a heap of tears on the floor.

Dr. Kowalski had tried to help me with my anger. At one of our last sessions he'd listed "work on anger management" as one of my goals. He taught me to ask questions whenever I started to feel angry. Would a reasonable person be angry in this situation? Is this worth my energy? How much of a threat is this, really?

Dr. Kowalski apparently had never experienced anger like mine, because his questions did nothing to help me. I knew a reasonable person wouldn't be angry about all these pointless minutiae. It was absolutely not worth my energy to get myself so worked up. But I felt so threatened by everything that my OCD paraded in front of me, and so drained from perpetual workaholism, that in the heat of the moment I could never tell what was a real threat and what was not.

But the phone currently ringing? That, without question, was a real threat. Because I'd never be able to get back to sleep. Without sleep, my life the next day, trying to manage my OCD, would feel like a scene from Dante's *Inferno* as he journeyed through the nine circles of Hell.

I ripped the covers from my body and launched myself out of bed, Fred and Abby simultaneously leaping off the comforter and scurrying for cover. My footsteps pounding like cannon fire, I rounded the corner into the kitchen and yanked the phone from its cradle. I'd give whomever had the guts to call me at this hour a piece of my mind.

All I heard was a dial tone. Whoever it was had finally hung up. It was just too much.

My guttural screams filled the kitchen. "I CANNOT DO THIS ANYMORE!"

I grabbed the curved metal handles of the chairs pushed under the dinette set Alex and I had purchased together—that I now used alone—and shook them as I raged.

"HOW MUCH MORE OF THIS WILL I FUCKING HAVE TO TAKE?" I bellowed, words forming and hurling themselves out with such violence that the back of my throat felt raw.

Shaking the chairs wasn't enough. I needed to *feel* the pain, so I slammed my foot into the hideous-strawberry-paper-covered kitchen wall.

I stood back, aghast. The jagged hole in the kitchen wall shouldn't have surprised me, considering the force that had created it. Stunned, I watched as eddying wisps of plaster dust pooled gently on the floor.

It was a gaping maw, lightless and foreboding. Appropriate, really, as I felt a similar darkness growing inside me, engulfing me.

What was happening? What was I turning into?

I slid down the opposite wall, tears obscuring the destruction in front of me. Stifling a sob, I grabbed the phone and dialed the number I knew by heart.

"Sydney, it's me," I choked. "I think I need help."

After a rift of a few years during college, Sydney and I had gone back to being good friends. She lived in Washington, DC, with her husband, an economist, and over the years I'd visited them whenever I was in town for work, and sometimes flew up to see them and their daughter Josie for fun.

But while Sydney was my oldest friend, it wasn't until The Night I Kicked A Hole In My Kitchen Wall that she knew about my OCD.

I reached out that night, knowing I had to tell someone, because the pain of my life had become too big for me to hold alone. Sydney had picked up the phone and listened to my entire story—for fifteen minutes, then thirty, then an hour—holding my hand tighter and tighter from afar as I dangled off a cliff, not wanting to fall, but not having enough strength left on my own to pull myself back up onto the ledge.

"I think you should try medicine again. You said it helped a little bit before, right?"

"But the side effects were so terrible. I don't know if I could go through that again."

"Shala. Listen to me. I want you to try. For me. Okay? Just try. Tell the doctor everything. Tell him what the other drug did. That was years ago; they might have better drugs now." Sydney's voice was soft and soothing. "You can do this."

I didn't respond.

"Shala? Please? For me?"

I felt Sydney's grasp, understood that her unwavering belief in me was the only thing pulling me up and over the cliff's edge to solid ground.

"Okay," I agreed, spent. "For you, I will see someone."

I hung up, paradoxically too worn out to sleep, and pulled out my laptop, writing a letter to my parents:

Dear Mom and Dad,

I've been sobbing for hours. Sobbing because I made a hole in the wall. Sobbing because I feel like such a slave to sleep. Sobbing because I'm tired of being me. I'm just tired.

Every day my OCD gets worse and worse. I'm trying every possible way I know to control it, but everything makes me withdraw further from society. I have to get eight hours of sleep. I can't do anything that would slightly cause me to worry, which means I have to be perfect. I feel I have to be so structured and rigid that I can't participate in everyday life anymore.

What a shame OCD is ruining my life. OCD makes you afraid to love anyone or anything, because the worry that accompanies love is more a punishment than the love is a reward. I feel so alone and scared and hopeless. I'm not quite sure of the point of my life, since I have to give up so much to maintain my sanity.

I *am* likely to kill myself, but it won't be labeled a traditional suicide, even though it will be self-inflicted. Cause of death: excessive worry leading to a constant anxious state—her heart just gave out.

Which doesn't matter anyway, since I've had to shut down my heart to control my world.

I held the letter now, as I looked at Dr. Honeycutt, my new psychiatrist. I'd chosen him similarly to how I'd chosen Dr. Kowalski: he took my insurance, wasn't too far from my home, and had an appointment available the very next day.

"So tell me what brings you in today," Dr. Honeycutt said, legs crossed, a look of intense interest crinkling the skin around his dark eyes.

It had been two days since The Night I Kicked A Hole In My Kitchen Wall.

"I have OCD," I said, trying not to cry.

Dr. Honeycutt scratched a note on a yellow legal pad balanced on his leg. "Okay. Tell me about your symptoms."

A tear crept down my cheek, as if it weren't sure it was okay to fall. I looked at my lap, where I held my letter, the paper softening in the grip of my sweaty fingers.

Then I felt it. Not just the tears, which had started to fall in earnest. But the barrel of a gun, pressing gently into my temple.

I've had it with you, my OCD sneered. *You blabbed to Sydney. Fine. What the hell is she going to do? But you are not blabbing to this guy. He has power. You tell him the wrong thing, and we're going to end up in an institution. The world is not tolerant of people like us. Don't you get that?*

Once again, Rule #1 flashed in front of my eyes.

"Fuck off," I said, the words barely audible.

Excuse me? said my OCD, incredulous.

I felt Sydney's hand holding mine across the miles, heard her say, "Shala? Please? For me?" Looking down at the letter in my lap, I took stock of all I'd lost. Of all I was going to lose. All because of my OCD.

Shaking, I repeated myself loudly in my mind, "I said 'Fuck off,' OCD. You've had it with me? I've had it with *you.*"

It was my first shot fired at OCD, in an anguished attempt to finally take back territory that for so long had flown my monster's flag.

More confident now, I fired the next shots, a machine gun sweeping back and forth, trying to do as much damage as possible as tears streamed down my face.

"I have every OCD symptom imaginable. It takes me twenty minutes to leave the house because I'm afraid I've left something on that will cause a fire. I avoid touching things I think have germs. I play scenes over and over in my head. I think I say weird things out loud. I have to be perfect or I might go to jail. I'm constantly cleaning and fixing and arranging things because they have to be just so. I worry that I'm going to kill other people inadvertently. I've checked the front door so much to make sure it's locked, I've pulled off the knob at least twice. I won't throw away anything that's recyclable because that would be irresponsible. I touch objects four times to make sure bad things won't happen. I see sickening images of animals being killed and tortured ..."

Dr. Honeycutt put his hand up, palm facing me, like a cop stopping traffic. I was crying so hard my nose was running into my mouth.

"Okay, I get it, you have OCD," he said, his abrupt gesture softened by the kindness in his voice. "So we need to get you on some medicine."

I fished a tissue out of my jeans pocket, noisily crumpling the letter in my lap, and wiped my nose. "But the medicine I took before, Medicine A, had so many side effects: insomnia, stomach pain, dry mouth. It was awful. I stopped taking it after just a few weeks."

Dr. Honeycutt shifted in his chair. He was so tall, he even looked tall sitting. "Well, that was several years ago. We now have a new drug called Medicine B. It's a more refined version of another drug we use for OCD. They are both called SSRIs—selective serotonin reuptake inhibitors. They're antidepressants, and we think this new version works better for OCD. And I'm going to prescribe you one twentieth of a therapeutic dose."

"One twentieth? Is that going to do anything?"

"Well, not at first. But it's the best way to avoid side effects. We're going to gradually up your dosage over the coming months until we get to something we think is therapeutic."

"And does it work?"

"It should. It won't make your OCD completely go away, but it should make it a lot better."

He handed me a prescription. "I've written on there when to increase the dosage. I'll want to see you back in three weeks."

I smiled at Dr. Honeycutt, giving my eyes a quick wipe with my tissue. This time I wasn't smiling to prevent bad things from happening, or because I was trying to make sure I didn't offend him, or because I thought I should.

I was smiling, as I slid my crumpled and somewhat soggy letter back into my purse, because I'd disobeyed a direct order from my OCD. And because I had, maybe all I'd written in my letter about my past and my present with OCD did not have to become my future.

Over the coming months, after I'd tucked my letter to my parents into my light-blue therapy folder, where it would stay hidden for more than a decade, I followed Dr. Honeycutt's instructions, taking liquid Medicine B until I was up to a high enough dose to take a quarter of a pill, then half, then three quarters, then a whole pill a day.

He'd been right. Titrating up so slowly seemed to inoculate me from unwanted side effects, while the wanted effects took hold and quieted my OCD. At first, it continued its strenuous objections to the entire treatment process, griping and complaining and threatening, but the longer I took Medicine B, the more it seemed as though my

OCD were talking to me from another room. Sometimes, my OCD's mouth was wrapped so tightly in the woolly scarf of my SSRI that I just couldn't understand what it was saying. I could hear it grumbling, but I couldn't make out the words.

In Medicine B, it appeared Dr. Honeycutt had given me the magic key to finally turn down the volume on WDNG, my radio station from Hell.

Without my monster's constant heckling, I found I could stop doing some of my rituals. I let go of the sillier ones first: trash-kissing, touching things multiple times, reciting incantations in my mind. Then, slowly but surely, I got better at some of the others. I wouldn't drive back to check for bodies every time I thought I hit something. I wouldn't ruminate on a bad work conversation the entire day, just for a few hours. I wouldn't think every time I touched something "contaminated" I'd necessarily end up prematurely dead.

As a result, I was also a lot less angry.

I was finally getting better.

At least, I thought I was.

But as in a garden hastily tended, weeds whacked but not uprooted, fallow soil concealed under a layer of mulch, chaos was lying in wait.

The Accident II

"Come on, Lee," I said as I tightened the girth of his saddle. "Let's go forget about work for a while."

Lee bent his head around and nibbled at the zipper of my fanny pack that held his treats.

"Yes, you can have one," I laughed. I opened the pack and pulled out a cookie, smelling its tangy artificial apple flavor as he took the treat gently with his whiskery lips, and we started walking to the lake.

Normally the barns where I boarded Lee had lots of riding space: fields, country roads, trails through the woods. But this barn, which I'd chosen for its small size and proximity to my office, did not. It only had a lake covering the span of several acres, encircled by a wide dirt track, on which I'd exercise Lee on weekends and in the evenings after work.

One of the only positive things I could say about my current work situation was that my office was just a short drive from Lee's barn. I'd left XcelleNet a few years earlier to work for Joan as marketing director at Cambia, a new start-up she was running. When it was acquired by a larger software company, we both moved on to different start-ups. I was currently marketing director for a company that sold GPS ankle bracelets used to track people in a sector of society that scared the pants off my OCD (even though I was still on Medicine B): the criminal justice system. I spent each day immersed in the world of parole, probation, and prison—with a special focus on tracking bracelets for sex offenders—all of which sent my monster into a fear-induced frenzy of "what if" worries:

What if we got this job only because we need to be prepared for what it's like to go to prison because that's where we're going to end up?

What if we've already done something bad and someday there will be a knock on the door and it will be the police coming to get us?

What if we lose our freedom and can never, ever do what we want to do ever again?

To make matters worse, I could tell that my boss, Gus, didn't think I was doing a good job. Gone were the kudos, the attagirls, the shots in the arm I'd always received from management. Gone were the sources of external validation and absolution that could overpower the internal sense, muted by Medicine B but still present, that I was somehow a bad person. Perhaps just like all those people in the criminal justice system who wore our ankle bracelets, too bad and dangerous to have their whereabouts unknown.

My OCD and I were, needless to say, nothing short of miserable.

Our misery did nothing, however, to quell my drive to work. While I didn't think of it as a true OCD compulsion, my Quest-fueled workaholism served the same purpose as a ritual—reducing my anxiety temporarily—by keeping my mind distracted. But my nose-to-the-grindstone ways had also taken their toll, and I was fried.

In that state, I had no business participating in risky activities, such as riding Lee, a horse who seemed to think himself a latecomer to the Kentucky Derby. My OCD, off worrying about its typical nonsense of highly unlikely hazards (for example, that I'd end up wearing a corrections-issued GPS ankle-tracking bracelet), ignored the true risk facing me every time I mounted up. It missed the opportunity of a lifetime to give me a warning that, for once, would have been useful.

Lee was not a Thoroughbred, the typical racehorse, but an Arabian, a breed used thousands of years ago as a desert war mount, one who could race into enemy encampments and endure long, harsh treks across barren landscape. I loved the fact that Lee had his breed's passion for running. I could feel his ancient Arab blood coursing through his veins as he took off and raced across rolling fields, down country roads, or around sandy arenas, his powerful legs a blur.

As much as I loved the energy of Lee's sprints, dust sanding my face, the percussion of hooves pounding the dirt, if I were honest, his bolting off also scared me. Because many times, I just didn't know how to make him stop. Perched precariously on his back, I could feel myself tense when he went into high gear. I'd lean over in a protective posture, my enthusiasm for the adrenaline-pumping thrill ride battling my anxiety about going *so* fast, with absolutely nothing between me and the hard ground whipping by below.

I'd fallen off Lee several times. Everyone who rode frequently fell off now and then. I'd also taken lots of lessons to learn how to communicate to Lee what I wanted.

"Your posture sucks!" one of my favorite instructors, Katie, would always yell as I rode around the arena during my lessons, Lee tossing his head impishly while he ignored my commands. "You need a posture bra, girl!"

Which I then dutifully purchased. A white cloth contraption with a lot of wide Velcro® straps, the posture bra was supposed to pull my shoulders into line so that I'd have an upright stance when in the saddle. But the bra was painfully uncomfortable, and I'd left it to get lost in the back of my underwear drawer after only a few strained wearings.

So I maintained my slouched posture while riding, leaning over as Lee galloped, always pulling hard on the reins in an effort meant to slow him down, but seeming to make him go that much faster.

Lee and I reached the lake, the air crisp with the slightest hint of a chill, the dirt track barely touched by the rain showers earlier that afternoon. I mounted up and, starting out at a walk, Lee and I made a couple of loops around the water. With my legs, I urged him into a trot, and as I posted up and down, he jogged along the track that was edged with detritus from last autumn's fallen leaves.

My helmet seemed a little loose, so I slowed back to a walk, adjusting the strap under my chin. Shortening my reins, I gave Lee the cue to canter. As we glided forward, I listened to the rhythmic ta-ta-TA, ta-ta-TA, ta-ta-TA of his hooves as they hit the sandy dirt track.

Then I felt it. That infinitesimal movement signaling he was about to pick up the pace and launch into his *other* gear. The gear where the sound of three measured hoofbeats turned into the brisk blur of a snare drum, indicating Lee had shifted into a flat-out gallop.

Without meaning to, I tensed up. "Whoa, Lee," I pleaded, as I shortened the reins still more, pulling back sharply.

He sped up.

Beginning to panic, I leaned forward, pulling on the reins again, commanding, "Whoooooaaaaaa!" But we rocketed even faster around the tranquil lake. It seemed as if Lee wasn't understanding me. It would be years before I realized Lee was giving me exactly what I was requesting.

I remember thinking as we came around the bend, in the moment that it all went wrong, as Lee's hooves slipped in slow motion on the skin of leaves ringing the lake—leaves that were dry on top but slick as ice underneath—how strange it was to see the upturned U-shape of Lee's shoe. I've never seen his shoe before while riding, I thought, as his legs skidded out from under him and all thousand pounds came crashing down onto the ground. Everything went dark as the force of the impact flattened me beneath my beloved horse.

The last time I'd been knocked unconscious, I'd also been crushed. This time, in The Accident II, I'd woken up before being whisked to the hospital in an ambulance, before being lifted onto a wide, flat board by five burly firemen who'd first secured some sort of stabilization device around my neck. Now, lying flat on my back on a gurney, I watched squares of bluish fluorescent lights winking in and out of my vision as I was rushed from the ambulance to the emergency room and then to Imaging for a full body CT scan.

As I lay perfectly still for the scan, I realized how much luckier I'd been this time than last. How nothing seemed to be broken. How Lee was completely fine, having righted himself and run back to the barn, alerting the barn owner by his riderless saddle that something had gone terribly wrong, that his rider was lying lifeless in a heap beside the lake. How my helmet had saved my life, as I'd hit my head hard enough to completely dislodge the helmet after it cushioned what otherwise would have been a fatal blow.

I left the hospital that night with a concussion, two black eyes, a twisted ankle, and a promise that I would hurt for many days afterward, as the entire left side of my body rebelled at the grievous insult it had just endured.

My body was not alone, however, as my mind also rebelled. It was as if the force of the impact had not only knocked me out but had also woken me up. I couldn't stop thinking, "What the hell am I doing with my life?" My second death-defying experience made me realize that for the last twenty years I'd been running on auto-pilot, operating from the unspoken guidebook of life that said I was supposed to graduate from college, get married, have kids (well, skipped that one), and pursue an ever-upwardly mobile existence with another degree, higher-level job titles, and more responsibility. The result of all this lemming-like striving? Something resembling happiness. That's what had been implicitly promised, anyway.

So why, after following these instructions as diligently as I could, was I still so very miserable?

Two months later, I decided to end part of the misery and leave my job at the prison-focused ankle-bracelet company and take some time off. I was having my last meeting as a marketing director with Gus, a discussion I'd dreaded, as he'd made it plain to me when I'd resigned three weeks prior that my departure felt like a betrayal.

"I appreciate all the work you put into the transition, Shala. You did a nice job with that," Gus offered, starting our final meeting by extending an olive branch. Fractured sunlight streamed through the blinds, spotlighting dust motes as they danced over Gus's desk.

Startled, I managed a perfunctory, "Thanks. I don't like to leave loose ends." It would have been more truthful to say, "My OCD, even with a sock in its mouth from Medicine B, won't allow me to leave things a mess, especially when there's no way for me to come back and fix it." But that was way more than I was going to share with anyone, especially Gus.

"You're going to take what I say next, Shala, the wrong way, I think," said Gus. He looked at me from across the desk, stacks of paper thrown into relief by stark shadow patterns created by the descending sun. Gus, a successful man twenty years my senior who'd sold at least one business venture for a personal gain of multiple millions of dollars, could be intimidating. But now he looked a little sad.

Here it comes, I thought, bracing for another rebuke for leaving them in a lurch, especially when I wasn't even leaving for another job.

"Look. I'm just going to say it. You need to find something else to do. Marketing is not your passion. You don't care about it. To be successful, you need to *want* to explore what you're doing, read about it, think about it when you're not here. You need to love what you do. I've watched you, and you don't care about marketing. You need to go out and find your passion."

Dumbfounded, I spent the rest of our meeting trying to process what Gus was saying as I stared at the shifting sunlight and shadow on the wall. Was he now not only withholding praise, but also blatantly telling me I wasn't good at my job? Was he telling me to throw in the towel, to give up because I was clearly so incompetent? Was he actually glad I was leaving, so he could find someone more passionate about generating sales leads to replace me?

Had I been in a better place mentally and emotionally, I would have heard the kindness, the wisdom, the truth in Gus's words. Instead, I heard him tell me I was failing at my Quest, my lifelong goal, and those were words I couldn't take in. Because who would I be, if I weren't succeeding at my Quest?

CHAPTER 10

The Most Dangerous Appliance

The clown fish bobbed hypnotically up and down in his anemone. I watched the anemone's tentacles, like miniature, gauzy, off-white pool noodles, repeatedly hug and release the orange-and-white fish. The saltwater tank, humming rhythmically at the back of the doctor's office waiting room, was mesmerizing. Almost soporific. Or maybe that was just because I hadn't slept the night before. Or the night before that. Or the one before that.

Which was, of course, why I was sitting in this doctor's office.

"Ms. Nicely?" a young woman in blue scrubs called my name from the other side of the room.

I followed her down a well-lit corridor, where nautically themed art adorned the textured taupe walls. She opened a door and indicated I should take a seat on the exam table.

"Dr. Ananda will be in in just a moment," she said as she left the room, sticking a manila folder in the plastic rack on the outside of the door.

My BlackBerry started ringing as the door closed. I saw it was Stephanie, the marketing writer I'd hired for one of my clients, and knowing the doctor could walk in at any moment, I sent the call to voicemail.

After taking six months off from working in technology after The Accident II, I'd started my own business on a whim when a former colleague called to inquire if I knew anyone who could do marketing strategy for his small tech start-up. Pushing Gus's words, still raw and painful, to the back of my mind, I'd volunteered that I could help him, giving birth to Nicely Done, LLC. One year and ten clients later, I was working from home, running my very own marketing consulting firm. I found the work rather tedious and mind-numbing, and only having to walk from one room to the next to go to work in the morning (or in the afternoon, or evening, or middle of the night) was a boon to my workaholism. But it paid the bills, and I did like working for myself.

Having silenced my BlackBerry, I took out the Sleep Summary I'd typed up, a page-and-a-half bulleted list of all my observations about my symptoms, just in time to see the handle turn on the exam room door and the doctor walk in.

"I'm Dr. Ananda," he said, shaking my hand. "What can I do for you today?"

Relief swept through me, now that I had an opportunity to share my new hellish experiences with someone who might be able to help me. "I'm having the wildest sleep issues. I'm worn out all the time. It's absolutely killing me." I handed him my typed-up summary. "Here, there's so much going on, I made a list of what I'm experiencing."

"Wow," he said, looking impressed. "I wish all my patients would do this."

It would be a dead giveaway that they have OCD, I thought, as he sat down in a chair across the small, antiseptically white room and started to read.

I'd compiled the bullet points on the page into sections that included my insomnia history, the medicines I was taking for OCD (Dr. Honeycutt having added Medicine C, another antidepressant, to my Medicine B, as the SSRI by itself eventually made me so sleepy I could barely function), the medicines I'd tried for sleep, and the section I thought was the crux of the entire problem: dreaming.

Not nightmares in the traditional sense, my dreams had become fantastical, Technicolor® productions on par with *Moulin Rouge!* or *Chicago.* My nocturnal slumbers were active affairs: lively conversations with people from my life that seemed to go on for hours, complicated mysteries involving multiple puzzles only I could solve, or drawn-out encounters with notable figures who included Jesus Christ and Severus Snape. Even worse, when I woke up, I felt like I'd been *doing* these things all night long. It was exhausting.

I'd never been able to successfully sleep in the same bed with anyone, and Corey, my boyfriend, was no exception. I'd met Corey, a software developer, through a dating service when I worked with Joan at Cambia, and we'd moved in together in my house. He knew how lightly I slept, a problem I attributed to my OCD, hypothesizing that in my monster's mind, the best way to keep me alive was to make sure I'd never sleep through a potential threat, no matter how insignificant. "A butterfly could sneeze and it would wake you up," Corey teased me occasionally, as he headed off to his bedroom and I headed to mine.

Sleeping in a different room, however, currently benefitted Corey as much as it did me. Because now I seemed to need to act out my dreams. A month before, I'd woken up sitting upright in bed, slamming my fist against the headboard. A week later, I'd shattered the silence by waking up to the sound of my own screaming. But nothing could top what had happened the night before I saw Dr. Ananda.

I'd been sitting up in bed, a soft glow illuminating the ceiling. A gossamer strand, luminous yet strong, hung above me: the string of a ghostly pendulum, with a fluffy pink mass for a bob. It swung back and forth, back and forth, its arc tiny and precise. I stared at the furry pink blob. Cotton candy? No. A cupcake? Yes! It was a cupcake. My mouth started to water as I watched it hover.

As I sat, entranced, I noticed that the pendulum's pivot seemed to be lowering the cupcake as it ever so gently moved through the air.

Huh, how strange.

Wait, what are those things sticking out of the cupcake?

Little black things.

Little hairy long black things.

Suddenly, comprehension dawned.

Oh my God! It's not a cupcake—it's a spider!

I bolted, pulling away as the spider rappelled through the air, coming ever closer. Swearing, I pulled at the sheets, trying to extricate my legs, but they seemed wrapped so tightly in layer upon layer of cloth that I couldn't escape, no matter how hard I tried.

Surrendering to the spider's inevitable descent, just hoping to keep my face as far from it as possible, I leaned back so far—and so fast—that my head collided with the headboard.

Which woke me up.

Turning on the bedside lamp, I found that my legs were indeed wrapped up in the sheets. I was sitting up in the same position I had been in the dream. It appeared I'd acted out the entire cupcake/spider scenario while I was fast asleep.

While I'd not put all the details of this particular incident in my bulleted list, I could tell Dr. Ananda understood the seriousness of my nocturnal issues as he finished reading and looked up at me, concern creasing his forehead. "How long has all this been going on?" he asked.

"Several months. I'm not sure exactly when it started, but it's been a while."

"Tell me," he said, scratching his stubbly chin with his fingers. "Do you have any family history of Parkinson's?"

Parkinson's? Why in the world was he asking me about that?

"No, none."

"And how long have you been taking the SSRI?"

I thought back, remembering my first tearful meeting with Dr. Honeycutt. "Four and a half years."

He sat down, nodding. "I can have you do a sleep study and run some other tests, but I'm not sure we need to do that. I think I know what's going on, and it's one of two things."

I scooted forward to the edge of the exam table. Finally, some answers.

"The first potential cause is that you may be experiencing symptoms of early stage Parkinson's disease."

My OCD perked up, alert. Parkinson's wasn't something it had ever worried about before.

"Sometimes people who go on to develop Parkinson's report the type of dreaming and acting out of their dreams that you're experiencing, but I don't think that's what it is, with no history of Parkinson's in your family."

I sat on the table, barely breathing.

"Instead, I think you're experiencing a rare side effect of your SSRI. It's called REM Sleep Behavior Disorder. It essentially means that you act out your dreams. But because I think it's a side effect, if you stop taking Medicine B, I'm guessing your sleep will go back to normal."

Astonished by his suggestion, I opened my mouth to speak, but no words came out.

Stop taking Medicine B? Pull the sock out of my monster's mouth?

I swallowed and found my voice. "What about other SSRIs? Would I have this problem with them, too?"

"Probably," he said, "although I can't say for certain. All you can do is work with your psychiatrist to taper down off Medicine B and see if all this dreaming and nighttime activity stops. If it doesn't, come back to see me. But I bet getting off Medicine B will fix your problem."

Visiting with Dr. Honeycutt the next week to share Dr. Ananda's theory, I could tell he thought the sleep doctor was full of it.

"That would be so unusual..." he started to say.

"But come to think of it," I interrupted, "that's why I stopped taking Medicine D! Because of the dreams."

A year or so ago I'd mentioned to Dr. Honeycutt that my OCD seemed to be breaking through the SSRI barrier a little too much for my liking. He'd suggested I add Medicine D on top of Medicines B and C. After a few nights on Medicine D, I flounced into the kitchen one morning, bottle in hand, while Corey was eating breakfast.

"They should call this stuff Terror in a Bottle!" I shouted, incensed.

"Why?" Corey asked, eating cereal at the kitchen table while Lily, our terrier, stared fixedly at his bowl.

"Because it sucks, that's why! I've never had such dreadful nightmares. I don't care what Dr. Honeycutt says about this making Medicine B work better. It's not worth it."

Now Dr. Honeycutt peered at me over his reading glasses. "Medicine B is working really well for you, Shala. I'm concerned that if you stop taking it, your OCD symptoms will come back."

It was a concern I shared, which left me with an agonizing choice. I could keep taking the lifesaving drug that had pulled me back from the brink of OCD-induced self-destruction, but live with a crippling new sleep disorder that left me so chronically fatigued I couldn't manage the OCD symptoms I still had. Or I could stop taking Medicine B so I could sleep, and in doing so, pull the sock out of my monster's mouth.

I didn't like either choice. But I knew if I continued to be as sleep-deprived as I was, my OCD would come back anyway.

So I tapered off Medicine B and found that both my doctors were right.

My sleep got a lot better.

And my OCD got worse.

As I tapered off Medicine B, I tried to distance myself from my monster's taunts, which were becoming louder, more innovative, and at times, almost comical.

Take the refrigerator, which my OCD had recently elevated to persona non grata, a designation usually reserved for appliances that used heat. The fridge was cold, very cold, and all of a sudden that scared the bejesus out of my monster, as I learned one day when I opened the fridge for a snack.

Absentmindedly staring inside, I tried to figure out what I wanted. Yogurt? Gatorade? Cheesecake? No, I wanted a granola bar, which wouldn't even be in the refrigerator.

Shutting the fridge door, I opened the pantry beside the ill-fated wall I'd slammed my foot through all those years ago, when my OCD had been completely out of control. I pulled a granola bar out of its bright green box and headed back past the fridge on the way to my home office.

That's when I heard it.

Hey! You. Yes, you! Wait. Don't leave. I think Fred might be in the refrigerator!

I stopped. I'd never thought of that possibility before. Could Fred actually be in the refrigerator?

I'd found Freddie at an animal shelter in Chicago sixteen years earlier, where volunteers had named him after Freddy Krueger from *A Nightmare on Elm Street* because he was so wild. I'd decided he'd be the perfect playmate for equally wild Abby, my little black kitty who'd been shredding everything within claw's reach in my apartment.

Fred and Abby were my children. They meant the world to me, and if anything were to happen to them, I didn't know that I'd survive.

My OCD, never one for subtlety, was going for the jugular.

I turned to the fridge and opened the door. There was, of course, no question that I'd do so, because if Fred were in the refrigerator, that would be bad. It was cold in the fridge, so cold he might freeze to death. Refrigerators were probably soundproof, so I wouldn't hear his plaintive little meows, crying for his mommy to rescue him as he scratched in the frigid blackness, shaking with cold, trying to get out, as one by one his little organs stopped working and he died, frozen and alone.

My OCD loved these graphic details because the deeper it could lure me into its story, the more likely I was to do its bidding.

With the fridge door standing open, I leaned down, gazing over all the shelves, checking once, twice, three times, four times to make sure Fred wasn't there. The granola bar wrapper crackled loudly, protesting, as I gripped it in my now sweaty hand.

Standing up, I closed the door and stood rooted to the spot.

It's worth noting that I did not, however, open the freezer. That thought didn't even cross my mind. Because that would have been ridiculous. Freddie getting into the freezer, a much narrower compartment, seemed outside the realm of possibility. Anyway, he'd have jumped out instantly if he got into the freezer, because it would have been *too* cold.

But the fridge, all of a sudden, had become the most hazardous appliance in the house, a clear and present danger to my fur child's long-term survival.

I opened the door again.

Leaning down a second time, I moved things around with my free hand. I pushed back the bag of apples, hearing them clunk heavily as they hit the side of the fridge; slid the milk out of the way as it sloshed and splashed in its plastic jug; and shoved a lone eggplant to the side, its shiny purpleness now out of my line of sight.

No Freddie.

Not content with the knowledge that he wasn't on the lower level, I used both hands to move a sack of flour on the upper shelf, accidentally dusting the inside of the fridge with both flour from the outside of the bag and crushed granola from the wrapper I was still clutching. As I realized the mess I was making, I saw a little pink nose appear below me as Fred leaned into the fridge to see what I was doing.

"Hey, Fred," I said, nonplussed.

"Hi, Mom," he seemed to say back. "Whatcha doing?"

"I'm looking for you."

"Oh, okay," he seemed to say, drawing back, nonchalantly turning and making his way into the room that had formerly held the pool table, but now was Corey's study.

I stopped, dead in my tracks, and shut the door.

What was I doing?

Fred was clearly *not* in the refrigerator, because he'd just walked by.

But I didn't move. I couldn't move.

I knew Fred was fine, yet I stood spellbound at the refrigerator, absolutely, positively unable to walk away.

Corey, having heard me talking in the kitchen, walked in and stared at me.

"What are you doing?" he asked, looking perplexed.

I turned to look at him. I couldn't speak. I was part frightened, part embarrassed, and part enjoying the fact that I could see the little game my OCD was playing with me. Even though I didn't quite know how to get myself out of this predicament, I was getting to the point in my relationship with my monster where I could admit it was really good at its job.

Trying not to laugh, I said, "I know you're going to think I'm crazy, but … is Fred in the refrigerator?"

Corey, used to my OCD's nonsense, said, "Well, I don't know—let's look!" and shouldered me out of the way to open the fridge. He stuck his head in, made a few movements like he was looking around, and said, "Nope, not there. Which makes sense considering he just walked by my desk."

I stared at Corey and burst out laughing. Then he started laughing, too.

"You know," I said, catching my breath. "I should write a book about all this. Everything I've been through with OCD. Because there's got to be a story in here somewhere."

"That's a good idea," Corey said. "Maybe it would help other people to hear what you've been through, how you manage."

I paused, considering this, and a flash of insight struck.

I grinned. "Oh my gosh! I could call it 'Is Fred in the Refrigerator?'"

Corey beamed. "That's great! I love it! You should do it!"

Perhaps it was time to share my story. Perhaps it was time to really start breaking Rule #1.

PART III

CHAPTER 11

Changing the OCD Mind

I scanned the soaring room called Regency D, amazed to see how many people were milling around looking for seats. A hundred, maybe two hundred? Glancing down, I recognized the overlarge, multicolored designs swirling off into the corners of the giant conference room, the carpet reminding me of the many Las Vegas hotels I'd visited for marketing tradeshows. As I searched for a place to sit, I thought whoever sold these garishly patterned carpets to conference centers around the country must be one helluva salesperson.

Taking a seat near the middle, I turned and gave the woman beside me a quick, closed-lip smile. I'd promised Sydney I'd find someone to eat with by lunchtime today, but since it wasn't even eight o'clock in the morning, I figured I had a little time. I put my backpack under my chair and surveyed the front of the room, taking in my surroundings at the 17th Annual International OCD Foundation Conference.

It was pure luck that I was here on this sunny July day in 2010. Corey and I had been finalizing plans to attend his family reunion in Vermont when I remembered from *Kissing Doorknobs* that there was a nonprofit in Connecticut focused on OCD. I'd continued to mull over the idea of writing *Is Fred in the Refrigerator?*, and if I was going to be in this organization's neck of the woods, maybe I should look them up and perhaps even stop by.

A quick internet search updated me on the foundation's where-abouts—they'd moved to Boston—but more interesting was the fact that at the end of the same week as the family reunion, they were hosting a conference about OCD in Washington, DC. Corey and I determined that it made sense for me to leave the reunion early to check out the event. Maybe I could obtain some useful information for *Fred*, and even meet other people who had OCD.

Syd, upon hearing my plans for this adventure, immediately volunteered her house as my lodgings. When I'd arrived the night before the conference, after we'd had a chance to catch up, she'd sat me down for a heart-to-heart.

"Look, Shala," she said, her thick blond hair grazing the tops of her shoulders. "I know these past couple of months have been really hard, and you've been really depressed, but I think you should put yourself out there and try to meet some people at this conference."

I saw Syd's look of quiet compassion and felt tears forming, an all-too-frequent occurrence of late. "Really hard" understated what my life had been like since March. "Completely devastating" would have been more accurate.

Because in the course of one week, Freddie had gone from seeming fine to dying, right in front of my eyes. I'd taken him to a special cat clinic after my regular vet didn't give me what I considered an educated-enough answer about why Freddie had rapidly lost a huge amount of weight. While he was hospitalized at the cat clinic, on our fifth agonizing day of trying to figure out what was wrong with him, he suddenly seized up right in front of me, unable to breathe as he lay convulsing on the polished-steel exam table. My uncontrollable cries of "Freddie!" ripped through the air as the vet tried to help him, then announced within less than a minute that administering euthanasia drugs was the only way to end his suffering. I sobbed in paroxysms of grief as my baby was snatched from my arms by a cruel universe, the very one my monster had been warning me about my entire life.

It was my worst nightmare come true. The unspeakable images of animal suffering I'd been seeing for years, laid bare in all their grim reality right in front of my disbelieving eyes.

Beginning the day I lost Fred, I took out my previously moth-balled veil of depression and wrapped it tightly around my suffering, replaying Freddie's final moments in my mind. I flagellated myself for not having acted sooner, for having been such a workaholic that I hadn't noticed something was gravely wrong with Fred. The mental wounds I created, my self-imposed sentence in a prison of grief, made the veil even more necessary, as I felt too raw to expose myself to the outside world. I was too incapacitated to even don the Disneyesque façade I'd so adeptly assumed to hide my anguish in the past.

As I sat on the daybed with Sydney, listening to her advice, I just wanted to slip on my veil and cover my still-weeping wounds.

"I know you," she continued softly, handing me a tissue from a cheerily paisley-printed box. "I know you've gone to conferences where you didn't do anything socially, just attended sessions, didn't talk to anyone, because of how you were feeling. This conference is an opportunity. I want you to promise that you'll talk to people, that you'll find someone to eat lunch with. Okay?"

I nodded as Sydney hugged me tightly, my free hand grabbing more tissues from the happy paisley box. I'd do as she suggested, because I knew keeping promises made to Syd had always been in my best interest.

Now that I was sitting, unshrouded, at the Hyatt Regency in Crystal City, surrounded by a surprising number of other people interested in OCD, I granted myself parole. I allowed myself to feel a little better, to give myself the mental space to take in what the presenters, and the other people I'd meet today, had to say.

A woman stepped up to the podium to introduce the day's first speaker, Dr. Reid Wilson from North Carolina, coauthor of *Stop Obsessing!: How to Overcome Your Obsessions and Compulsions*. As I'd browsed sessions online before the conference, trying to choose which to attend, I'd been struck by the title of Dr. Wilson's talk: "The Art of Persuasion: Changing the OCD Mind."

He's clearly never met my mind, I thought. But I decided to shove my skepticism to the side, because I was intrigued by a sentence in the session description, "How do you alter your course when it feels like your heart, mind, and soul are committed to finding comfort and certainty?" I hoped he had an answer, as I certainly didn't.

"We all know," Dr. Wilson began, looking confidently into the audience as stragglers took their seats, "that ERP is the gold-standard treatment for OCD."

What?

My heart stuttered, missing a beat.

What did he just say?

I tried to make sense of his words. ERP. Enterprise Resource Planning software? That was the only ERP I knew of, pulled from the archives of my time at XcelleNet, and it didn't compute. Was he saying software was the treatment for OCD?

In that moment, my vision changed, narrowing so I could only see Dr. Wilson—and so he was talking only to me.

"ERP. Exposure and Response Prevention therapy. You expose yourself to obsessions and then prevent yourself from doing rituals. This will, of course, make you really anxious, but over time your anxiety will come down and your brain will learn that those obsessions aren't something to be afraid of. Through repeated practice, that's how you get better from OCD."

The hands on the clock of time stopped, as if my entire life were and would always be only this moment. Dr. Wilson continued to speak, but I couldn't hear him. The echo of "gold-standard treatment for OCD" ricocheted across my consciousness, turning my world on end.

There was a treatment for OCD?

One that worked?

You mean, I didn't have to suffer?

Realizing I had to hear and remember every single word this man uttered, I ripped my backpack out from under my chair, tore it open, grabbed my notebook, and started furiously writing down everything he said.

He said I had to refuse to be comfortable or certain. That I had to move toward the threat. Invest in it. Risk losing something I cared about, such as my beliefs. And be willing to tolerate the pain.

I was scribbling so fast my hand began to cramp, but I didn't care.

He said I needed to *want* to be anxious. That by doing so, I could change the game my OCD was playing. He said I couldn't win by trying to push away intrusive thoughts or anxiety, because in doing so I was playing by the rules of OCD's game, one it would always win.

Holy shit. This guy *had* met my mind. He seemed to be *in* my mind. In ten minutes, he'd communicated a better understanding of my monster than I'd heard in all the hours I'd ever spent in therapy. He'd also described a seemingly paradoxical yet effective way to deal with it that actually made sense.

He continued, talking about a part of the brain called the amygdala that detects threats, and he said my amygdala needed to learn for me to get better. He said if my prefrontal cortex was telling my amygdala "This is dangerous!" then that made getting better harder, so instead I could say, "I want this" and "I can handle this," and that would allow me to get focused and win.

"Your OCD says, 'If you don't wash your hands, you will get sick,'" Dr. Wilson offered.

Yes, but how the hell does he know that?

"If you hear that, of course it feels like you can't handle it. But if you say instead, 'If I don't wash my hands, I will be uncomfortable,' well, now we've got something you can handle."

I scribbled intently, and as Dr. Wilson talked, I noticed two things occurring I was sure had never happened before.

The small, timid part of my mind that wasn't controlled by my monster, as it listened to this master-of-all-things-OCD speak, began to smile and sit up a little taller.

My OCD, on the other hand, crossed its arms protectively, turned its back on this show of confidence, and with a little bit of a shiver, said, *Hmpf*.

Oh my gosh. My OCD was scared!

"How do you know when you're practicing?" Dr. Wilson finished. "Your OCD will be saying, 'This is a very bad idea!'"

I nearly bounded over to my next session. My jubilant gait reminded me of the euphoria I used to feel, so far in the past, when I'd run at the University of Illinois, every fusion of my sole to the pavement a further melding of my soul to my beloved university. Except now, each union of my sole to the crazy casino carpet at the Crystal City Hyatt Regency felt like one step closer to not a melding but a mending of my soul.

Practically flying into my chair for the next session, I enthusiastically introduced myself to the woman sitting next to me, Rebecca, who happened to be from North Carolina.

"OhmygoshIjustsawthemostamazingspeakerfromNorth Carolina," I gushed, too excited to breathe, as the next speakers began their talk.

"Today we're going to give you tools for battling the Doubt Bully," said Jeff Bell, one of the team of speakers for this talk titled "Strategies for Increasing Motivation." "I'm going to tell you a little of my own OCD story today—including how my daughters called it 'Octopuses Chewing Doubt-Nuts' when they were younger."

Holy crap, he has OCD!

Jeff proceeded to tell a packed room how he'd beat his Doubt Bully, in the first story of its kind I'd ever heard: "It was a hot, sticky night in August 1997. I remember thinking to myself, 'This is perfect. There will be no relief tonight from this heat wave. There will be no relief from the boiling cauldron which is my life at this juncture.' And I was in a bad place. I was angry ..."

He had gotten angry, too!

"... I was bitter. I was dejected. And I was ready to quit. Because no one or nothing could could fix me."

I felt tears well in my eyes as I realized this person also had felt he was too broken to fix.

Jeff said he'd wound up in a hammock on that sultry night, blurting out to the mighty heavens, "Show me how to turn around this crazy life and I'll share my story with anyone who will listen!" It was what he called "his bargain with the universe," his Greater Good that had allowed him to successfully overcome his OCD.

As I gathered up my things at the end of this eye-opening session, I turned to Rebecca. "Do you want to have lunch with me today?"

Her face lit up. "Sure! In fact, I met some other women in the first session who talked about going to lunch, too."

"Great, let's find everyone and all go together!"

After the next session, Rebecca and I met by the registration desk, and a group of five of us went to lunch at a small soup-and-sandwich place around the corner from the hotel. Had anyone been watching our little gang, no one would ever have guessed we'd just met. All first-time conference attendees, we shared an instant bond in the parasitic monsters we harbored, and we reveled in meeting, for the first time, other people who 'got it,' who understood monsters in all their fury. Ensconced in a high-backed wood-paneled booth, we swapped our stories, all of us breaking Rule #1, hesitantly at first, then with utter abandon. We saw heads nodding with understanding of OCD's toll on self, friends, and family; foreheads creased in consternation at the inept therapies offered; mouths turned up in laughter at ridiculous compulsions unveiled.

All eager to get back to the conference for the start of the afternoon sessions, we hurriedly exchanged contact details, promising to stay in touch and to find each other the next day.

I'd chosen the next session I wanted to attend, "The Bee Trap: Storytelling in the Treatment of OCD," because the word "storytelling" jumped out at me. In 2000, my mom had finished her second master's degree, this one in storytelling from East Tennessee State University. She and I had spent many cold early October days huddled together in sweatshirts in sprawling tents that seated a thousand people, listening to some of the nation's best storytellers at the National Storytelling Festival in Jonesborough, Tennessee. My mom's passion for storytelling and its power to convey a memorable message had rubbed off on me.

Dr. Allen Weg also clearly understood the power of storytelling, as he'd written an entire book, *OCD Treatment Through Storytelling: A Strategy for Successful Therapy*, on the same subject as his talk. I was fascinated by all the entertaining stories he shared explaining OCD and its treatment. "The Horror Movie" was a favorite, reminding me on a positive note of all the horror flicks I'd watched with Doug in high school and on a negative note of my OCD's gratuitously violent fascination with scenes of torture, murder, and gore. Dr. Weg explained through the story that anyone who willingly sits through a horror movie enough times will eventually see Freddy Krueger coming around the corner as a big yawner.

More impactful, however, than "The Horror Movie" was Dr. Weg's recommendation as he answered questions near the end of his session: "Oh, and if there are family members out in the audience, don't help your loved ones with rituals. It just makes things worse."

Wait.

What?

Don't have Corey help me with rituals?

I don't get it.

Corey's help made my OCD better. If I dragged Corey along before we left the house—together eye-balling every outlet, every appliance, every door to ensure things were unplugged, closed, or locked tight—I could knock my anxiety level down by about half. It was beautiful. While my monster still didn't trust my senses, it mostly trusted Corey's. It also liked knowing that if anything happened after Corey had checked, it would decidedly *not* be my fault.

At the conclusion of Dr. Weg's session, I rushed to the front of the room to ask this storytelling OCD expert my burning question.

"Dr. Weg, I loved your presentation, but I don't understand something. You said loved ones *weren't* supposed to help with rituals?" My intonation was raised, leaving no question that I thought, for all his degrees and experience, the good doctor had surely misspoken.

"That's right," he said, smiling amicably at my expression of incredulity.

"But—" I stammered "—that's how I get through my day! Things will take forever without my partner's help! I'll never get out the door on time!"

His face softened, brimming with compassion, as he leaned closer to me to reply. "I know it feels that way. But that's part of getting better. If you find a good ERP therapist, he or she will walk you through how to help your partner gradually pull away accommodations."

Accommodations, I thought, turning the word over and over in my mouth, like a sommelier tasting a fine wine and finding it a little too unoaked for his liking. I thanked Dr. Weg, my world tilting off its axis once again.

I attended one more session on using mindfulness and meditation as an adjunct to ERP. This last presenter talked about how cultivating mindfulness was like guiding a terrier to sit for an extended period. I envisioned how long my own exuberant one-eyed terrier Lily, who practically vibrated with energy when asked to sit, would stay in one place, "Go get it!" being her preferred command. The presenter said every time the terrier starts to wander away, you gently say "Sit!" again and bring her back. Doing that over and over again—except with one's mind—supposedly cultivated mindfulness.

Again I visualized Lily, who had springs in her toes, and I thought the task sounded impossible, for a dog *or* a mind. As I got up to leave, I mentally filed away the talk under Things to Look into Muuuuch Later After I Have Learned How to Do ERP.

As I rode the Metro from Crystal City to the Smithsonian station for a break on the National Mall before the support group I wanted to attend that evening, I reviewed my notes, unable to believe how much I'd learned in eight hours. It was as if I'd entered another dimension, the piercing, dissonant *Twilight Zone* theme stuck on a loop in the back of my mind.

I didn't have to live like this.

I could get better. Really get better.

I'd done countless hours of therapy, clawing and scratching and battling my way back to sanity, but now I recognized that I'd been fighting an asymmetric war. For years, I'd been using Civil War infantry battle lines, marching regiment after regiment of rifle- and bayonet-toting foot soldiers to grisly, painful deaths. But no more. Dr. Wilson, Jeff Bell, and all the subsequent presenters had given me the intelligence I'd been missing before, introducing me to a more modern, surgical, and effective method of conquering OCD: willingly sneaking into my enemy's territory and ambushing it from behind—modern guerrilla warfare powered by ERP.

As I ascended the escalator that would put me onto the National Mall, I considered my options for the next half hour. My parents had taken me on numerous childhood summer vacations to the national museums, so I knew the lay of the land. Perhaps I could nip across the green and take a nostalgic whiff of the swampy, sweet smell of ancient dinosaur bones in the Museum of Natural History. Or I could go into the American History Museum and watch the giant pendulum swing its lonesome arc above the majestic marble floor. So many choices, I thought, as I reached the street above.

Then I saw it.

A display on the lawn of the Mall bearing the acronym "PETA."

People for the Ethical Treatment of Animals.

I looked away.

Because I always looked away when I saw ads or displays featuring PETA. Because what they showcased looked just like the appalling scenes of animal torture I'd seen in my mind ever since I was a child.

I stopped, a cold chill washing over my body, even though the temperature must have been more than eighty degrees. A crumpled National Zoo brochure, sporting a colorful photo of the zoo's distinctive painted animal tracks leading to exhibits, somersaulted in front of me, heading toward Smithsonian Castle.

Wait a minute, I thought, as the brochure flitted away.

PETA displays look exactly like what I see in my head.

An idea, like a lightning bolt, flashed across my consciousness.

Maybe I could try that Exposure and Response Prevention thing—right now.

The world became quiet, with only two sounds remaining: those of my footsteps crunching on sandstone-colored pebbles as I slowly approached the PETA exhibit, and that of my OCD, cocking its weapon.

It no longer looked scared, as it had during Dr. Wilson's session. It looked pissed.

What are you doing?! it screamed in my ear.

Slowly, I moved as close as possible to the stanchions delineating the edge of the exhibit on the Mall. I saw it then: a poster of a dog in surgery, its belly split open, organs wet and glistening, washed in a purple sepia haze. I widened my eyes, as if involuntarily mirroring the ghastly surgical incision.

Do not do this unless you are going to do something to undo what you've seen! You've got to replay it, rethink it, make it into a movie with a happy ending—anything—but goddamn it you have to do something now! My OCD, incensed, slammed the barrel of its pistol into my temple. The metal was so cold it burned, seemingly branding my flesh with my betrayal.

"I want to do this. I can handle doing this. Just keep looking," I mumbled to myself, quivering as I reached for the plastic chain that hung from one stanchion to the next, something to anchor myself to this spot, this exposure, this reclamation of territory from my monster.

If you do not stop looking at these posters, you are going to cause some animal to die! Do you hear me? Do you understand me? Do you want to be the cause of any more death?

I stammered under my breath, finding it hard to think, to breathe, to remember words. "The presenters said—they all said— they said—don't do any rituals. Just be with the fear. Just hang on. I can do this, I can handle this. I want to do this ..."

If you don't do something now, it's going to be one of your pets who dies! Do you want that? Listen to me. Doooooo yoooouuuur rituuuaaaalllll!

I inhaled and balled my fists, my fingernails eating into the flesh of my palm.

"Nooooooooo!" I screamed in the theater of my mind, for the first time in my life spinning around to fully face my audience of hecklers. I took another deep breath, then replaced their merciless voices with those I'd heard at the conference, filling the theater with my cry of freedom:

THIS. TIME. I. AM. NOT. DOING. A. RITUAL!

A tourist bumped into me as he passed, camera in hand, but I stood resolute, refusing to remove my gaze from the posters. The jostling dislodged the barrel of OCD's gun, however. I could still feel it, but it shook against my temple.

Well, what do you know? I thought, simultaneously exhilarated and terrified. My OCD was shaking, just like I was.

We stood there, my OCD and I. I moved around from time to time, taking in the other nauseating, sepia-toned posters. As I stood and stared—for five, ten, fifteen minutes—my anxiety began to dissipate.

As my fear went down, so did the barrel of OCD's gun.

It was as if my OCD had been getting its strength from my fear of the fear, from my doing rituals to keep myself from being scared—and without that, it couldn't even hold up its weapon.

The longer I remained there, eyes locked on those posters, the less frightened I felt. After what seemed like an eternity of standing in front of the exhibit, I came to the realization that the images were still revolting, but I was no longer scared.

I looked down and saw that OCD was staring at the ground, its gun swinging loosely by its side. As another crumpled brochure skipped past, OCD aimed the gun at it and pulled the trigger. The gun clicked impotently as the brochure tumbled, crumpled but whole, toward the Washington Monument—that pillar of strength standing tall as the sun dipped its toes in the Tidal Basin.

Sighing heavily and unable to meet my gaze, my OCD dropped its gun on the sandstone pebbles and buried its face in its hands.

A tear ran down my cheek as I recognized for the first time the charade in which I'd been participating.

My whole life, my OCD has been bluffing.

There have never been any bullets in its gun.

I turned around and headed back toward the Smithsonian Metro station, exhausted but triumphant. My recovery from OCD had finally begun.

CHAPTER 12

Playing a New Game

This will be a mental game.

Those were the words projected onto the screen in bold font, above images of chessboards, basketball hoops, and playing cards.

I looked around the small, windowless room at my cohort. Eight of us in total: three men and five women. All staring at Dr. Reid Wilson as he advanced to the next slide, launching us into our two-day weekend OCD treatment group.

Two months had passed since the OCD conference, and my remaining time at the Crystal City Hyatt, after my unexpected first ERP exercise on the National Mall, had continued to be a whirlwind. Unexpectedly, it turned out that one of the most inspiring workshops during the final two days of the conference was a session not related to getting treatment, but giving it: "Careers in OCD: Which Path Makes Sense for Me?"

A few months prior to the conference, I'd been toying with the idea of leaving marketing for good. After Freddie's unexpected death, and thoroughly miserable and bored in my marketing consultant role, I'd started seeing a psychologist, Dr. Longview, who specialized in administering career assessments.

"I received your assessment reports back, Shala, and there were several scales on the MMPI, or Minnesota Multiphasic Personality Inventory, where you had significant findings," said Dr. Longview, as he leaned back in his chair, an abstract painting of guitars behind him. "You scored in the ninetieth percentile on demoralization, the ninety-ninth percentile on low positive emotions, and the ninetieth percentile in dysfunctional negative emotions, such as worry and obsessing. And your results on the Birkman Career Assessment were also quite interesting. I think they explain why you're so frustrated in your current job."

"Frustrated" was an understatement. In the past, I'd hidden my anger from therapists, but Dr. Longview had a front-row seat to my rage. I dropped the F-bomb so many times during my first meeting with him ("If I have to fuckin' put one more campaign into that fuckin' marketing-automation software, I'm going to fuckin' scream. They could pay me $400 a fuckin' hour to do it, and that wouldn't fuckin' be enough!") that he probably thought I was a sociopath.

I'd told Dr. Longview I had OCD, but he probably wasn't familiar with what "having OCD" actually meant, as that wasn't his area of expertise and my façade of normalcy masked my case's severity. I'm convinced he'd added the MMPI to my list of assessments because he thought my combination of anxiety, depression, anger, and frustration was not a result of OCD, but was symptomatic of a much deeper psychopathology.

Now leaning forward in his chair, Dr. Longview said, "The Birkman shows that your top areas of interest are outdoor, social service, and literary. The top job family for you is what we call 'knowledge specialists,' which, for example, include counselors, psychologists, physicians, and lawyers. In fact, sales and marketing, as well as management, fall in the bottom ten percent of jobs you'd be interested in. Further, you feel you lack a sense of mission or meaning."

It was tangible proof of what Gus had tried to tell me in the final conversation I'd had with him as his marketing director: "You need to love what you do. I've watched you, and you don't care about marketing. You need to go out and find your passion."

I'd thought a lot about finding my passion since I'd received my Birkman results. I'd even made a special effort to spend time talking with Corey's sister-in-law Deborah, a social worker, during the Vermont reunion the week before the OCD conference. I'd been mulling over the idea of doing social work, of helping other people, ever since social service had come up on the Birkman as a top interest area. Sitting under a sprawling picnic shelter one afternoon as adults set up food and kids played tag in the woods around the shelter, I'd asked Deborah about her work and why she chose it.

"It was a calling," she stated without hesitation, looking into the heavily forested Vermont mountains that rose sharply around us. "I link people to resources. I'm their advocate. And I feel like what I do matters. It makes a difference."

As I walked into the panel on careers in OCD at the conference, I held onto her words and all I'd learned from Dr. Longview about what I needed in my profession. For two solid hours I listened to the panelists share thoughts about how to have a career in the field of OCD. One of the panelists, Dr. Jonathan Grayson, had run the GOAL (Giving Obsessive-Compulsives Another Lifestyle) group I'd attended the prior evening, and during the group he'd shared a tidbit that had stuck with me: that the goal of ERP therapy is to live in a world of uncertainty and be happy anyway. So I perked up during the next day's panel discussion when he proffered another tantalizing nugget: "You will *never* get bored doing this work." Hearing his words, my thoughts began to spin, forming the nucleus of an idea.

What if *I* went back to school and became an OCD therapist?

Because clearly, there weren't enough of them out there. Not if I'd been in and out of therapy for twenty-five years and had never heard of ERP until yesterday.

And what better way to put all I'd been through to good use? What better way, other than writing *Fred*, to create meaning?

Wasting no time, the week after the conference I applied and was accepted to a graduate program for a master's degree in mental health counseling.

As Dr. Wilson moved to the next slide, I saw it said in big black letters:

What are you playing for?
What's your prize for winning?

That's easy, I thought. I had come to the treatment group to take my life back from OCD, but I also wanted to learn from one of the world's leading experts how to treat OCD so I could help others take back their lives, too.

As I'd left the conference on Sunday—my OCD still with me but quite confused over how to deal with my newfound knowledge of its charade—there was no question in my mind who would teach me how to beat OCD. Dr. Reid Wilson. He was the one who'd told me about ERP as I sat in Regency D, the hands of time halting in tribute to the significance of his words. He was the one who'd told me I could handle my anxiety, that I wanted to *want* to face my fears. Knowing from my experience at the PETA exhibit on the National Mall that standing up to my OCD was what would make me better,

I wanted to do Exposure and Response Prevention. But after all I'd been through in therapy, having seen six mental health practitioners just since I'd been diagnosed with OCD (three psychologists, two psychiatrists, a social worker, and a partridge in a pear tree), none of who seemed to even know that ERP existed, I was *not*, at this point, going to face my fears with anyone who wasn't a nationally recognized OCD expert. I wasn't wasting more time or taking any chances. No matter what it took, I was going to North Carolina for treatment and to learn from the best.

Fortunately, Dr. Wilson offered a two-day OCD treatment group, and I'd signed up immediately after the conference. Invigorated by my early ERP success on the National Mall, I'd decided I wasn't going to wait until the group to do more ERP. Stopping as many rituals as I could, I'd been pushing the limits of my OCD's comfort zone again and again.

And it was working. I could tell I was getting better. In fact, Dr. Wilson had the group participants take something called the Yale-Brown Obsessive Compulsive Scale, or Y-BOCS, shortly before the group convened, and I was pleased to see I was already in the "mild" range in terms of OCD severity. But my score in no way diminished my perception of the monumental task in front of me, as I knew that if I'd taken the Y-BOCS in any of the years preceding the OCD conference, I would have been in the "severe" category every single time.

My OCD, due to my newfound infatuation with ERP, was at long last experiencing some of the demoralization it had always inflicted upon me, but it wasn't just going to raise a white flag and surrender. It had too much to lose. Instead, it redoubled its efforts, resorting to scaring me with one of its worst fears: rabies. My OCD had a vast repository of knowledge about rabies, a fatal disease that vied with HIV/AIDS for the number-one slot on its Top Ten Most Miserable Ways We Could Die.

In the short month I had been in grad school, I had already discovered a colony of feral cats on campus and, animal lover that I was, had begun feeding them before my classes. Wasting no time, OCD pressed its advantage when I dropped the feral cats' water bowl one night before I'd refilled it, splashing used water all over my face and directly into my eyes, nose, and mouth. *You just gave us rabies!* it screamed, coming unglued. Wrapped up in OCD's fatalistic but scarily believable fairy tale that ended with my dying a tragic death, surrounded like Disney's Snow White with adorable (but rabid) woodland creatures, I didn't do ERP. Instead, I spent hour after hour on the Centers for Disease Control website researching how likely it was I could get rabies from that potentially saliva-infected water. OCD: 1. Shala: 0.

Dr. Wilson had requested that I send my list of anxiety-provoking situations to him prior to the group, in order from most to least threatening. Unsurprisingly, situations triggering fears of rabies were at the top.

As he continued to go through the slides, however, Dr. Wilson didn't seem to care much about what scared my OCD.

"This is not about the content," he declared, crossing his arms and looking at us. "What do I mean by that?"

No one responded.

"Shala," he asked, turning to face me where I sat in the center of the arc of participants. "You know I know this answer, because I saw your list, but will you share with the group what your OCD is afraid of?"

I heard Sydney's voice, telling me to "put yourself out there," the sage words she'd spoken before I attended the life-changing OCD conference.

Knowing Dr. Wilson wouldn't force me to speak and not wanting to miss this opportunity to do an exposure by breaking Rule #1, I said, "I'm afraid of rabies and losing things and that I'm going to burn down the house and that I'm going to get sick and die."

"Excellent! Thank you, Shala. That's content. All the stuff your OCD makes up to scare you, it's content. This treatment is not about your particular variety of content." He looked around the room as he said it, his gaze encompassing all of us, to ensure we understood that none of our "content" made our OCD immune to therapy.

"This treatment is instead about purposely choosing to feel a generic sense of uncertainty and anxiety."

The group continued for several hours, with Dr. Wilson digging into the details of the counterintuitive stance it took to beat OCD. He said it was our frame of reference that was most important, that we needed to treat all this as a game as we practiced purposely creating anxiety and doubt.

Just before our first lunch practice session, he handed out notecard-size scorecards.

"Write what you're going to practice doing to create doubt and anxiety on these scorecards. Then give yourself points. Points for purposely creating it. Points for wanting to be uncomfortable. Points for saying you want your anxiety to stick around or to be intense."

The participants around me rustled through bags, getting pencils and pens, as cards passed down the line and we started to jot down practice ideas.

Talking over the noise, Dr. Wilson continued, "Now, to help you think of this as a game, there are prizes."

I stopped writing. My ears perked up.

Prizes?

A new opportunity to receive tangible proof of my worthiness? Tell me more.

"This is ultimately, of course, about getting your life back. But we're adding some additional prizes, just to make it fun. Whoever gets the most points during our two days together will win one thousand dollars." Dr. Wilson projected a thousand-dollar bill onto the screen while he waved a ten-dollar bill in the air.

"Whoever gets the second most points gets five hundred dollars," he continued, showing us an image of a five-hundred dollar bill and waving five dollars in his hand. He then pinned the ten-dollar and five-dollar bills to a flip chart with our names already printed down one side.

He needed to say no more. I was going to walk out of that treatment group with the ten-dollar bill in my hand. If this was a game, I was going to be the winner.

Ever since that fateful day on the National Mall, I thought of my OCD as an entity separate from me, yet always by my side. When upset, it now acted like a child—a sobbing, "the sky is falling!" Chicken Little—instead of like a goth teen rebel. When it wasn't worried, I imagined it to be quietly knitting, miniature needles clicking away.

The more I envisioned my OCD as a pathetic little creature waddling along behind me, whining about all the things that could kill us, dragging the tissue it used to wipe its runny nose, the more it seemed to have the characteristics of one of Lily's favorite dog toys. A bright orange squeaky rubber ball with big clownlike feet, it perfectly personified my OCD. Years after my time in Dr. Wilson's group, I even purchased a sunglasses-bedecked version of the toy for my desk. I taped a tissue to it; my mom fashioned a blue, half-knitted blanket attached to a teeny ball of yarn; and my dad produced pint-sized knitting needles to insert into the blanket's top. My OCD's new personification was complete.

For my first treatment-group practice session against my real-life OCD, I decided to go back to my hotel room. Having a small kitchen in my room turned out to be a bonus, I discovered, as I sat with the group writing down practice ideas on our scorecards, because I could simulate everyday anxiety-provoking situations in my room using the kitchen appliances, including a miniature stove and fridge. The mini fridge currently stored a sandwich I'd brought in a cooler on my drive from Atlanta the night before, then ignored in favor of a greasy burger and fries. I figured for this first practice session, I could go back to my room and eat the sandwich while I did some appliance exposures.

As I sat on the hotel bed and ate my homemade sub, my OCD piped up, saying, *You really shouldn't sit directly on the bedspread. I've heard they're filthy.*

I heard the sonorous boom of a room door swinging shut down the corridor as I considered what my OCD had said. Since I'd started doing ERP, OCD often employed a new strategy of presenting what sounded like well-reasoned arguments to get me to do what it wanted.

"You're right, OCD. Thank you," I said, as I got up, turned to face the bed, and put my sandwich directly down on the bedspread.

I gave myself points as OCD screamed, *NOOOOOO! That's disgusting! What if we get sick and die?* It started to cry, snot beginning to drip out of its nose. It had been on edge lately, and it didn't take much to set it off.

"Good. There's my obsession," I parroted anxiously from what I remembered about what Dr. Wilson had told us to say. "I'm not answering that question, OCD. I WANT to not know."

I reached down into my purse and handed my OCD a tissue. I heard the buzzing click of a lock disengaging nearby as someone inserted a flat plastic key into a hotel room door, but the sound was overcome by the swelling timpani beginning to pound in my chest. My OCD was anxious, and my emotions were unfortunately tied to those of my disorder.

All of a sudden, I had to pee. Probably anxiety, I thought, as I put the sandwich down on the bed and began to walk across the room.

OCD abruptly stopped crying. Its focus had shifted, and it now stared in the direction I was heading: the bathroom. And I knew instantaneously what it was thinking.

All thoughts of peeing pushed aside, I grabbed the sandwich, ran into the bathroom before I could change my mind, and put my hoagie directly on the floor, right in front of the toilet.

The drumming in my chest accelerated as I stood up. My OCD wailed, *What are you DOING?!* But I continued my systematic torture, as I reached down again, picked up the sandwich, and took an enormous bite.

NOOOOOO! OH MY GOD! My OCD started to throw a complete tantrum, its little arms and legs flailing as they beat the floor. But it hadn't seen anything yet.

I grabbed my scorecard from the bed and gave myself points for creating doubt, wanting anxiety, wanting it to stick around, and wanting it to be intense.

I turned to face my OCD. I knew it so well. I knew exactly what scared it. Exactly what it wouldn't want me to do. Why not use that knowledge right now, in this very moment, to threaten my OCD? Why not use it to win this game?

Ignoring all the echoing sounds of passersby in the hallway outside, I took a deep breath, gathered all my resolve, and mentally threw down the gauntlet, telepathically letting my OCD know what I was about to do.

It stopped flailing and sat up, taking me in, a look of incredulity and rage on its face. *You wouldn't!* it rasped, barely able to breathe as it contemplated my new threat.

"Oh, yes I would." A triumphant note emerged through the tremor in my voice.

I picked up the sandwich, pulled it apart, and put the lunchmeat, cheese, and bread separately down on the bathroom floor. Then, as my OCD stared open-mouthed, I remade the sandwich and shoved the entire thing into my mouth.

I was at a ten out of ten on the anxiety scale, the crescendo of kettledrums vibrating from my very core. But I also felt joyous, as my OCD stood up and staggered, its eyes rolling into the back of its head, and passed out onto the floor.

As I returned to the group that afternoon, I felt like for the first time in a decade I could once again hear my personal soundtrack, *St. Elmo's Fire*, John Parr's voice surfing gloriously on a fanfare of trumpets, belting out the title song's final, powerful lyrics about feeling alive. Because the more I pushed myself out of my comfort zone—out of my OCD's comfort zone—the more alive I felt.

After my little sandwich sucker punch to my OCD, I'd slapped it across the face, waking it out of its stupor, and pulled it stumbling from the room, where I refused to check to see if the stove I'd quickly turned on and off was really off. I left the room a giant mess, towels and my personal belongings all over the floor, something a "responsible guest" wouldn't do. Seeing a dog in the lobby, I dragged my OCD, now kicking and screaming toward it, and asked its owner to let the pup lick my face. Covered in dog slobber, I threw away a perfectly recyclable Coke bottle and said under my breath that I wanted my mom, dad, and Corey to die. I threw OCD unceremoniously into the car, backed up without checking afterward to make sure I hadn't mowed someone down, and drove to Dr. Wilson's office, more anxious, but also more invigorated, than I'd been in years.

There was no question I had the most points of anyone in the group after round number one. And I decided I liked this ruthless little game. While poking my OCD produced anxiety that at times felt overwhelming, it would eventually subside. My OCD would also recover quickly and proceed to warn me about some other impending doom, but according to Dr. Wilson, that was okay, as it just gave me more opportunities to practice.

That night after group, as I had dinner with Rebecca from the conference, who lived in the area, I continued my assault on OCD's senses. Sitting outside at a pizzeria, I kept my scorecard on the table and used every opportunity I could find to earn more points. I put an artichoke heart on the table then ate it. I upped the ante, putting my piece of pizza on the ground, stepping on it, and then eating it. I wouldn't use a straw with my water, drinking directly from the place where I was sure the waitress had held the glass. I took my shoe off, turned it over, kissed the bottom, then went back to eating pizza. I rubbed my fingers on the chair, table, and ground after dinner, then used them to apply lip gloss. I felt sorry for Rebecca, who I think might have been a bit sickened by what I was doing, but I didn't care. I was having fun torturing my OCD.

Back at the hotel after dinner, when OCD gave me thoughts of my beloved dogs Bella and Lily being tortured, I decided to just let those thoughts be there. In fact, why not change them up just a little and insert me into the scenes as the one doing the torturing, doing the killing?

Do you like that, OCD, you little bastard? My anger was bubbling over, fiery and molten. Dr. Wilson had been the first person in my life to acknowledge that of course I was angry, that of course all of us in the group were angry. And that we could *use* that anger at our OCD to fuel our recoveries.

I poked and prodded my OCD, channeling my anger to turn my disorder's own savagery against it, until it once again lay on the hotel room floor, sobbing and begging piteously for mercy.

Mercy I was not about to give it. Not after all it had done to me. Not after all it had taken. Relationships. Confidence. Joy. Happiness. Peace. Sanity. Possibility. Hope. And almost my very life.

Emboldened by my own bravado, and to ensure my OCD had no misunderstanding of who was now in charge, I decided to take its penchant for barbarity one step further. I flipped open my laptop, logged onto the hotel's wireless network, and opened the one website I knew would send my OCD over the edge.

PETA.org.

With my first glimpse of the photos on the website, I inhaled sharply, transported back to the National Mall. To those nauseating purple-sepia posters I'd used in my first successful battle with OCD.

What I beheld now, however, was almost worse than the images from the Mall. A video of emaciated black cattle slipping and sliding on concrete floors slick with their own excrement. People milling around, completely oblivious to the animals' suffering, shoving them with prods into the sides of metal enclosures, not caring if one of them fell, if one of them moaned in tortured anguish.

Within seconds of taking in this heinous spectacle, I started to cry. Big, throaty sobs. Because I'd grown up with cattle on our farm. When I was a kid, I'd name every one of them Herman. I loved their big soft noses and their gentle lowing sounds as they grazed on the grass and clover. I knew we were raising beef cattle, that eventually they'd all be hamburger. But that seemed to happen in a distant world, far away from me, and in a way I couldn't, wouldn't, let myself imagine.

Now, I wouldn't let myself hide from this reality. I kept watching, as my OCD, who was also bawling, walked over to me, dragging a tissue. It tapped gently on my arm and held up the slightly damp tissue, a peace offering. I took it, and OCD sat down beside me, gently putting its hand in mine.

Together we sat, one minute becoming five, ten minutes becoming twenty, as we wept tears of sadness over the world's cruelty, the cruelty we just couldn't control, and the uncertainty that it could be happening anyplace, anywhere, and to anyone, now, in the past, or in the future.

The next morning in group, Dr. Wilson asked for volunteers to share what they'd done for practice the night before. Weary but also exhilarated from my night's adventure, I tentatively raised my hand.

"Shala?" Dr. Wilson prompted, giving me the floor.

I recapped my dinner with Rebecca as my group mates nodded and smiled, approving of how I'd poked my OCD.

"Then I—I—" I stammered and looked down.

I heard Syd's voice, telling me "put yourself out there."

I looked up at Dr. Wilson and forced myself to speak, to make real this experience I'd lived last night, this experience of purposely creating doubt and anxiety in the service of reclaiming my life.

"I made myself look at the PETA website and it was horrible with cattle being tortured and people not caring and the cows were slipping and falling but I made myself watch it I wouldn't look away ..." I put my head in my hands, unable to go on, and dissolved into sobs of both grief and relief.

Silence.

Then, "Do you think she's working hard?"

I looked up, wiping my face with my hand. Dr. Wilson had posed the question to the other group members, who all nodded in solidarity to our shared cause.

I left the group that evening with the ten-dollar bill in my pocket. Dr. Wilson was right. I had been working hard. In fact, I'd never worked harder in my life than I had during those two days. And with my workaholic, Type A history of overachieving in service of my Quest, that was saying something.

But this time, for the first time, my desire to win had actually netted me something worth having: a chance to take back my life.

CHAPTER 13

Adversity to Advocacy

Don't walk down that aisle! screamed my OCD as we passed shelves of brightly colored shampoo bottles in Target. *I see price tags on the floor! If we come near them, we'll have to pick them up because otherwise someone might slip and fall and die and it would be all our fault!*

I sighed. Even though I was learning to tame my monster, at times it was still, well, a monster.

"Great idea, OCD," I said, purposely turning my cart down that aisle, stepping on the price tags that had popped off the displays as I looked at my shopping list to see if I needed shampoo.

Nooooooo, my OCD howled, collapsing into a heap on my shoulder.

After my exhilarating Exposure and Response Prevention triumphs on the National Mall and at Dr. Wilson's group, I'd tried to turn my life into one giant self-directed push-yourself-out-of-your-comfort-zone exposure. Had I lived anywhere near Durham,

North Carolina, where Dr. Wilson practiced, my therapy would not have been self-directed, as I would have attended weekly therapy sessions with him. But that wasn't an option, and from my jaded perspective on therapy, no one in Georgia would be able to help me. I'd therefore decided to be my own therapist and, outside of going to Dr. Wilson's group, conduct my own OCD therapy.

As I went through my days, I took almost every opportunity to do the opposite of what my OCD wanted, such as walking down a Target aisle littered with price tags, despite my monster's bitter protests about the wisdom of my actions.

We stepped on the price tags! That was irresponsible! Someone is going to slip and fall and crack their head open and die because of us!

My OCD was such a drama queen, and with my emotions directly tied to those of my monster, I viscerally understood its fear as it raged. "Yes, OCD," I said calmly, belying my heart-pounding angst as I stepped on yet another little plastic tag. "Someone may slip and fall and die, and it may or may not be all our fault. But I want to be anxious and uncertain because I want to beat you, OCD."

My OCD pounded its little fists on my chest in anger and frustration, my heart racing in time to my monster's thrashing as I recited my "scripts," the statements I'd come up with to talk back to my OCD, to keep myself from participating in my mental rituals.

Since the conference, I'd read books written by many of the people I'd heard speak at that life-changing event. I'd liked Dr. Jonathan Grayson's explanation at the conference that the goal of ERP was to live in a world of uncertainty and be happy anyway, so I purchased his book *Freedom from Obsessive-Compulsive Disorder: A Personalized Recovery Program for Living with Uncertainty.* In it, Dr. Grayson detailed how to use "exposure scripts" to combat "mental compulsions," the official term for the pas de deux I'd danced with my OCD most of my life. At their core, these exposure scripts were filled with uncertainty. I highlighted them as I read Dr. Grayson's book (emphasis mine):

> There is no way for me to truly protect my wife and son from myself. I just have to live with *the possibility that*, just like everyone else, *I could lose control* and kill both of them tonight ...
>
> When I'm driving on the road, I know *there is a possibility* that I have hit someone ...
>
> When I leave home, I have to make sure that I start with my left foot, *so Mom might die*....

Aha! I thought as I put down my highlighter. My fears weren't about bad things happening. They were about *not knowing* whether bad things were going to happen. Another way to think about what Dr. Wilson had said: OCD is not about the content. It's about uncertainty.

"To keep myself from doing mental rituals, I need to talk back to my OCD, telling it that whatever it's threatening *may or may not* happen, and embracing the general uncertainty of the situation," I said as I closed Dr. Grayson's book, summarizing in my own words what I'd learned. As I digested this key understanding, I felt simultaneously anxious and liberated. Anxious because it dawned on me that almost everything in life was uncertain and I didn't have much control over anything. Liberated for the very same reason.

If I said them repeatedly and out loud, my scripts—such as "Someone may slip and fall and die, and it may or may not be all our fault. But I want to be anxious and uncertain because I want to beat you, OCD"—mostly kept me from picking up my mental toe shoes and dancing the "What if?" pas de deux with my obsessions. I also thought of my scripts as a form of exposure to possibilities my

OCD didn't want to contemplate. Exposure scripts were the mental equivalent of purposely grabbing a potentially germy doorknob: I was exposing myself to the concepts OCD didn't want to mentally touch, that it would rather push away. My scripts forced OCD to come face to face with ideas that scared it, while keeping me from hearing the terrifying tales it tried to spin to convince me of the need for doing compulsions.

Scripts allowed my OCD and me to get used to the uncertainty, the discomfort, the lack of control in life. Invariably, after I'd focused on wanting the general uncertainty inherent in the "may or may not" statements and the anxiety they caused—for five, ten, fifteen, forty minutes, whatever it took—I'd start to feel better, and my OCD would sit back down on my shoulder, its fit of pique having passed, and knit quietly until the next time it sensed clear and present danger.

My OCD still carried its gun, of course, tucked out of sight. It knew I knew the truth about the gun's lethality, so it drew the weapon only in the direst of circumstances, the ones that also transformed it from a harmless, whimpering orange ball into my adult version of the goth-like, heavy-metal-loving rebel of my youth, which I now not so affectionately called the Triad of Hell.

As I conceived it, the Triad of Hell spun three characters into one: Gollum from *Lord of the Rings*, obsessed with his precious ring— or in my life, with anything that could bring harm; the *Looney Tunes* Tasmanian Devil, hypervigilant, whirling around searching for the next thing that could kill us; and a *Harry Potter*-styled dementor, utterly preoccupied with scenes of soul-destroying death and destruction.

Doing ERP whenever OCD felt threatened would initially swell OCD's fury, as it was sure whatever exposure I did would lead to our premature death. Eventually, though, it and I would calm down as we habituated to the uncertainty of a situation, and I'd have some peace until the next time it cried and pulled on my shirtsleeve, grousing in my ear and begging me to keep it safe. Or until it felt we were in grave danger, which was when it transformed into the Triad of Hell, an event that still occurred much too frequently.

Perhaps OCD still bothered me too much because I wasn't always as successful at using ERP to eliminate rituals as I hoped. Sometimes I did prevail: for example, when I walked by price tags on the floor and didn't do any rituals such as pick them up, move them, or sneakily get someone else to do so. ("Oh, miss? You work here, right? I thought you'd want to know that in the shampoo aisle, some of the price tags have fallen down," I'd angelically offer as my OCD transferred our responsibility for catastrophe to the poor store clerk. Because hey, it wasn't *our fault* if she didn't listen and get rid of that obvious tripping hazard!)

But other times, I wasn't so successful.

Like the times I'd drive by the body of a cat on the side of the road, blood pooled like overturned paint on the fading gray asphalt, and my OCD would perk up, yelling in my ear, *I think I saw that animal move! I think it's still alive! It's suffering, Shala! We have to check to see if it's alive, because it would be so scary to be a helpless animal lying beside the road, unable to move as car tires fly by! You have to DO SOMETHING!*

Listening to my OCD's fears, I'd turn the car around and slowly drive by again. I was doing the opposite of ERP, giving into my disorder, looking for movement I knew I wouldn't see, shame blazing in my cheeks as I hated myself, hated my anxiety, but most of all, hated my goddamn OCD.

I had no idea, when I started my master's program in counseling, what effect it would have on my monster. I was enthusiastic, full of hope, and oblivious to what I was walking into. All I knew was that I was finally embarking upon a career that excited me because I was going to be helping people with OCD.

As I entered the cavernous atrium of the counseling building on orientation day, I saw two women with equestrian-themed bags sitting at a large round table across the room. Guessing they must be fellow horse lovers, I walked over, sat down beside one of the women, and introduced myself.

"Hi, I'm Shala."

"Hi, I'm Therese," the one closest to me said. "You excited?"

"Yeah, I am," I replied, for some reason feeling more nervous than I remembered being when I started business school.

"What kind of counselor do you want to be?" she asked.

Don't do it.

My OCD, standing on my shoulder, leaned in closer and whispered, *No one has to know why we're here. Don't tell her information she doesn't need and ruin this chance to start over, this chance to be perfect. Don't tell her about me.*

My OCD couldn't resist sharing its opinions when it felt threatened, and I suddenly realized that this counseling program scared it. It was intimidated by all of the unknowns of starting a new career, especially one that had regulations and ethical considerations and state licensing and responsibilities for other people.

Not wanting to give my OCD a chance to share any more of its fears, I rattled off the answer I'd prepared for this very question: "I want to treat OCD. I have OCD, and mine went untreated for more than thirty years, so I want to help people get treatment faster than I did."

Now she's going to think we're crazy! She'll probably never talk to us again! I felt my face flush as my OCD put its hands on its hips and glared at me with exasperation.

"Wow! That's great," said Therese, seeming to ignore the red tinge I felt on my cheeks. "I want to do trauma work. And probably equine therapy. I have horses."

As Therese and I began talking about our horses and OCD continued fuming at the fact that I'd once again broken Rule #1, I realized this was not going to be easy. OCD was going to try to punish me for embarking on what it considered to be an incredibly hazardous career.

I couldn't wait to begin graduate classes on cognitive behavioral therapy, or CBT, the category of therapy under which Exposure and Response Prevention fell. There must be a lot of CBT classes, I thought, as I paged through the program handbook during orientation.

I could only find one, however, an elective matter-of-factly called Cognitive Behavioral Therapy. I figured I must have missed the others when I skimmed through the handbook. This was a mental health counseling program, after all, one accredited by the Council for Accreditation of Counseling and Related Educational Programs, the standards board for the counseling profession. So it couldn't be possible that this program taught future practitioners how to treat mental health conditions but didn't offer courses in CBT.

It turned out, however, to be not only possible, but reality. As I progressed through the program, I heard few mentions of CBT and none at all of ERP unless I was the one mentioning it.

I found this disconcerting, and once I started my psychopathology class about how to diagnose mental illness, I spent an afternoon scouring the *Diagnostic and Statistical Manual of Mental Disorders*, the diagnostic bible for the mental health profession, to find guidance on what I thought would go hand in hand with diagnosis: treatment. But I couldn't find treatment information anywhere in the manual.

"Excuse me, Professor," I asked at the next class. "Where do we find a listing of the types of therapies used to treat all these disorders?"

I waited with bated breath, sure he'd clear up my confusion, point me to the section in the book I must have inadvertently overlooked.

"There isn't one," he replied. "There isn't agreement in the field about the best way to treat any of these disorders. So this manual just focuses on diagnosing them."

While I found this news shocking, it did serve to explain my twenty-plus years of ineffectual experiences in therapy. No wonder I'd been offered every type of psychological intervention for my OCD—except the one that actually worked.

When I attended my first Anxiety and Depression Association of America (ADAA) conference, I learned that researchers did studies on the very phenomenon I witnessed as a student and had experienced as a patient: the lack of use of exposure therapy. Their studies aimed to pinpoint why therapists didn't use ERP, when it was proven to be one of the most effective treatments for anxiety and the most effective treatment for OCD. I talked with other clinicians sitting next to me at various ADAA sessions, and I heard from social workers, psychologists, marriage and family therapists, and other counselors that they hadn't been taught CBT or ERP in grad school, either.

It seemed it wasn't only my program that wasn't focused on CBT or ERP, or what I came to learn were called *evidence-based* treatments—therapies backed by scientific evidence supporting their use for the treatment of particular disorders. This gap in knowledge transfer seemed to be a pervasive trend in the field of psychology at large. It was a chasm that unfortunately swallowed two innocent groups: mental health professionals, who could leave graduate school unaware of how to effectively treat people with OCD or other mental disorders, and clients with mental illnesses who, like me, could suffer needlessly for years, even decades, as a result.

My own experiences in therapy solidified my conviction that both providers and clients would benefit enormously if we could bridge the knowledge gap, if more graduate programs across all mental health disciplines would teach treatments for mental disorders that had been shown by science to work for many or most people. But with the dawning recognition that this bridge was not yet a reality and the realization that the elective CBT class listed in the handbook wouldn't be offered during my tenure as a graduate student, I decided I'd have to train myself to become a cognitive behavioral therapist specializing in the treatment of OCD. So I found a treatment manual, wrote a syllabus for my own independent study of anxiety disorders, and asked an adjunct professor I respected to supervise me (even though he confessed I'd know more on day one than he did about the treatment of anxiety disorders). Not only would I teach myself, I'd decided as I designed my course of study, I would also try to be part of the bridge-building solution by sharing what I learned with as many people as possible.

I made it my mission to educate everyone with whom I came in contact in the mental health world about OCD and its treatment. When a well-meaning professor offered a decades-old technique called "systematic desensitization" as an effective treatment for anxiety, I hesitantly raised my hand.

"While that can be effective," I offered, "I've been doing a lot of reading about exposure therapy lately, and I think it's been shown to be more effective."

In my group therapy class, where we were required to take part in a semester-long therapy group, I let down my guard, sharing with my groupmates details about the damage OCD had inflicted upon my life and how long it had taken me to find the appropriate treatment.

Shortly thereafter, when a PhD student did a guest presentation in our psychopathology class, he quipped with a laugh, "You can always recognize the people with OCD—they're the ones doing things over and over again," one of the people who'd heard my story in our therapy group, Andrea, knew what my reaction would be to his comment about the disorder that had almost ruined my life.

"You okay?" Andrea said to me during a break, true concern etched into her mahogany complexion.

"No—I'm not okay," I stammered, feeling the prickly pain of indignation fill my chest. "How dare he talk about OCD like that, like it's something cute and funny? Especially to a counseling grad school class."

"I know," she said, putting her hand on my arm. "I think you should talk with him about it. Tell him about OCD. He needs to know."

Before class resumed, Andrea beside me, I pulled the PhD student aside.

"I have OCD," I said, trying to mask the way I'd felt his comment had invalidated my suffering. "It's about a lot more than doing things repeatedly. It's a debilitating mental illness. I know you didn't mean any harm, but especially in this setting, it's nothing to joke about."

I wanted people to understand the anguish caused by OCD and why it was critical to offer people with the disorder the opportunity to do exposure therapy. I'm sure I became known around school, for better or worse, as "Little Miss OCD," but I didn't care. I was driven to help others find the right treatment faster than I did.

I'm convinced it was this passion that landed me my clinical internship, a coveted spot at The Anxiety & Stress Management Institute in Atlanta, where, in 2011, about a year after I'd learned about ERP, I started seeing clients who had OCD.

It meant the world to me to be in a position to offer people with OCD the chance to take their lives back through Exposure and Response Prevention therapy. It was no surprise, then, that shortly after I started seeing clients, my OCD found new ways to use my budding passion against me.

Don't you think you were a little too tough on that client who didn't do his ERP homework? Now he's probably totally demoralized and will never get better, and that will be all your fault!

Wait! What if that client who just left was suicidal? What if you missed it? What if he kills himself because you didn't notice something or assess the situation correctly or were just completely incompetent? Then we won't be helping people. We'll be killing them!

As I began my clinical practice, when OCD threw these particular types of obsessions my way, I'd call my incredibly patient supervisor, Donna.

"Okay, here's the situation," I'd start, launching into a hurried explanation of exactly what I thought had happened and what I was worried about, always finishing with, "So what do I do?"

It was hard for me to admit that many times *I* wasn't making these phone calls. That, as a therapist-in-training helping people overcome OCD, I let my OCD make these phone calls. Embarrassed about sometimes still being in the clutches of a disorder I was working to help other people overcome, I never mentioned my OCD in my initial overview of the situation to Donna.

"What's your OCD saying?" Donna would ask, knowing what this was really about.

Part ashamed, part relieved, I'd hang my head, admitting, "It thinks I was so rude to the client that she'll never come back, which means I'm an atrocious therapist." Or, "It thinks that because the client said what he did, I should have done a suicide risk assessment/ done it correctly/done it more thoroughly...and because I didn't, the client is going to die and it's going to be my fault."

She'd ask a few more questions about the details, and then she'd say the same thing she always said, "Shala, what you did was fine," concluding with the clinical reasons for her assessment.

I knew I wasn't the only new therapist with these kinds of concerns. Because I had OCD, however, I encountered these worries more frequently than my nondisordered colleagues, and when I did, I experienced the same physical sensations of fear that my clients with OCD felt every day of their lives. I tried to keep in mind that these new OCD challenges were really empathic reminders of why I'd become a therapist.

A few years after I'd started seeing clients, my OCD changed its focus. It moved away from taunts about how I was an incompetent therapist who was clinically harming clients to how I was probably sexually molesting them.

Shala, did you see the way that client looked at you? It was weird, like he thought you'd done something grievously wrong. Wait, I know! He was looking at you that way because you sexually molested him! It doesn't matter that you can't remember doing anything lewd. Maybe you looked at him suggestively! Maybe you did something else immoral!

What are we going to do? Now he won't get the help he needs and he might sue us and report us to The Board and we could lose our license and then we would never be able to work again and that would be confirmation that wearejustBAD!

My body would sit paralyzed in my office, shame and panic reddening my face, while my mind would begin the tedious pas de deux, trying to riddle out the truth of this seemingly serious yet ridiculous obsession. Until I remembered what I now did for a living.

Then I'd say, "I may or may not have sexually molested my client, OCD. I may or may not be a sexual predator. I may or may not be hurting people instead of helping them. Thank you for this opportunity to practice. I want to be anxious and uncertain because I want my life back."

My OCD was nothing if not smart, and it always went after what I loved most. Providing therapy for people with OCD was a calling. Not only did I personally understand the suffering OCD caused my clients, but as an ERP therapist, I could offer them hope in the form of a treatment that worked for most people. Which was, unfortunately, more than most of them had ever been offered.

"So what brings you in today?" I asked my new client, a physician in his thirties.

He stared at his hands as they twisted back and forth in his lap, an outward manifestation of an inner struggle. He looked up at me and opened his mouth to speak, tears beginning to pool in the corners of his eyes. He sat mute, apparently unable to put words to his torment.

I reached over and grabbed the tissue box, suddenly noticing the smell of mocha coming from our office kitchen. Handing the box to my client, I leaned back, the aroma of coffee and chocolate filling the void.

Wiping away tears, my client looked past me out the window to the wall of thick cypress trees, a barrier between us and the outside world. He sighed deeply as his hands continued to twist, the wadded tissue pressed between them, until he finally found his resolve.

"My wife and I have a baby, Charlotte. She's three months old."

He stopped, again dabbing at his eyes with the remains of the tissue. The coffee fragrance dissipated, its source most likely skirted into a therapy office by one of my colleagues.

"I keep thinking I'm going to kill her," he said. "That I'm going to wrap my hands around her neck one day and just squeeze ... I know these thoughts are just my OCD, but still ..." He let the sentence trail off as he leaned forward, putting his elbows on his knees, fisting his hands together as if to ball up and toss away his anguish.

"I was seeing this therapist," he continued. "I told her about my thoughts. She started by asking me all these questions, about whether I enjoy thinking these things, about whether I've actually put my hands around Charlotte's neck. I told her of course not, these thoughts aren't me, I don't *enjoy* them! Then she told me I should just stay away from Charlotte while I'm having these thoughts, let my wife do everything for her, and that should make the thoughts stop. But it isn't working. In fact, I think they're getting worse! And I don't want to stay away from Charlotte. She's my daughter. She's everything to me!"

He buried his face in his hands, overcome by disbelief that his mind could have become such a torture chamber.

It was all I could do, when I heard stories like these, not to cry with my clients for the suffering caused by a disorder so misunderstood and mistreated.

"So you know you have OCD," I said. "But staying away from the person who triggers your thoughts—your daughter—just makes things worse. You're having more intrusive thoughts and you feel you're being kept away from the most important person in your life."

"Yes!" he said. "And I know this is ridiculous. I know who I am. I'm a doctor. I help people. I know this makes no sense. I love Charlotte more than anything. And the horrible thoughts were hard enough to manage, which is why I went to a therapist, but now it's even worse than it was before. Which makes me think maybe I don't even have OCD. Maybe I'm a closet psychopath who's going to snap and kill his daughter someday, and maybe that's why the thoughts are getting worse!"

"So you're thinking that because your therapy didn't help, that might mean you don't really have OCD. That maybe you're just a bad person, a person who would hurt his own child."

He nodded, again mute.

I took a deep breath, trying to center myself, because stories like this were frustratingly all too common. People with OCD that went undiagnosed or misdiagnosed, who were told to stay away from their triggers, or who were given talk therapy to help them work through their "issues." People told to recognize that these thoughts were "just not rational," or to pray the OCD away, or to try to figure out the root cause of all this weird distorted thinking to make it disappear.

Part of my own recovery has been learning to relinquish my anger at the many detours I took on my circuitous therapy journey. I could point fingers in a multitude of directions: at therapists, at doctors, at the educational system that trained them, at my own desire to just "get through" therapy without taking the time to educate myself, and of course, at the biggest culprit, my OCD's fevered insistence that we never break Rule #1. But while anger felt justified, even righteous at times, it didn't help. It only served to change my story from one of a survivor to that of a victim. And I knew my best chance to help others would be to assume the mantle of a survivor.

But this session wasn't about me. It was about my client, about helping him understand that there were tools available to help him write his own survival story.

"It's common for OCD to do that, to tell you that you don't have it, that you're just a bad person. But that's not true, you have OCD," I said, offering reassurance. This was something I'd taper as we began exposure in later sessions, so as not to support reassurance-seeking compulsions, but it was crucial in this moment so he could feel acceptance, empathy, and hope.

"Your intrusive thoughts about harming Charlotte are unfortunately typical in new parents who have OCD," I continued. "But OCD is not about the content of these scary thoughts, about killing your baby. It's about the uncertainty of not knowing whether you would do something like that. OCD is based on the intolerance of uncertainty. Through Exposure and Response Prevention therapy, we can help your brain learn that it can handle uncertainty about these thoughts so that it stops showing them to you all the time. For as debilitating and devastating as OCD can be, it's also highly treatable."

His shoulders dropped, his relief filling the room as intensely as the aroma of mocha had done just moments before.

Relief is not easily accessible to those of us with OCD. According to the International OCD Foundation, it takes fourteen to seventeen years from the onset of symptoms to get the right treatment.

It took me twice that long.

Treatment is also not always successful. ERP works for the majority of people, but it doesn't work for everyone. Sometimes OCD also contributes to the very thing it makes its sufferers afraid of: death. Often co-occurring with substance-use disorders, OCD can lead its victims to accidentally kill themselves through overdoses or other substance-related accidents. Often co-occurring with depression, as well as other anxiety and/or OCD-related disorders, OCD can also contribute to suicide attempts and to people tragically taking their own lives, because they feel they can't deal with one more intrusive thought, one more draining compulsion, one more day of Hell on Earth.

It's a tragedy I've unfortunately experienced more than once in my career as a therapist. In these cases, in the seconds after I heard the devastating news of a suicide attempt or actual loss of life, my OCD's transformation into the Triad of Hell was lightning fast, as it swiftly morphed my disbelief into a swirling vortex of grief, fear, and shame.

Like an unsuspecting swimmer hit by a rogue wave twice its normal size, I'd feel suddenly overwhelmed by uncontrollable intrusive thoughts: What if I'd caused this? What if I could have done something differently? What if I could have prevented this but wasn't knowledgeable enough, experienced enough, or good enough to do so?

Thrashing around, gasping for air, on the edge of drowning in a frenzy of thoughts and feelings, I could sense one emotion becoming predominant, threatening to engulf me. Shame. Because my goddamn OCD could turn a tragedy into an obsession about me, when this wasn't about me but about precious lives almost or totally lost—forever.

In the aftermath of these tragedies, it took all my strength and support from colleagues, friends, and family to put one foot in front of the other as my OCD wailed and convulsed, spewing a self-obsessed diatribe of fear: *This job is too hard, too stressful, too risky. Why did we leave marketing, again? We should go back to marketing! We can't do this anymore, we can't work with people who are like us: people who are sick, people who are suffering, people who might hurt and even kill themselves!*

I refuse to give in to my OCD's fear. I refuse to let it control my life. For me, being a therapist can sometimes be an exposure, but that would be true for any career.

I sometimes tell my clients that OCD wants its victims to live in a big white box, with decontaminated, hermetically sealed packages of food shoved three times a day through a slot in the side. But that isn't living. Living entails risk, and there are risk-laden givens that everyone who helps others for a living must accept: that we cannot help everyone, that things can go wrong, that sometimes people tragically lose their lives.

But that's not a reason to stop helping. Instead, after the grief, after the exposure, after learning to live with the greatest of uncertainties in the wake of tragedy, I resolve to go back to work even more determined, even more unwilling to give up, even more devoted to turning my adversity into advocacy.

In my interview for grad school, the department chair asked, "You've had your own therapy, right? You're not wanting to be a counselor to 'fix yourself,' are you?"

I told him yes, I'd had my own therapy and no, I wasn't trying to fix myself. Because helping myself wasn't my intention for becoming a mental health clinician.

It has, however, been an unintended outcome. As I've watched my clients push themselves through the hard work of therapy, their strength and courage has motivated me to push myself and my OCD harder and farther than I ever have before.

So when I was offered the chance to do the biggest exposure of my life, I jumped at the opportunity.

CHAPTER 14

Owning Imperfection

I looked out over the audience from the stage in the ballroom of the Hyatt Regency Atlanta. How many people were there, sitting in chairs that had been placed atop that familiar, gar-ishly patterned casino carpet? Seven hundred? Eight hundred? A thousand? I didn't know.

In college, I'd become of fan of surrealism, and of Salvador Dalí in particular. A poster of his iconic masterpiece *The Persistence of Memory* had hung on my wall when I was a young adult. Now I felt as if I were standing *in* that painting, liquid clocks languidly sliding down as I took in the details of the most surreal moment of my life. Jeff Bell, the person who'd shared his story at my first International OCD Foundation, or IOCDF, conference, had just introduced me in his resonant, radio-perfect voice. Dr. Reid Wilson, the person who'd taught me how to take my life back, was in the front row, looking up at me expectantly. Time was playing tricks on me as it draped itself over my memories. Was it only three years ago that I'd attended this conference for the first time, and now I was about to give the keynote address?

Gathering all my strength, I took a deep breath and began. "It was a hot summer afternoon in 1975, and I was four years old ..."

It was also a hot summer day on this date in 2013, the day of the biggest exposure of my life. Because I was about to break OCD's Rule #1 again—in front of nearly a thousand people.

The idea of giving the keynote at the OCD conference had come to me a year earlier as I'd watched the 2012 IOCDF keynoter, an Australian woman named Liz. I realized, as I listened to her incredible story, that if I could break OCD's Rule #1 in front of a room full of people, I'd deliver a blow to my OCD from which it would never recover.

I'd been attending the IOCDF conference every year since my first conference in Washington, DC. The year after that first conference, I'd also decided to get involved with the IOCDF at the local level by cofounding an affiliate, OCD Georgia, with Dr. Becky Beaton, who ran the institute where I did my counseling internship. Through the process of getting our affiliate up and running, I'd come to know the IOCDF national office staff. When I broached the idea of doing the keynote, they were supportive, suggesting I send them a video of what I had in mind.

What I had in mind was a story. One reminiscent of the tales told at the National Storytelling Festival: a riveting, edge-of-your-chair, can't-wait-to-hear-what-happens-next story of life with my monster.

Becky and I started offering local educational events about OCD through OCD Georgia, in an effort to raise awareness about the disorder and its treatment. Several months after I'd heard Liz's keynote, I began organizing "OCD Unveiled!," an event featuring a local expert in OCD whom I'd met through a previous conference. After her presentation, I would tell the oral version of *Is Fred in the Refrigerator?* for the first time, then send the video of my performance to the IOCDF.

In the days leading up to "OCD Unveiled!" my OCD stood on my shoulder and began its usual litany of woe. *What will people think if you tell them all this? What if you're ostracized by everyone who sees it? What if word gets out that you have OCD and no one ever comes to you for OCD therapy?*

I chanted my exposure scripts between rehearsals of *Fred* and working on the logistics of the event. "I may or may not be ostracized, OCD. I may or may not end up clientless, and then all this time in graduate school may or may not have been a waste. But I want to do this. I want all my anxiety and all this uncertainty, because I want to get better."

My OCD vacillated between being the benign orange ball that mostly accepted the uncertainty of the situation, and the Triad of Hell that definitely thought this was a bad idea.

On the day of the event, as I told *Is Fred in the Refrigerator?* to about a hundred people, as I came to the part where I kicked a hole in my kitchen wall—a hole that had seemed to represent the gaping maw of darkness and hopelessness growing inside of me—I saw from the expressions of the audience members that I'd reached them with what I'd shared. Friends from work, from the barn where Lee lived, from all parts of my life, had tears in their eyes. They had seen into my life, and I could tell they'd understood.

A month or so later, after submitting to the IOCDF the video of my *Fred* talk, I received a phone call from Jeff Szymanski, the organization's executive director, telling me I'd been chosen to give the 2013 keynote address in Atlanta.

On the day before the keynote, I stood on the ballroom stage preparing to do a dry run of *Fred* for one of the IOCDF staff.

She hadn't asked for a dry run. After all, the staff had seen my video and had chosen me from all the applicants for the keynote, so they knew I could do this.

But by contrast, my OCD wasn't so sure. In the days leading up to our national debut, it seemed to have irreversibly morphed into the doubting, derisive Triad of Hell:

You haven't done a perfect runthrough yet! If you're going to tell this fuckin' story, you better damn well do it perfectly, do you hear me?! Because if you're perfect, at least your audience will have some respect left for you after you finish making us look like fools!

My potty-mouthed monster was a seasoned strategist. It knew that even though I was much healthier mentally, thanks to ERP, I still hadn't abandoned my Quest for distraction, perfection, and absolution. Using this to its advantage, OCD waged a ceaseless campaign to persuade me that without an immaculate performance, I'd be one more pitiable person who made a laughingstock of herself by sharing a little too much.

Convinced by the wiles of my disorder, in the week before my keynote I practiced *Fred* countless times. The more I rehearsed, the more hopeful my OCD became that its strategy to wear me down from perfectionism-induced overpreparation would run me into the ground before I could ever take the stage.

Months later, I'd hear TED Talk sensation and vulnerability and shame researcher Brené Brown define vulnerability as "uncertainty, risk, and emotional exposure. Showing up and being seen when there are no guarantees. Perfectionism is the twenty-ton shield [protecting us from being vulnerable]." Years later, I would read in her book *Rising Strong*, "When perfectionism is driving, shame is riding shotgun."

I'd used perfectionism my whole life to avoid being vulnerable, because being vulnerable meant that bad things might happen. Though Brené's work isn't about OCD, it beautifully illuminated not only my OCD's strategy to hijack the keynote that day, but also why my lifelong Quest for distraction, perfection, and absolution hadn't worked all that well.

However, without knowing these truisms, I was getting lost in OCD's content, believing its threats that if I messed up *Fred*, everyone would know I wasn't "good enough" and I'd be irrecoverably shamed. Thus, my "may or may not" scripts, urgently muttered in the twenty-four hours leading up to the keynote, weren't working because I wasn't accepting uncertainty. Instead, I felt like I was trying to plug holes in a leaking dam with my fingers. In the final hours before I was to take the stage, I thought I just might drown.

"I need to tell you, I'm not feeling all that hot, so I'm going to grab a stool and put it on stage in case I need it," I said, walking with Jeff Bell toward the ballroom at eight o'clock in the morning, fifteen minutes before the keynote would begin.

"Yeah? Are you okay?" Jeff, the emcee for today's events, stopped walking and turned to face me. He looked concerned.

"Yeah, I'll be all right. It was a rough night," I said, as I tried to smile, and we started walking again.

Jeff, who'd seen me rehearse *Fred* the day before, smiled back as we headed down the hall. "Shala, you're going to be great. Just let me know if you need anything, okay?"

I'd debated telling anyone how I was doing, but I figured at least one person should know I wasn't operating on all cylinders, in case I passed out on stage.

After I'd given Jeff this "heads up," I retreated back inside my head, compulsively trying to figure out how, when I felt so rotten, I'd pull off the perfection my OCD demanded.

My OCD was in rare form, buoyed by having given the crowning performance of its life the previous night, the apotheosis of its career as a monster.

After a nice dinner at my favorite seafood restaurant with Corey and my parents, I'd returned to the hotel room where my OCD, not Jeff Bell, was the emcee for the evening's activities.

Ladies and gentlemen, may I present Shala Nicely! Watch as she fails magnificently tomorrow, forgetting what she's supposed to say and looking like a complete idiot in front of people who previously respected her! Her family, her friends, her colleagues will all be there, so her fall from grace will be spectacular!

Trying to "may or may not" my way out of this harangue was still proving ineffective, and I developed a searing stomachache listening to OCD's spiteful emceeing.

Hoping that if all else failed, unconsciousness would shut down OCD, I popped one of the sleeping pills I'd begged from my doctor for this very circumstance. But it seemed the pharmacist must have put a sugar pill in the bottle because it had absolutely no effect. I lay in bed wishing for sleep, trying to tune out the sideshow in my head.

Isn't this wonderful, folks? Your keynote speaker is a fraud! She can't even manage her own OCD! And boy, how's she going to do after popping pills? She'll probably still be intoxicated tomorrow morning! Wait one moment ... let me check ... oh, yes! It already is tomorrow morning! One o'clock in the morning! She's going to be exhausted and sedated, folks, how about that? Let's give a rousing round of applause to our drugged-up keynoter!

After thirty minutes of OCD's nefarious narration, my stomach felt full of daggers. Abandoning the effort to sleep, I staggered to the toilet where I promptly threw up my entire dinner.

"I must have food poisoning," I moaned as I laid my head on the cool rim of the toilet, feeling so sick I didn't even recognize that putting my face on a hotel toilet seat was a damn good exposure I'd never even done before.

What a show we're getting tonight, ladies and gentlemen! Not doing so well at wanting her anxiety now, is she?

Returning to the bedroom, I flopped down on the mattress, trying deep-breathing (something I almost never did) to clear my mind. It didn't work. I looked at the clock. It was one-thirty.

What time does she have to be up? Oh, that's right! Seven o'clock. That means she's going to have five and a half hours of sleep, and that's if she conks out right now! How likely is that? Not all that likely!

I decided the pillow top on the mattress was too squishy. That had to be why I wasn't sleeping. I got up, flipped the mattress over, and remade the bed. Nope, still too mushy. I got up again, shoved the mattress onto the floor, and lay down on the box springs.

Let's hope there's no one in the room below, because our keynote speaker's gymnastics are probably waking them up! She just wants company for her all-nighter! But every hour she stays awake is another hour of sleep she's not getting, making her breathtaking fall from glory all that much more likely!

Realizing I couldn't sleep on a box spring, I pulled the mattress back onto the bed, hastily tucking the sheets back around it. I looked at the clock. It was two o'clock. I had to be on stage in six hours.

Feeling completely defeated by the very disorder I was supposed to talk about overcoming, I mentally gave up. And with that surrender, my OCD's strategy backfired right in its face as, finally burned out, I unknowingly said just the thing to pull the plug on the vengeful emcee.

"Whatever, OCD. At this point I don't give a shit. Maybe they can play the recording from 'OCD Unveiled!' instead of having me do it live. In fact, I think I have a copy of the DVD ..."

I woke before my alarm went off four hours later, my stomach still feeling as if knives were lodged in its depths. Realizing I probably needed to take some sort of stomach medicine to calm it down, I called the front desk to ask when the hotel store opened.

"Eight o'clock, Ms. Nicely. Will there be anything else?"

Yes, how about a new life, just for today? I opened my computer and searched furiously for the nearest twenty-four-hour drugstore. Somehow, I managed to locate one, go there, come back, take a shower, get dressed, and eat breakfast all before meeting Jeff Bell outside the ballroom at eight o'clock.

As I sat through the awards presentations that preceded my keynote, my OCD tried one final time to reassert control. My purse was on stage, under a cloth-covered table that Jeff and I were going to use when he interviewed me after my address. My cell phone was in my purse.

I think we left our cell phone on! What if it rings while we're speaking?

I took the bait, trying to figure out how to keep my cell phone from derailing the most important performance of my life. Leaning over to an IOCDF board member, who was sitting beside me, I confessed, "I don't know whether my cell phone is on silent, and it's onstage in my purse. Should I sneak around to the table and make sure it's turned off? I could turn it into a checking-compulsion joke!"

She looked at me compassionately, shook her head, and said, "No. It will be fine."

I have two memories of my experience sharing *Is Fred in the Refrigerator?* at the conference.

The first is that when I delivered one of my closing lines, I flubbed my words, saying "ERP" when I meant "OCD." Realizing my mistake, I stopped mid-sentence, smiled, said what I'd meant, then kept going. It was a tiny mistake, probably not my only one and one that likely didn't even register with the audience. To me, however, it was one of the most important moments of the keynote because it was imperfect. Imperfection was what my OCD had been afraid of. It had happened, and we'd survived.

The second memory is the people who came up to me afterward, sharing that they felt understood and a little less alone after hearing my story. While this feedback, of course, fed the part of me still craving acceptance and absolution, it gave me something much more valuable: a sense that my suffering had meaning. That sharing my story had, in some small way, made a difference.

I'd been right about the effect sharing my story would have on my OCD. After the conference, it didn't put much energy into enforcing Rule #1 anymore. Sometimes, in the months following *Fred*, as I'd start to tell someone about my disorder, my OCD would open its mouth to protest. Then it would remember that not only had I already told a ballroom full of people, but that I'd posted the video of *Fred* on my website for anyone to see. Deflated, it would go back to its knitting, resigned to the fact that this particular compulsion no longer mattered.

What did matter was that after all my OCD's worrying about the repercussions of doing the keynote imperfectly, the experience exposed my OCD as the one who wasn't "good enough." It wasn't good enough to keep me held hostage. It wasn't good enough to stop me from telling my story. It wasn't good enough to prevent me from using courage and meaning to triumph over fear and doubt.

I didn't know it then, but giving the keynote would have one more consequence—an unintended one, but one of vast importance. It started me down a path to understanding that my brain had made a fundamental error on the day of The Accident, one that forty-plus years later, I could correct.

CHAPTER 15

Belief

One of the traits that had made me a valuable employee in the tech industry was my Quest-fueled sense of urgency. Absolution, after all, had a shelf life. Once I'd proven my worth by making a long-awaited sale or generating a flurry of new marketing leads, it was only a matter of time before that accomplishment would pass its expiration date and I'd toss it unceremoniously into the trash. I also had this vague sense of dread, hovering on the edge of consciousness, that my days were numbered. That I needed to hurry and get things done because I just didn't have much time left. Life felt urgent.

In my new career as a therapist, I sometimes also felt behind, as if I didn't know enough to be qualified to help others. The euphoria of vanquishing my OCD through sharing my story at the keynote dwindled rapidly, leaving me with the notion that I was an impostor compared to other ERP therapists. I couldn't absorb information fast enough to close this knowledge gap. I felt I needed to *know it all now* and could hear my OCD goading me while I voraciously read book after book about OCD, psychology, and mindfulness. *Read faster! We don't know enough yet! And we don't have much time! HURRY!* The presence of unread books spilling from my bookshelves only served to make me more worried, as I heard my OCD complain that even if I read them all, more would line up to take their places.

It's not surprising, then, that I'd procrastinated in my self-prescribed clinical reading at times, not wanting to deal with OCD's frenetic approach to learning. But I'd decided that during my cross-country flight to Los Angeles for the IOCDF conference the year after I gave the keynote, I'd finally read one book that had been on my shelves for a while: Jeff Bell's *When in Doubt, Make Belief: An OCD-Inspired Approach to Living with Uncertainty.*

I made this decision hastily as I packed my backpack in my office the day before the conference, my OCD beginning to whimper frantically from my shoulder that we needed to choose the "perfect" book for our trip, as we couldn't waste four hours of reading time. Scanning my shelves, I saw Jeff's book, decided that it might or might not be the perfect choice but I was taking it anyway, and threw it into my backpack as I walked out the door.

As I read in my window seat on the way to LA, OCD sat quietly on my shoulder, knitting away while the plane skied smoothly across the snow pack of clouds. Every now and then, however, its needles would stop their tinny clicking, audible even over the din of the plane's engines, and worry out loud: *What if we aren't remembering all the main points? What if we don't finish it by the time we land in LA?*

"I don't know, OCD. I want to not know the answers to those questions," I'd reply, rapping it on top of its orange ball of a head with the end of my highlighter, hoping I was annoying it as much as it was annoying me.

Even though I'd been in recovery for years and felt so much better than I had in the past, I still experienced a constant buzzing feeling of hypervigilance that OCD's impatient attitude didn't help. It was as if I were walking around, day after day, with a target on my back. A giant bull's-eye that seemed to say to the universe, "We know something bad is going to happen any minute now, and we're the one it's going to happen to!"

The target on my back was the bedrock of my OCD's view on life. Bad things had happened in the past, and they were going to happen in the future. It was only a matter of time. The world was dangerous. It was out to get everyone, but most of all, it was out to get us.

I was a couple of pages into Chapter Four of Jeff's book about what "making belief" meant when OCD piped up again, talking over the voice of the pilot who was warning us of turbulence ahead.

I don't like Jeff. His book is stupid. I think we should stop reading it.

I turned my head to look at my disorder, its little arms crossed in defiance as it stood resolutely on my shoulder.

"That's rude, OCD," I said. "And because you said that, I'm going to keep going."

Hmpf, we'll see about that, it threatened, trying to jump down onto the book to get in the way of what I was reading, but I blocked its path with my highlighter and read the next sentence: "Albert Einstein is said to have remarked that the single most important decision any of us will ever have to make is whether or not to believe that the universe is friendly."

I felt the plane shake a little, a gentle rumbling under my seat.

I read the quote again and then, a few lines down, Jeff's assertion that "no belief is more significant than the way we choose to view our world."

OCD was still trying to jump onto Jeff's book, so I pushed it firmly back up onto my shoulder and highlighted all of what I'd just read, then read the words once more.

I could choose to believe that the universe is friendly?

The plane lurched from side to side, the promised turbulence coming to fruition, but I kept reading, my eyes glued to the pages as the book shook in my hands. My OCD started to pace on my shoulder, ignoring the turbulence and grumbling ever more loudly. It was no wonder that my OCD was doing its best to keep me from reading, because both Jeff and Einstein were saying I didn't have to believe my monster.

They weren't saying bad things didn't happen. After all, Jeff was a radio news anchor, so he shared troubling events happening all over the world on a daily basis. He also wasn't saying that choosing to believe the universe is friendly would suddenly mean only good things would happen. Instead, he was suggesting that for every example of an unfriendly universe, anyone could come up with a counterexample of a friendly universe, and vice versa. The "reality" of the tone of life was unprovable, so we could choose what to believe. Thus, said another Einstein quote a paragraph down from the first: "There are only two ways to live your life. One is as though nothing is a miracle. The other is as though everything is."

When I'd performed *Fred* the previous year, I'd concluded the story of The Accident with, "I have some scars that you can't see. Scars buried deep within my mind. Because my mom and I almost died that day, and my brain learned the world was a very dangerous place." It was a belief I'd taken for granted: that I had no choice but to protect myself from the inevitable perils of life.

Jeff was saying it was an OCD-empowering mistake to ignore the possibility Einstein's words offered.

"I don't have to see the world as dangerous," I whispered to myself as I put the book down, patches of rough air causing the cup of Coke sitting on my seatmate's tray table to hiss and fizz. I stared out the window in wonder at this paradigm shift. "I can choose to believe the universe is friendly."

My OCD, who had started to jump up and down belligerently on my shoulder, as if it were the one causing the turbulence, came completely unhinged upon hearing my words.

It is NOT! it screamed.

"Yes. Yes, it is," I said, testing this new paradigm for how to drop the hypervigilance and live life without an undercurrent of fear.

You cannot say that! my OCD screeched. *You are putting us in jeopardy! Only hypervigilant people stay safe. Only people who don't feel too happy. Saying the universe is friendly is letting down your guard. It's asking for trouble! You are going to kill us!* It started blubbering.

I handed my OCD a tissue and patted it on its little orange head as the plane shook again, knocking my disorder off its clown-like feet as it plopped heavily on my shoulder.

"I don't care, OCD. We are going to try this. I'm going to choose to believe the universe is friendly."

After a few days of trying on my new belief at the conference, of doing the not-for-the-faint-of-heart exposure of letting down my guard and telling myself the world wasn't out to get me, my OCD's tantrums subsided, and I began to feel better. Less hypervigilant. More able to be in the present moment. More like I was enjoying life. As if, for the first time, the bull's-eye on my back had magically disappeared.

By Saturday evening of the conference, I'd come to understand the power inherent in this simple change in belief to remedy a decades-old, OCD-enabling perspective.

Jeff was at this conference, once again emceeing the keynote, and I decided he needed to know about the miracle he'd created by bringing this empowering choice to my attention.

At the social Saturday night, I saw him leave a small group of people with whom he'd been chatting and knew this was my chance to thank him.

"Jeff?" I said, running up to him, hoping to catch him before he was nabbed by some other eager conference-goers.

"Shala! Hi!" He beamed and gave me a hug, his white oxford shirt untucked, sleeves rolled up, a more relaxed look than his coat-and-tie emceeing attire.

"I read your book *When in Doubt, Make Belief* on the flight here. What you say about the universe being friendly? It's amazing. I've started telling myself that it is, and it's completely changed how I feel. I used to be so tense and hypervigilant, and just by choosing to think differently, I feel so much better! I want to buy books from you for my clients, because they have to know the difference this one choice can make."

"That's great, Shala!" he said in his booming voice, leading me over to a stand-up table beside the dance floor. "Let's grab a beer and you can tell me more."

With that invitation, I told Jeff all about the past year, about life after the keynote, about building a therapy practice, about my passion for helping others. We left each other's company that night with an understanding of our shared commitment to advocacy. The next week, I received a box of autographed books from Jeff that he refused to let me purchase, ignoring all my emails asking how much I owed.

Empowered with my new belief, I took a good look at my life and realized how many decisions I'd made because of my OCD's view that the universe was out to get me.

I'd purchased a house I didn't like because my OCD told me it was "fine," that I didn't need a house that was more to my tastes, because buying what I'd actually wanted would have been tempting fate. I'd never purchased a new car, always buying used cars from family members. I'd chosen almost all of my furnishings from piles of extended family hand-me-downs because my OCD had intimated that having worn-out things was protective. After all, in my OCD's distorted reality, the universe punished people who did what they wanted, who bought what they liked, who flaunted happiness. I recognized that choosing whether or not to have old stuff was a champagne problem, but I finally realized that for me, it was a manifestation of a deeply rooted set of warped beliefs.

A few weeks after the conference, I decided to put my new set of beliefs into practice and buy a new car, one to replace my eleven-year-old Honda. I was determined that I wouldn't buy the car my OCD thought I *should* buy—a solid, reliable, "safe" car—but would instead buy a car I wanted.

I pondered for a week what car would create the most fate-tempting exposure. What was the happiest car ever made? I knew in my gut what my answer would be, and without considering any other options or taking more time to think (things my OCD told me I *should* do), I bought what was to me the happiest, friendliest car on Earth: a fire-engine-red 2014 Volkswagen Beetle Convertible. I drove it home from the dealership with the top down, singing at the top of my lungs to Pharrell Williams' "Happy" blasting from the speakers.

"You should fork over a few hundred bucks a month to my credit union for this car," I suggested to Jeff as we drove south from the airport in Atlanta.

"Why? Because picking me up at the airport got you a ticket? Because that's not my fault. This car is a ticket magnet."

When I'd learned that Jeff would be coming to Atlanta a few months after the Los Angeles conference, I'd offered to pick him up at the airport. Not realizing there was a cell phone lot where cars could wait for arriving passengers, I'd been inching along the lengthy pickup area, waiting for Jeff. My car was a bit too visible and I'd lingered a bit too long, however, and when Jeff had finally appeared, it was to find me standing beside my car, waiting to get my you-loitered-too-long-in-a-no-standing-area ticket from an Atlanta police officer.

"No," I laughed. "Because it's your fault I bought this ticket magnet."

"Oh, really?" Jeff said, looking at me over the top of his sunglasses. "Why is that?"

"Because I bought this car as an outward expression of how I now believe the universe is friendly."

Taking off his shades, he said, "Are you serious?"

"Yup, dead serious."

As we drove along the roads of Atlanta, I explained how in the months since the conference I'd been trying to embody the universe-is-friendly attitude in my actions and approach to life. I could tell from Jeff's expression that he was impressed with my dedication to living my new belief, and while he was in town, we spent several hours talking about the tragedy that was OCD, how it savaged its sufferers, and how it tragically sometimes took people's lives, figuratively and literally. We discussed how we might hitch our advocacy wagons to spread the word more widely about OCD and its treatment, especially the power of belief.

My new commitment to believing the universe is friendly wasn't always easy, however, because at times it did feel unfriendly, and not even in an OCD way.

I had christened my new car Lilybug, after our terrier Lily, the most joyful being I'd ever known. But cancer had stolen Lily's exuberant presence from Corey and me during my counseling internship. My mother's lung cancer had also been a most unfriendly shock, as had the same disease attacking her mother, my Nana, a decade before. Shortly after we lost Lily, Lee developed both of the most feared horse diseases: laminitis, requiring icing, x-rays, special shoeing, and endless months of confinement as the pain in his hooves slowly subsided; and colic, necessitating emergency surgery at the University of Georgia, where they flipped him over in an enormous operating theater and removed ten feet of his intestines. While the grim reaper mercifully spared my mother and Lee, it tragically claimed Nana, Lily, and Fred, and then, several years later, Abby, as its own.

However, regardless of potential evidence to the contrary, I was convinced that believing the universe was a friendly, supportive place was going to be key to my staying out of OCD's grasp, and I worked to maintain my staunch commitment to my new belief. Which then led to what felt like a most unfriendly outcome: the end of my partnership with Corey.

As I talked with Corey about my new perspective on life, he and I discovered that we'd unfortunately lost more than our precious pets over the past several years. Somewhere in the time we'd been together, we'd also lost the relationship we'd once had, in no small part because when we'd started dating, I'd still been stuck in the Gravitron, unsure of who I was or what I wanted out of life. Corey and I determined that we'd probably been staying together because, like my hand-me-down furniture, our relationship was "fine." But it also wasn't what either one of us wanted. So after eight years, we separated, and we finally sold the house that I'd never really liked.

I was coming to understand that recovering from a disorder that had dominated my life for so many years was a little bit like doing a tricky puzzle. Tricky in that it seemed, when I poured out all the little cardboard pieces and turned them over, puzzle-side up, that I had everything I needed. But as I put the puzzle together, continuing to choose from the remaining pieces, I recognized that what I had left wasn't going to complete the beautiful picture of a life free from the grips of OCD.

My puzzle was incomplete. A bunch of pieces were missing.

The process of finding those pieces was taking time. Four years, in fact, since I'd first learned about ERP. But I was about to find one of the most important puzzle pieces, one I'd unknowingly had all along.

CHAPTER 16

Shoulders Back

"We watched a great TED Talk that I think you might find interesting," my dad said, as we talked on the phone one evening in early 2014. "It's called 'Your Body Language Shapes Who You Are,' and it's given by a researcher out of Harvard named Amy Cuddy."

My parents, voracious readers and consumers of educational programming, were always a fount of useful information. But neither my parents nor I knew how influential Dr. Cuddy's talk would turn out to be for me.

What she proposed made sense. When people are feeling powerful, she said, they open up their stances, making themselves bigger. But when they aren't feeling so mighty, they close in on themselves, hunching over. A person's body language communicates how she is feeling. But more important is that the opposite is also true: people can influence how they think and feel by their choice of body language. Cuddy's research has shown that if someone adopts a "high power pose" for two minutes, that changes levels of some key hormones, making the person feel more powerful.

As I finished her talk, my mind whirled with the beginnings of an idea. Wasn't that one of OCD's biggest moves, striking a power pose? After all, that's exactly what it was doing when it changed into the Triad of Hell, right? Wasn't it making itself bigger and scarier?

Couldn't I do the same thing?

Deciding to try out my theory when OCD started to bellyache about my potentially having left the stove on at home after I arrived at my office one day, I stood up, threw my shoulders back, put my hands on my hips, and adopted the same haughty, arrogant tone that OCD used with me.

"I may or may not have left the stove on when I left the house this morning," I said. "My house may be burning down right now. I may kill all my pets. But I want this anxiety and uncertainty because I want to get better."

Huh, I thought. It was sort of funny, standing here like Wonder Woman while speaking imperiously at the wall. I said my script again, as forcefully and powerfully as I could.

"I may or may not have left the stove on. I may or may not be burning down the house and killing all my pets. But bring it on, OCD, BRING IT ON!"

I continued saying variations on my script for two minutes, throwing my shoulders back as far as I could. It was incredible. Standing tall and speaking powerfully did seem to make me feel more powerful.

I started doing power poses every time I talked back to my OCD, to give myself that little boost of confidence, to make myself feel bigger and more powerful than my still somewhat ornery disorder.

It was working. I was on to something.

About a year later, Dr. Wilson helped me understand why.

I'd not only hunted down Jeff at the Los Angeles IOCDF conference in 2014, I'd also made sure to attend a roundtable discussion run by Reid (otherwise known as Dr. Wilson. I'd finally asked him a few hours after I'd given my keynote if he'd mind if I called him by his first name. Amused, he'd said, "What have you been calling me 'til now?"

"Dr. Wilson," I'd replied.

"Oh, I hadn't noticed," he'd said, and I'd been calling him Reid ever since.)

Looking at the people seated in a circle around him during the roundtable, Reid said, "You need to act like the content is irrelevant. I'm not saying you'll believe it is or that it will feel like it's irrelevant, but I'm saying you need to *act as though* it is."

Years earlier I'd learned from Reid that OCD's content—all that mental garbage about rabies, AIDS, not pleasing people, and so on—was meaningless. Now he was adding a twist, one he would describe in detail a few years later in his book *Stopping the Noise in Your Head: The New Way to Overcome Anxiety and Worry*. He was saying I needed to make a conscious effort to *act as though* what OCD was saying didn't matter, a subtle but tectonic shift in how to approach my monster.

"If my OCD is worried I've offended someone and I throw my shoulders back, I'm acting as though I'm okay with not being in control of what that person thinks," I said to myself as I walked down the casino-carpeted hall after Reid's session, processing what he'd said. "If I give credibility to what OCD threatens, I'll act scared, meek, as if I've done something wrong. But if I'm acting *as though*, I'm going to act confident. I'm going to throw my shoulders back and act like what OCD taunts me about doesn't matter."

I decided to try something new. Whenever my OCD bothered me, I would simply throw my shoulders back and go on with my day.

I could hardly believe the power of my new exposure strategy. One small posture change brought my OCD to its knees.

After adopting this technique, I rarely needed to use my "may or may not" statements. They were required on those infrequent occasions when my OCD was able to trick me into getting lost in its storytelling and I mindlessly began the pas de deux of mental rituals. Once I started mentally dancing with my OCD for any length of time, I found it challenging to stop without saying "may or may not" statements out loud. Doing so was using OCD's content against it, forcing it to face feared thoughts without the crutch of mental rituals, until it recognized that what it was worried about was indeed just uncertainty—uncertainty over which we had no control.

The majority of the time, however, when something triggered my OCD, the union of "shoulders back" with "acting as though" worked beautifully. Because in throwing my shoulders back, I was owning the uncertain truth of the "may or may not" statements without having to verbalize them or give any credence to the stories OCD was telling.

One day a few months after Reid's roundtable, as I rode Lee on leaf-strewn forest trails, lulled into thought by the white noise of his hooves sweeping and crushing fallen leaves, I thought about all the strides I was making by putting my shoulders back as an exposure strategy.

Then it hit me.

Shoulders back.

I heard echoes of my old riding instructor as she yelled, "Your posture sucks, Shala!"

Of course! Lee had been running away with me because of my posture—because I'd acted like prey! I'd sit on Lee, anxious and tense, hunched over and small, telegraphing through my stance that I was scared. Horses are prey animals. Their main defense is running. If one of the herd acts scared, they all run. It's their best chance of staying alive. I was Lee's herd when we were riding, and I was acting like something was about to kill us every time I tensed up and leaned forward.

We'd had The Accident II because I'd been doing the opposite of putting my shoulders back.

"Shoulders Back," I said out loud, patting Lee gratefully on the neck. I'd finally learned the simple yet powerful strategy that my horse had been trying to teach me for almost a decade.

Shoulders Back turned out to be especially effective for fighting what I finally recognized was its own class of intrusive thoughts that had long driven my Quest for perfection and absolution: people pleasing. My obsession with making everyone happy led to my most egregious compulsions: my constant reassurance-seeking through the accumulation of accolades, approval, and accomplishments.

But people pleasing met its match in Shoulders Back.

You might have offended her, Shala!

Throw shoulders back. Act as if I'm on top of the world.

That person might be upset with us. We should apologize!

Throw shoulders back. Act as though everything is fine.

We don't have as many clients as that therapist does. We're not as good as she is. Maybe this is the beginning of the end of our career!

Throw shoulders back. Act like what OCD is saying is garbage.

Shoulders Back would leave my OCD standing speechless, mouth agape.

For years I'd been trying to control how other people thought of me, looking for my own absolution in their approval, and as a result, I'd abdicated power over my own self-worth. If I only thought well of myself when I was sure everyone else did, I gave everyone else power over my emotions, my value, and my self-esteem. In trying to please everyone to earn praise that would make me feel worthy—a Sisyphean task—I ensured that I'd almost never feel good about who I was, giving more power to my OCD, whose obsessions only made me want to please everyone more. It was a vicious, demanding cycle that Shoulders Back completely disrupted by helping me realize I had no control over other people or their thoughts.

When I first started doing Shoulders Back, I thought that acting "as though" meant I wasn't supposed to care what people thought of me; after all, in doing Shoulders Back I acted like I didn't care, right?

But then I watched Brené Brown's talk "Why Your Critics Aren't the Ones Who Count," which helped me understand the distinction was not so black and white. "Not caring what people think is its own kind of hustle," she says. Simply not caring means making oneself invulnerable, thus forestalling the possibility to connect meaningfully with others.

For me, it can be a double-edged sword. If I try not to care what others think, as Brené says, I become stoic; I disengage and lose the ability to connect. But if I care too much about others' opinions, I try to be a people-pleaser, masking my vulnerability with a veneer of perfectionism, thereby distancing my true self from others.

The goal is to be somewhere in the gray, embracing uncertainty. With Shoulders Back, I embody acceptance of being unsure what others think and why. It can still hurt when people don't think positively of me, but I can recognize that what anyone else thinks is not under my power, or my OCD's power, to control. As my sage friend and Alcoholics Anonymous veteran Bob once told me, and I now understood: "What other people think of me is none of my business."

Even with Shoulders Back, however, there was still a part of me that believed what other people thought about me was very much my business: the appearance-obsessed, whispering salesman who'd started soliciting my buy-in back in college. Because although he'd never regained the strength he'd had during my time at the University of Illinois, he was still with me, and I was finally about to learn his name.

CHAPTER 17

Fading Echoes

"You need to eat that, Shala."

I looked at the chocolate-chip cookie. It was huge, probably five inches across its plastic-wrapped diameter. M&Ms peeked out across the craggy surface like multi-colored crocus flowers bursting from a forest floor.

"I know. I will," I replied to Jeff Bell as he gathered his backpack to head to work.

"Good. You'd better. See you when I get off the air, okay?"

Spreading out my things on the small wooden table in the café, I watched Jeff leave. We were in the financial district of San Francisco, not far from KCBS, the radio station where Jeff worked as a news anchor during afternoon drive time.

I'd been coming to San Francisco frequently during the first few months of 2015 to use Jeff's father's sailboat, otherwise known as "The Boat" in Jeff's memoir, *Rewind, Replay, Repeat: A Memoir of Obsessive-Compulsive Disorder*, as a writing retreat and also to work on

Jeff's and my new advocacy venture, Beyond the Doubt. Sometimes, though, it was a little chilly on The Boat, and I'd stay at Jeff's house instead, commuting into the city with him on the ferry, and I'd write in cafés while he was on the air.

I picked up the cookie, the plastic crinkling merrily, and thought about how this particular goody had ended up in my hand. As we'd waited in line to pay for our sandwiches, Jeff had said, spying the cookies in the display, "I love those! I'll buy one for each of us." I froze, unable to offer what should have been thanks, and I knew Jeff had seen "the look" flash across my face. The wow-that's-a-big-cookie-and-I-don't-really-want-to-eat-that look.

I hadn't had disordered eating for more than twenty years, but remnants remained, surfacing unbidden at the most inopportune times. It was hard to hide those remnants, like "the look," from Jeff. He could spot a compulsive behavior, whether monster- or salesman-induced, from a mile away. Thus, his "You need to eat that, Shala" as he'd left me to my own devices with a cookie that the salesman absolutely didn't want me to eat.

As I'd learned to treat OCD, I realized I needed to know how to treat the mental illnesses that often accompanied the disorder: social anxiety disorder, depression, panic disorder, trichotillomania, skin-picking disorder, generalized anxiety disorder, hoarding disorder, phobias, and body dysmorphic disorder, or BDD.

At the first IOCDF conference I attended as a therapist-in-training in 2011, I went to a workshop called "Cruel Reflections: What you need to know about treating Body Dysmorphic Disorder," given by Dr. Sabine Wilhelm, a BDD expert. She explained that in BDD, people become obsessed with a perceived flaw or imperfection in their appearance. This obsession leads to a variety of compulsions, which can include mirror-checking, camouflaging the perceived defect, comparing oneself with others, or even surgery to try to remedy the flaw. One of my key takeaways from the workshop was that people with BDD typically have less insight into their disorder than people with OCD, because people with BDD tend to believe more strongly what the disorder tells them.

A year later, as I was reading Dr. Wilhelm's *Feeling Good About the Way You Look* in preparation for working with a client who had BDD, I considered how debilitating it must be to have body dysmorphic disorder. The shame, the worry, the perceived constant judgment from others. Fortunately, BDD, like OCD, has effective treatment: cognitive behavioral therapy that includes cognitive work, exposure therapy, and some other components, and after graduation I purchased Dr. Wilhelm's new *Cognitive-Behavioral Therapy for Body Dysmorphic Disorder* treatment manual, coauthored with Katharine Phillips and Gail Steketee. Pressed for time, I read everything except Chapter Sixteen, titled "Weight, Shape, and Muscularity," as it didn't seem particularly relevant to the clients I was currently seeing.

Another year later, about four years into my training on treating BDD, I recognized that two of my clients were presenting with a combination of OCD, a mild eating disorder, and BDD, so I determined it was time to read that chapter. Plopping down on the paisley-patterned turquoise, green, and brown rug in my office, I leaned against my overstuffed armchair and cracked open the book, letting its cover rest against my legs. I started reading, and for the first time, I saw aspects of myself described in the pages about body dysmorphic disorder.

"You should also ask the patient about excessive, compulsive behaviors such as the following: exercising more than one hour a day more than six times per week, continuing to exercise even when injured, or missing important activities in order to exercise."

I'd run every day when I was at the University of Illinois, no matter what. Nothing could have kept me from running, from participating in that sole-pounding exercise that had seemed necessary to my soul's survival.

"... if a patient is obsessed with body weight/shape (e.g., a protruding stomach) but does not meet criteria for an eating disorder, BDD would be the more appropriate diagnosis ..."

I'd been obsessed with my knees and thighs in college. I'd had disordered eating that didn't meet the criteria for an eating disorder. While my disordered eating thankfully hadn't survived college, I still hated my knees and had never been able to let go of my negative thoughts about my thighs. From my kneecaps to my groin, my legs looked the same to me as they did when I was at the University of Illinois, and I continued to do everything I could to disguise what I didn't like.

"Oh my God," I gasped, the book sliding off my legs and onto the rug. "I have BDD."

All of a sudden, the events of twenty-five years earlier, hazy and scattered, sharpened into focus. My disordered eating habits had never met criteria for an eating disorder because their goal wasn't to make *me* thinner. The goal was to make *my knees and thighs* thinner. My eating issues had never been a standalone eating disorder. They were instead a BDD compulsion: a way to try to sculpt my knees and thighs into the shape the salesman wanted.

The salesman who now had a name: body dysmorphic disorder.

As I continued to read, I marveled at how I'd been exposed to the concept of BDD for four years now, and it had never crossed my mind that I might have it. But that's because of the very nature of the disorder: people with BDD believe what the disorder tells them. My salesman wanted me to believe he wasn't a perception or a disorder, but reality: my knees were just fat and ugly.

In fact, as I did research for this chapter and read the updated DSM-5 diagnostic criteria for BDD, I found that it says, "Note that distressing or impairing preoccupation with obvious appearance flaws (for example, those that are easily noticeable/clearly visible at conversational distance) is not diagnosed as BDD; rather, such preoccupation is diagnosed as Other Specified Obsessive-Compulsive and Related Disorder."

See! I'm not BDD! cried the salesman in protest. *I'm just reality telling you that we are deformed. But I have a solution! We can fix it!*

Not until reading about compulsive exercise as a ritual of BDD did it dawn on me why I'd become a compulsive runner. I'd been trying to meet the demanding standards of a disorder that was never going to be satisfied.

I heard the café staff yelling orders at each other behind the long, glass-fronted counter as I took a bite of the cookie. I was a little nervous eating it. Not because I thought it was going to make me fat, but because I hadn't eaten a snack that decadent for a while. Now that I knew I had BDD, I recognized that if I didn't do the exposure of occasionally consuming junk food, I would once again begin to hear the faint whispers of the salesman echoing through my mind.

After learning I had BDD, I used the treatment manual to do cognitive behavioral therapy on myself. In situations where my knees were visible and the salesman was concerned other people would notice and think less of me, I learned to question these distorted thoughts, replacing them with more rational views, such as "It's unlikely people are focusing on me; they are focusing on what's important to them." I've tried to retrain myself in the use of mirrors, widening my perspective to take in my whole reflection instead of laser-focusing on the appearance of my knees. However, recognizing the compulsive trap looking in a full-length mirror can still be, I took the one leaning on my bedroom wall and put it in the closet. When I've become better at taking in my whole reflection, I'll put it back. I've also worked to stop the ritual of staring at other women's knees and comparing them to my own, a long-standing compulsion that started in college.

However, my treatment for my own BDD is still very much in its infancy for one simple reason. Of all my psychological issues, with the exception of my time at the mercy of the salesman in college, dealing with BDD has not been my priority. OCD has been my priority.

Recently, the salesman has used this to its advantage to try to reclaim some of his former college-days glory.

"What are your goals for training?" Tammie, my new athletic trainer, asked me at our first meeting in 2016. A vivacious, enthusiastic woman about my age, Tammie had blonde hair that fell loosely down her back and an intense gaze that conveyed how much she cared about her job.

"My doctor recently told me I need more muscle mass. I've belonged to this gym for three years, but I clearly don't know how to build muscle, so I decided to hire a trainer," I said.

I'd met with the head of training at the gym the previous week. He'd taken me through a series of fitness evaluations that were frankly embarrassing. I could barely do one push-up. I thought my abdomen might rip in two as I tried to hold a plank. The results shocked me, as I'd been swimming laps several times a week for a couple of years. After the revealing evaluation, I'd signed on for a year of training with one of my gym's master trainers, Tammie.

"We can definitely get you more muscle," Tammie said, making notes in a dark-blue notebook. "Anything else?"

"My upper-body strength is abysmal," I admitted, flexing my arm in the manner of a weightlifter showing off his biceps.

"Okay, we'll do upper body. Is that it?"

Tell her. Say it! Tell her what we want!

The salesman had been mostly slacking off since I left the University of Illinois, but I still felt his presence. He wasn't as ambitious, nor as convincingly effective as he'd been in college. As my weight went up and down over the next two decades, he'd pipe up occasionally, offering tips and tricks to hide my flaws, or he'd gaze nostalgically at the smooth attractiveness of other women's legs, fondly remembering the days when he could effortlessly close every deal he put before me.

Signing the training contract, however, had been like giving the salesman a double shot of espresso. Instantly energized, he began to offer insistent, whispered ideas about how I could best utilize my time with this expert in fixing how people looked.

Tell her what we really want! It's not too late. We can do it. Twenty-five years later, we can finally have beautiful, smooth legs!

The salesman became my ventriloquist, and I gave voice to its words. "I don't like my knees. The flabby skin above them. Can you tone that up? Can you make it go away?" I grabbed the flesh above my kneecap with my hand to emphasize my point, to communicate that I needed—the salesman needed—her answer to be "yes."

Her long blonde hair swinging rhythmically behind her, Tammie shook her head and answered, compassionate but firm, "No, we can't change that. That's the way you are. It might tone up a little, but not in a noticeable way."

Out of practice at handling objections, the salesman stammered, giving me a moment to recognize that I had a choice in how I approached training. "That's okay. I actually have body dysmorphic disorder about my knees and thighs," I admitted. "It's probably good we can't change how they look, as that's just part of my disorder, wanting that."

Still, the gym is a danger zone for the salesman. Floor-to-ceiling mirrors in the aerobics rooms, toned women walking around, motivational billboards featuring buff models plastered on the walls. I go anyway, but I have rules to keep me from succumbing to the salesman's whispered entreaties. I can lift weights three times a week, which is Tammie's prescription, and no more. I can do an average of about two and a half hours of cardio a week, the current recommended guideline for adults, and no more. I try to use helpful self-talk as I see myself in the mirror in Zumba® or Body Works classes: "I, like everyone, am imperfect, and I am enough. I'm going to love myself for who I am."

The echoes of the salesman's whispers are fading, but my BDD clearly needs more therapeutic attention, which I will give it. I've tried to be compassionate with myself that I'm still at the beginning of this part of my recovery. After all, working on my recovery from my BDD has not been my focus. I've spent so much of my life crippled with its cousin, OCD, that the echoes of my BDD have seemed, since college, like background noise, haunting but tolerable.

I had severe BDD in college, my thinking so distorted that I warped my eating to try to meet my disorder's urgently whispered demands. But the salesman has rarely been as powerful as the monster that is my OCD. In college, fearful that my disordered eating was going to bring undue negative attention, my OCD essentially took control of the situation, shutting down my rituals with food. It did the same thing with my excessive drinking in my twenties. While I don't think my drinking was ever at the level of an addiction, my OCD still didn't approve, and it turned off the taps for fear that my too-frequent bouts of intoxication would cause me to lose the aura of normalcy so important in its over-controlled world. My OCD was and probably always will be king; the other disorders—as well as any harmful coping mechanisms, such as drinking, which I've used to deal with them—were supplicants before the all-powerful monarch.

I have met a number of people with this combination of issues: OCD, BDD, disordered eating that may or may not meet the criteria for an eating disorder, and depression, and each person's presentation is a little different. For some, BDD is the star of the show, the accompanying disorders humbled in its presence. For others, it's the disordered eating or eating disorder that takes a leading role, OCD and BDD kowtowing to its whims. For people like me, OCD is the prima donna, self-important and always hogging the spotlight. Regardless of which disorder's name runs first in the credits, however, when these disorders are left untreated, depression is almost always there: always winning for best supporting actor, always propping up whoever is trying to run the show.

Squirming on the wooden chair, a furnishing clearly not meant for long-term seating, I took another bite of the M&M cookie. My anxiety had subsided, and I ate the rest of it contentedly, listening to the loud voices of waitstaff ricochet off the café's brick walls.

While the salesman may not be as strong as my monster, they're both childlike in their need for constant reminders of who's boss, and I often use food to assert my dominance. I order dessert I don't want every now and then. I rarely buy low-fat foods and almost never those that are fat-free. I have drinks with colleagues and sometimes a glass of wine by myself while watching Netflix. I eat chips and fries and candy bars. Sometimes I do a two-for-one reminder, buying an outrageous indulgence and eating it with unwashed hands straight off the floor. I don't do this all the time, but enough to remind my BDD and my OCD that they're not in charge—I am.

Working on overcoming BDD is now a priority in my life. I choose clothing specifically because it upsets the salesman. In fact, every outfit I wore at a recent IOCDF conference was purposely above the knee, giving me an opportunity to practice Shoulders Back, acting as if the BDD content were irrelevant and developing new, healthier beliefs about my knees, thighs, and myself as a result.

I'm going to continue to push myself because I want to show the salesman that the FUD factor as a sales pitch now falls flat. Because fear, uncertainty, and doubt don't have to be problems, and if they aren't problems, then I don't need whispered echoes of *"You can fix this"* as solutions. I can lean into fear, uncertainty, and doubt using cognitive behavioral therapy for BDD, remind myself that my salesman is selling smoke and mirrors, and embrace who I am, as the whispered echoes fade into the distance.

Smoke and mirrors have pervaded my life. Having OCD and BDD can be like living in an amusement-park funhouse, where shifting floors and distorted mirrors dizzyingly warp reality, making it a challenge to stand up straight, to know which end is up, to live life without repeatedly being knocked off balance.

It would be a lot for anyone to handle, so I'm going to be self-compassionate and give myself a break, knowing that, to try to control the bedlam in my head, I developed a lifelong addiction. One that, over time, had become as much of a problem as the chaos it was originally supposed to manage.

CHAPTER 18

Ending the Quest

"Shala?" my OCD asked, pulling gently on the sleeve of my purple fleece.

"Yes, OCD?"

I didn't mind that OCD was talking to me. It didn't bother me as much anymore, not in the way that it used to. I was consistently aggressive with it, as aggressive as it used to be with me, doing my best to throw my shoulders back and act as if what it was saying didn't matter.

I also poked it regularly, doing daily exposures such as refusing to apologize to friends whom my OCD was sure I'd offended, or leaving things all over the house in disarray on purpose. My OCD could sense weakness, and if I gave in to its demands in the slightest—checking on the pets before I left to make sure they were still inside, or hesitating to pull my gaze away from the rearview mirror in a leftover habit of looking for bodies strewn along the road behind me—it would seize the opportunity and try to once again make my life a living hell. It took energy to manage it, especially without medication, but most days, I was successful.

"I don't think we should write this next story, Shala."

I stopped typing and looked at my OCD staring up at me, a lonesome tear beginning to peek out from underneath its overlarge sunglasses. Reaching over and handing it a tissue, I tried to be as kind as possible as I said, "I know you don't, OCD, but this story is really important."

"But if you write it, people will think we are mentally ill!"

Snot dripping down its face, my OCD started to cry in earnest.

My poor OCD. I smiled slightly as I replied, "Well, technically we do have a mental illness or two."

Blowing its nose noisily, it stopped crying long enough to share its latest doom-filled litany of woe.

"Maybe it's okay to write about it if we've made progress, but this chapter will show everyone we still have problems that we're just figuring out how to solve, and if people know that, they won't like us or trust us or think nice things about us and we'll be ostracized and you won't have a job anymore and we'll be lonely and *probablyendupstarvinganddead*!"

Pulling another tissue out of the box, I held it up as my OCD blew its nose again.

"Yes, OCD, all of that may happen. But this story is important because people need to know what it's really like to live with life-long mental illness. And we have several! There's you, and the body dysmorphia salesman, and every once in a while there's depression, too. And the group of you can be a pain to manage sometimes."

I could see frown lines forming on OCD's forehead. It didn't like hearing the truth: that living with it could be challenging.

"Did you know that having a monster like you is the tenth leading cause of disability in the world?"

My OCD, looking a little shamefaced, had the decency to lower its head, a tacit acknowledgement of its latent, life-destroying power.

"What's worse, OCD, is that depression is even more powerful than you are. It's the number one cause of disability. And most people with an untamed monster have depression, too, so most people going through treatment for OCD deal with two of the top ten most disabling conditions simultaneously. That's not easy. And no one is always successful."

"But you treat mental illness! You *should* be successful!"

Realizing I'd get nowhere with this, but feeling a bit sorry for my OCD and its worries, I held out my hand so OCD could jump onto it, then raised it up so I could look my disorder directly in its eyes.

"There are no 'shoulds,' OCD, you know that. Should is the language of shame. There is only what is. I'm going to write this story. Because people need to know that recovery is a process, a long one at times, and it isn't perfect, and that's okay. We are all works in progress. Even those of us who help others for a living."

Sitting down with a little thump on my palm, my OCD blew its nose and put the damp tissue on my hand. Looking woeful and somewhat beaten, it said in a plaintive little voice, "Are you sure?"

And there was the crux of my OCD's issue. The issue I'd always help it face, over and over and over again. That there was no "sure." Trying to achieve certainty was the domain of fools, and I was no longer the court jester.

"No, I'm not sure. I'll never be sure about anything. But I'm going to do this anyway."

Lowering my hand to the floor, I nudged my OCD off. It hopped down, waddled over to the corner, and picked up its knitting.

With the rhythmic clicking of needles in the background, I turned to my computer and began to type.

"So are you telling me you don't even let people pick the meals they want to order, you just pick them yourselves?" I said into my iPhone, a little too loudly. I was speaking with customer service for a meal-delivery service company, a company from whom I now regretted ordering. Bella, my anxious ten-year-old Lhasa Apso rescue with three working legs and bullet shrapnel in her shoulder (from an unknown horror that occurred before I rescued her), looked at me plaintively as she put her front leg on my office chair. She didn't like it when I raised my voice.

"No, ma'am. You can pick them yourself," said the customer service representative, a young man who sounded very far away and who spoke with more patience than he probably felt.

"Then why did it just skip that step and send me an email, telling me my order was placed?"

I recognized that this was actually OCD talking. It had dawned on me over the past few years that my OCD didn't like things that didn't make sense, because in its over-controlled, ideal world, things should always make sense. But I felt the annoying need to voice my OCD's concerns, to point out that something was amiss that required fixing, as if this were some sort of life-imperiling emergency that demanded immediate attention.

Bella continued to look at me, her big brown eyes worried. Something was making me upset, and did that mean she was in danger, too?

"I don't know, ma'am, but I can show you how to change the selections. If you'll just click on ..."

I went to the area of the website he was indicating, fuming. Fuming because I was giving in to my OCD and because I didn't have time to be making this call. I'd ordered a meal-delivery gift for a friend, but the gift code hadn't worked when my friend or I tried it, and now I was wasting precious time sorting it out when I had client notes to write up, a clinical book to read, this book to write, phone calls to return, emails to answer.

"It would have been easier to go grocery shopping myself and then drop the ingredients off at their house," I snapped, again sharing my OCD's snarky thoughts, as I navigated to the page where I could indeed choose the meals for my friend's delivery.

Bella dropped down to the floor and rolled over, a nonverbal request for reassurance that everything would be okay.

I reached down to scratch her fluffy cream-colored belly, a bright turquoise suture line running down her abdomen where she'd been spayed. She licked her lips, still unsure.

As I absentmindedly rubbed Bella's tummy, I thought about how ridiculous this all was. Yes, I was giving in to my OCD, which I needed to stop doing in these situations, but why did I have to get angry to boot?

This wasn't life threatening. It didn't even matter. I'm sure whatever meals their system picked would've been fine.

But the situation still made me mad. And on top of that, I was angry at myself for being angry in the first place.

"I can see on my side that your meals have been chosen," I heard the rep say through my earbuds, interrupting my thoughts. "The delivery will be next Wednesday. Can I do anything else for you, ma'am?" he asked, probably praying I'd say "no."

"No, thank you. You've been very helpful," I said, sheepish.

I hung up, feeling like an idiot. What was wrong with me? Why did I have to get so upset about things that didn't even matter?

Leaving Bella lying on the floor, I straightened up and went back to my unending to-do list on my Mac with a heavy sigh, without realizing that the answer to my question was staring me right in the face.

I looked up at the wooden octagonal ceiling, an octagon-shaped skylight framed in the center. Light streamed in from the skylight and the floor-to-ceiling windows on either side of what looked like a fireplace, before which the speaker, Rick Hanson, was sitting.

I was at Spirit Rock Meditation Center just north of San Francisco for my fourth all-day workshop on how to be more mindful.

It had been seven years since I'd first seen a presentation on mindfulness and OCD at my inaugural IOCDF conference. The talk I'd mentally filed away under Things to Look into Muuuuch Later, After I Have Learned How to Do ERP. I'd changed my tune a lot since then.

Even before that first OCD conference, my dad had been conducting a years-long meditation-is-worth-continued-exploration-for-people-suffering-from-anxiety campaign, sending me articles about its benefits from various newspapers and magazines.

Finally convinced, after finishing business school, I'd started attending a local weekly meditation gathering and signed up to join these meditators for a weekend retreat. It was held several hours outside Atlanta in a rustic center surrounded on all sides by forest, with only one tiny gravel road leading back to civilization.

The retreat had started out innocently enough, but I realized, as I sat in a circular, high-ceilinged, wood-paneled room during the last "meditation" of the day, that this particular group and I weren't destined to gel. I put the word "meditation" in quotes here because as I sat cross-legged on a little black cushion, watching people get up one by one and spasmodically gyrate by themselves in the center of the room, I thought "drinking the Kool-Aid" might better describe the night's activities.

After several false starts—fortunately none quite as disconcerting as my Kool-Aid drinking faux cult experience—I'd developed an almost daily meditation practice a few years after I'd discovered ERP. I'd even cowritten a book about the subject and its cousin, self-compassion, called *Everyday Mindfulness for OCD: Tips, Tricks and Skills for Living Joyfully*, with my buddy Jon Hershfield.

Mindfulness and self-compassion had become pillars of not just my OCD recovery, but of my life. Mindfulness means being okay with the ways things are, even if in the present moment I'm experiencing a bunch of annoying obsessions and urges to do compulsions. Self-compassion, I learned from the work of scholar Kristin Neff, is accepting how I feel, recognizing I'm not alone, and being nice to myself. For instance: "I'm feeling anxious right now about writing this chapter. I bet many authors feel this way as they're writing. I'm going to give myself a break, accepting this first draft the way it is, and then watch *Madam Secretary* to reward myself for my hard work."

My discovery of self-compassion was revolutionary in changing my view of myself. I'd been self-critical my whole life because OCD was so demeaning, and I'd unconsciously made its perspective my own. Which is not surprising, because having lifelong, untreated OCD is akin to living for decades with an abusive partner. I'd internalized the mistreatment my partner constantly delivered: I must deserve it, or it wouldn't keep happening. Learning to be mindful and to step back from thoughts and see them as just that—thoughts, not facts—combined with being able to give myself compassion, combatted my mind's innate tendency to be, at times, an abusive jerk.

I'd decided to try Rick Hanson's Spirit Rock workshop because I loved his work. His book *Buddha's Brain: The Practical Neuroscience of Happiness, Love, and Wisdom* had helped me better understand why everyone, not only people with OCD, struggles with staying positive more often than we'd like to admit.

Jeff came with me to Dr. Hanson's workshop. I'd come to the Bay Area to see Jeff receive an award for his advocacy work, and we'd decided to attend Dr. Hanson's workshop while I was in town. It probably would have been better for Jeff to stay at home, however, as he was a "little bit moldy," as my mom would have said. Suffering from a raw sore throat and the beginnings of congestion, he sat beside me in stocking feet (having left his shoes, like the other attendees, in small, white cubbies in the main-entrance hall) and tried not to look like his throat was on fire.

Don't touch him, he's diseased. My OCD had climbed up on my shoulder and was whispering into my ear.

I leaned over and put my hand on Jeff's arm in what seemed like a show of solidarity for his predicament but was really a "fuck you" to my disorder. (I'd just written a blog post for Jeff's and my *Psychology Today* Beyond the Doubt blog called "The Hidden Power of Swearing at Your OCD: Three ways to use the art and science of cursing to power up your recovery," so I was trying to practice what I preached.)

Hmpf, my OCD said, sliding back down to the floor and picking up its knitting.

Jeff widened his eyes and gave me a strained grin, apparently concluding my hand gesture must have been an attempt to ensure he hadn't fallen asleep.

I realized, in that moment, what an achievement it was for me to be sitting here without an ounce of OCD-induced mental pain in the presence of Jeff's sickness. I could go blessed days when I didn't hear a peep out of my OCD, thanks to Shoulders Back. In fact, what I'd discovered was that if I put my shoulders back far enough, my OCD slid right off my shoulder and onto the floor, its little knitting needles tinkling as they hit the ground. I liked having my OCD on the floor. It was much harder for me to hear what it was saying from down there.

Giving Jeff's arm one more pat, I turned my attention back to Dr. Hanson, who was taking questions from the audience.

A woman stood up, long black hair framing an intense expression visible from across the room. "How do you balance contentment and ambition?" she asked, holding the microphone that volunteers were passing among audience members.

How indeed? I hadn't been paying all that much attention to the Q&A session until then. Until someone asked the question that had been the crux of my problem with workaholism for my entire life.

<hr />

My workaholism had risen to new levels over the past few years. I'd cofounded Beyond the Doubt with Jeff, and we ran in-person workshops, an online e-course called *Thriving With OCD*, and a daily motivational email program for people with OCD called *KeyWords*. I ran a full-time CBT therapy practice. I'd cowritten *Everyday Mindfulness for OCD* with Jon. I went to at least three national conferences a year, presenting at most or all of them multiple times per conference. I was writing this book, and Jeff and I had started cowriting a novel. Finally, I was trying to have a life outside of work that included meditation, time with friends and family, reading for fun, riding Lee, and spending time with my pets.

I was burning out. I didn't want to be working this hard.

I can think of a few short periods in my life when I did enjoy working around the clock. The adrenaline. The rush of giving it my all to beat an impossible deadline. The camaraderie of laboring on teams with other workaholics who all wore the fatigue, the dark under-eye circles, the caffeine-induced hyperactivity as badges of honor. And most importantly, the much-needed respite from my OCD's constant harangue of doom, death, and destruction.

When I was twenty-six, I'd purchased and read Richard Carlson's and Joseph Bailey's book *Slowing Down to the Speed of Life: How to Create a More Peaceful, Simpler Life from the Inside Out*. The book had been my beacon, one I never gave away in cleanouts of old stuff, always available on a readily accessible bookshelf. I hadn't ever been able to implement its advice, but the fact that it existed gave me hope that maybe someday I could stop the relentless drive to compulsively work.

Instead, I picked up more bad habits. Multitasking. Working longer hours. Working on the weekends. Drinking endless cans of Coke to pep up my flagging energy stores. (I'd stopped drinking diet soda years earlier.)

Workaholism, the very thing I'd created to manage my monster, had become its own monster, the result of the Quest I'd started in high school for distraction, perfection, and absolution.

I'd ardently tried, in classic workaholic fashion, many things to stop my workaholic ways. I'd joined Workaholics Anonymous, buying the books and attending phone meetings, but quickly lost interest. I'd developed a complicated spreadsheet to track all my hours, but it didn't change how many I worked. I'd taken time off, such as when I quit working for Gus's company, only to go right back to my old ways at my next job. I'd forced myself to take quarterly weeklong "breaks," then sneakily read two or three clinical books while I was "on vacation." I'd read self-help books on mindfulness, stress, happiness, anxiety, and OCD, but none seemed to hold the answer to how to stop working compulsively.

When Corey, with whom I'd remained the best of friends, sent me a link to Emmy Rossum's song "Slow Me Down," I watched the video on my iPad, seeing myself all too clearly in her poignant lyrics about running around, racing through life, rushing to get to the next thing—none of which I wanted to do anymore. But my ambition, my Quest, seemed to have a drive all its own. So there was no more important question than the one Rick Hanson was about to answer: How do you balance contentment and ambition?

I opened my journal, a beautiful book covered in blackened silver filigree, pen poised in anticipation, as I waited for Dr. Hanson to answer.

He explained that the likelihood of long-term success was not associated with being driven or intense, but with developing a core of positive emotion. He explained that when people experience the fight-or-flight response—that ancient reaction that gets us away from danger—in combination with negative emotion, they feel stress. But if they experience the fight-or-flight response paired with positive emotion, the result is instead engagement, enthusiasm, or delight.

"[A] cat can chase the mouse without hating the mouse. [A] person can hit that top spin in tennis with full aggressiveness without being angry," Dr. Hanson said. "And one of the keys to it is not letting yourself be invaded by negative emotion."

As I wrote, "People can be intense, aggressive, and goal-directed without being angry," I took in the weight of his words and what they meant in my life. I quickly scribbled a note in my filigreed journal—"Workaholism fuels negative emotions - > anger"—then pulled on Jeff's sleeve to get his attention, pointing to what I'd just written.

"Makes sense," he whispered around his throat-numbing cough drop.

It more than made sense. It was as if I'd been driving down a rainy road without windshield wipers, and suddenly, they started working and I could see the road ahead.

I hadn't been able to get a handle on my workaholism because I'd never before realized it was what made me irritable, resentful, and angry. My monster and the soul-draining weariness it caused had fueled much of my anger pre-ERP, but now that it was much better behaved, I couldn't blame OCD for all my negativity. Working compulsively, on the other hand, infused me with negative emotions—hostility, bitterness, annoyance—because I didn't want to be working so hard and I couldn't seem to stop.

I thought about my recent irritated outburst at the meal-delivery customer service rep. I'd been incredibly busy that day with no margin for extra tasks. Without setting boundaries around my work, intoxicated by my addiction, I'd said "yes" to too many things and continually pushed myself to the edge of exhaustion. Thus, I felt threatened, fully in the fight-or-flight response. I was seething with resentment that turned to anger, the "fight" side of fight or flight, when pushed to add a phone call that I didn't even have an extra five minutes to make.

Being in fight or flight—which is essentially what also happened anytime I was in an active OCD episode—made my amygdala, the brain's threat-detection center I'd first learned about years ago from Reid, extra jumpy, lowering its threshold for what it considered "threatening." So if I entered a conversation in fight or flight, my amygdala would already be giving a lot more ammunition to my OCD, and without recognizing what was happening, I was much more likely to say "yes" to my OCD's demands that I point out the senselessness of the problem.

A toxic teabag seeping slow-acting poison into my cup, workaholism at first seemed to quench my thirst for a little peace from the mayhem of OCD. Then it had temporarily sated my craving for admiration. Praise. Absolution. The potential fulfillment of the Quest. Until, of course, I was thirsty again, which happened all too quickly. Not until I heard Rick Hanson's words did I have the epiphany that workaholism intensified not only my Sisyphean cravings, but their attendant poisonous emotions.

As Dr. Hanson announced a break and stocking-footed attendees started padding by our chairs, I suddenly remembered *Type A Behavior and Your Heart*, the book my dad had tried and failed to entice me to read as a teen. I'd asked to borrow Dad's copy as a young adult, skimming parts of it, seeing my own behavior jump out of the pages. The forty-plus-year-old copy now resided permanently on the shelf above *Slowing Down to the Speed of Life* in my office. Dad and I had talked about Type A Behavior occasionally, one recovering Type A to another, and as Jeff and I rose from our chairs, I flashed back to a tidbit Dad had shared with me more than a decade ago.

"Did you know that they're doing research on the components of Type A behavior that cause coronary issues? That they're finding it's the hostility that may play a crucial role in the development of heart problems?"

Hostility. My workaholism was fueling my anger and hostility, and hostility *was* toxic.

Now I had three motivating reasons to fix this.

If I could stop working so hard, I could reduce negative emotions like anger, which clearly would be good for my health.

If I weren't getting angry, I'd be much less likely to do the annoying please-let-me-point-out-how-whatever-is-happening-makes-no-sense compulsion.

Finally, without the weight of negativity, I also had a better chance of developing a core of positive emotion—of accessing joy and delight.

As Jeff and I started to leave the soaring room, attendees murmuring quietly in small groups, respectful of this sacred space, a kaleidoscope of fragmented ideas abruptly coalesced into a coherent, beautiful solution. Stunned, I spun around to face Jeff.

"I know how to fix my workaholism," I said, suddenly breathless, as Jeff pulled a bright blue Golden State Warriors sweatshirt over his head.

"Okay," he said, reaching into his jeans pocket for a cough drop and fiddling with the crinkly wrapping. "Tell me."

"I get annoyed because I don't want to be compulsively working. But I've never known how to stop. I've never been very motivated to stop, because it seemed to provide so many benefits. You know, recognition, accolades, that kind of thing."

Jeff nodded, putting the cough drop into his mouth and crossing his arms over the Warriors logo, his forehead creased as he listened.

"I can't believe it's taken me so long to recognize what I'm about to tell you ... but I can use exposure therapy to beat my compulsive working, to stop my Quest for distraction, perfection, and absolution. I can take on less, say 'no' to things, take time to just do nothing. I can leave things undone and do things imperfectly on purpose. I can use Shoulders Back to accept that I don't have control over what others think. It will make me super anxious, but that means it's the right thing to do."

"That's a helluva exposure, Shala, especially to take on all at once," Jeff said. "But it would likely be very effective."

I took a breath. I could barely keep up with my own thoughts.

"I know," I said. "I need to recognize the lie that workaholism tells me: that it will make me free through the Quest, through keeping my OCD at bay, through providing the twenty-ton shield of perfectionism that will keep me invulnerable, through assuring I get admiration that will prove my worthiness. But that's not freedom. That's being in chains."

Shifting his stance, the blue of his sweatshirt in stark contrast to the white wall behind him, Jeff asked me the same question we taught everyone in all our Beyond the Doubt outreach programs. "Why do you want to do this, Shala? What's your Greater Good? How does this help you find your own purpose or enhance your sense of service to others? How will this motivate you?"

"Because I don't want to get angry at stupid stuff anymore, as it's not good for me or anyone else, and it just makes me more likely to do those annoying this-doesn't-make-sense compulsions that are frankly embarrassing and just strengthen my OCD.

"If I can do these workaholism exposures and end the Quest, it will help me walk our talk: to live in a world of uncertainty and be happy, be joyful, anyway."

Since that eye-opening workshop at Spirit Rock, I've been doing three anti-workaholism exposures most every day. In true black-and-white OCD fashion, I approach almost everything like a workaholic, so I have plenty of exposure options to choose from: Not scheduling extra client appointments during times I'd planned to do something for myself, like ride Lee or go to the gym. Not forcing myself to stay in the office until late at night making phone calls that could be returned the next day. Leaving typos in my write-ups of client sessions. Only vacuuming part of the house. Sitting on the couch and staring into space for what seems like endless spans of time, until my initial anxiety melts into relaxation.

Most of these exposures poke both my workaholism and my OCD's "just right" issues, as leaving tasks incomplete feels "just wrong." The happy news is that these two-for-one exposures are succeeding. I'm less anxious about work, as I'm learning it's okay to not do everything *today*. I'm more easily able to relax, especially on weekends, as I give myself permission to just be instead of running around trying to do every errand that pops into my head. I'm less irritated because I'm putting less pressure on myself, realizing I can say "no" to requests and the world won't come crashing down.

Ending the Quest will take years—and the Quest may never officially end, as my brain has forty years of compulsive habits to unlearn. But that's okay. Exposure is part of my life, and my daily anti-workaholism exposures are empowering. They enable me to wrest back another part of my life from the grips of both my OCD and my well-intentioned but faulty coping mechanism created to control it.

The hardest but most important part of this journey to end the Quest will be fully embracing Shoulders Back and self-compassion. I live night and day with my biggest critic, my monster, but as Teddy Roosevelt says in the famous "The Man in the Arena" passage of his "Citizen in a Republic" speech, a speech I learned about from Brené Brown:

> It is not the critic who counts; not the man who points out how the strong man stumbles, or where the doer of deeds could have done them better. The credit belongs to the man who is actually in the arena, whose face is marred by dust and sweat and blood; who strives valiantly; who errs, who comes short again and again, because there is no effort without error and shortcoming... and who at the worst, if he fails, at least fails while daring greatly, so that his place shall never be with those cold and timid souls who neither know victory nor defeat.

What counts for me is being in that arena, fighting fiercely and enthusiastically to break free of the prison that is obsessive-compulsive disorder, sometimes stumbling, sometimes falling, but always, always getting back up and fighting for my freedom again.

The process of recovering from lifelong mental illness is often two steps forward, one step back. OCD frequently tells me that had I done something differently, the outcome would have been faster or better, but that's one of its biggest lies. Perhaps if I'd found an ERP-trained therapist in Atlanta after going to Reid's group, I would have shortened my time in the arena of "getting better," this years-long journey that is still in process. But perhaps not. Things are as they are. I am who I am. I am where I am. I'm in the arena, fervently and self-compassionately working to break the compulsive shackles that keep me from being free.

And that work has created a delightful, unintended conse-quence: a brand new Rule #1.

CHAPTER 19

A New Rule #1

"Want some homemade pizza to take with you?" Nicole asked, as I hugged a heavy bag of horse supplements to my chest.

"Yeah, sure," I replied, awkwardly draping the top half of the bag over my arms as it tried to slip my grasp, and she ducked back into the house.

The feed store had delivered hundreds of bales of hay to the barn where Lee lived, but for some reason they'd put Lee's bag of supplements on the front porch of the house belonging to the barn owners, Nicole and Blake. I'd had a full day of seeing clients and couldn't get out to the barn until nine o'clock in the evening to pick up the bag and let Lee out for some grazing.

Nicole came back out, holding a foil-wrapped triangle. "Here," she said, balancing the pizza slice on top of my precariously held bag.

"Thanks." I said. "Hey, you've got to come over and see—"

"Wait!" interrupted Nicole. "Did you hear that?"

We both looked up, listening to the still night air, punctuated by an intermittent, high-pitched chirping.

I looked at Nicole as she stared up into the trees, from where the chirping emanated. "Bats," she said, answering my unspoken question.

"Oh, wow," I said, trying to sound excited, as my OCD simultaneously said, *Shit.*

Bats were on one of the lists kept by my OCD, this one titled Very Dangerous Things We Should Always, Always Avoid.

I may have been in recovery, but my OCD was my OCD. It would always have these kinds of lists. My OCD, which had climbed up onto my shoulder with its knitting project, now froze, its needles still. Whenever the knitting needles went silent, I knew we were in trouble. That OCD had picked up on a subtle cue that what was happening was important. That it needed to stop what it was doing and pay attention.

Such had been the case my first year of graduate school in counseling. My friend Kylie had flounced into class one night, dropped into a chair beside me, and said, "My son had to get rabies shots this morning."

As soon as Kylie had said "rabies," my OCD had ceased knitting, slowly and gently putting down its needles so it could give Kylie its full attention.

"What happened?" I asked, instantly scared, channeling my OCD's emotions.

"I found a bat in his room when I went to wake him up. When I called a pest-removal company, they told me he had to get rabies shots because he'd spent the night in a closed room with a bat. That it might have bitten him and he wouldn't have known, because bat bites can be undetectable. And bats are big carriers of rabies. Any exposure to them warrants rabies shots."

"Oh my gosh," I said, recognizing I hadn't taken a breath the whole time she'd been talking. My OCD was paralyzed, too, listening intently to every word she said.

"Yeah, we had to go to the ER this morning. That's where you get rabies shots. And he has to go back. It's a series of shots. You need to get multiple doses in order for it to work."

I'd heard the faint sound of a pencil scribbling when Kylie stopped talking. My OCD had broken its silent reverie and was writing the word "bats" beside "rabies" on the number-one spot on its list of fears.

Holding the foil-wrapped piece of pizza Nicole had given me, I walked back to my car, my OCD tapping on my shoulder and whining, *Shala, we shouldn't be out here! This is dangerous, there are bats!*

I retrieved Bella from my car for an evening walk while I put Lee out to graze and ignored my OCD. Poor little thing, triggered again.

Bella and I walked past where Lee was grazing by the horse trailers toward the main barn. I looked down at my black Birkenstock barn clogs as I waited for Bella to finish sniffing by the gray railroad ties delineating the parking lot. It was getting so dark that I could barely see my shoes. I could barely see anything other than Bella, who was stark white in contrast to her dark surroundings as she nosed around in the grass.

Suddenly, I felt a cool leathery presence, bounded by something furry, wrap itself around my left arm. It flopped several times, struggling, and then was gone.

I yelped, stopping in my tracks, and immediately knew what had happened.

A bat had flown into me. I had just been exposed to a bat.

"You're joking," Nicole said, as I talked with her on my cell phone while I walked back to my car. "A bat did not just run into you!"

"No, I'm not joking, and yes, it did. And now I'm going to the emergency room."

"Why?"

"Because I've been exposed to a bat, and I have to go get rabies shots."

"Rabies shots? No way!" I knew she was probably thinking this was my OCD. Over the many years I'd boarded Lee at Nicole's barn, she'd become an expert in what my compulsions looked like and could spot one in an instant.

I heard Blake in the background as I put Bella in the car. Holding the phone between my ear and shoulder as I shut the car door, I heard Nicole say, "Really? Wow. Okay," and then she came back to me. "No, you're right. Blake said getting rabies shots is the right thing to do."

As I drove away from the farm, I felt confident I was making the right choice.

Well, at least I thought I was. Until I got to the hospital.

"Did the bat bite you?" the physician's assistant asked, while my nurse, Al, typed away at a computer in the corner.

"I don't think so," I said, but then my OCD piped up, using my voice to speak, "But the CDC says that any bat exposure warrants rabies shots."

He walked over to me and quickly examined the top of my arm. "Well, I'm going to have to call the CDC to have the vaccine released."

It's funny, I hadn't even looked at my arm after the bat flew into it, because I didn't want to have an argument with my OCD about whether a bite or scratch was there.

"I don't see anything," he said, looking at me expectantly.

He was the first person to have questioned my decision to get the vaccine. Upon my arrival at the ER, one of the front-desk staff had emphatically said, "Oh, yes, you did the right thing. You'll get five shots tonight and then three more in follow-up visits. You don't want to mess around with bats." Then, in the waiting room, I'd read the Centers for Disease Control and Prevention webpage about bats and rabies, embarrassingly caught in a Catch-22 of doing a reassurance compulsion to prove to myself that I wasn't doing a compulsion by coming to the ER. Managing OCD could be a little hairy at times.

"Here's the thing," I said, trying to sound reasonable and not channel my OCD, who was screaming, *We HAVE to have these shots!* "I don't know if I got scratched or bitten. But I know someone who was in the same room with a bat overnight and had to get rabies shots, even though they don't know if the bat came close to him. This bat ran right into me!"

Backing toward the door, with a skeptical look on his face, the PA said, "Okay, I'll make the call to the CDC," and he walked out of the room.

I leaned against the hospital wall, shaky, feeling overwhelmed by the frantic pounding of my heart as my OCD sobbed, *What if they don't give us the shots? We are going to die!*

Too tired to deal with my OCD's tantrum, I gave into its fear, wondering what it was going to be like to die of rabies. But after a few minutes, I recognized I was wallowing in OCD's worries, and I tried to sit up so I could do Shoulders Back. As I did so, I raised my left hand to my shoulder to readjust my hospital gown, exposing the underside of my arm. The place where the bat had collided with me.

That's when I saw the scratches. Eight or nine of them in a chaotic pattern crisscrossing my skin.

I raised my right arm to look at its underside. No scratches.

I picked up my left arm and looked at it again. "Hey, Al?" I said, motioning with my free hand to the nurse. "Can you please come look at this?"

Al walked over and looked down. "Wow, I didn't see that before. Is that from the bat?"

"I don't know. Maybe. This is the arm the bat ran into."

"Well, I saw on the computer that the PA ordered the shots. Your rabies vaccine is on its way."

My OCD collapsed in a heap on the floor, overcome with relief. I closed my eyes and waited for my shots to arrive.

It wasn't until my third visit to the ER that anyone brought up the subject of how much all these rabies shots were going to cost.

"Don't freak out," the woman from Billing said, as she stood beside my hospital bed with her rolling computer cart. "Your charge for today is two hundred and fifty dollars."

From talking with Kylie, whose son had had the shots, I knew they would probably cost between one and two thousand dollars. But rational knowledge, of course, has absolutely no bearing on OCD.

When the woman from Billing said "two hundred and fifty," I heard my OCD start to panic, the initial stage of its transformation into the Triad of Hell. *What if it's not just a few thousand dollars? What if it's more? We need to know RIGHT NOW how much it's going to cost!*

"I knew this wasn't going to be cheap," I said, ignoring my OCD and handing the woman my HSA card.

As she took it, I could feel my OCD starting to blubber. It began to pull on my shirttail, as it always does when it thinks I can't hear it.

We need to know! Ask her! Ask her how much it is!

In my defense, it was six-thirty in the morning. I'd been advised to come back early for my follow-up shots, to avoid the ER rush that apparently started each day around nine a.m. I was tired and not completely at the top of my game. Which is why I gave in to my morphing OCD's demands.

"Just out of curiosity," I said, trying to sound casual, as if the way I asked this question would affect its answer. "How much will this whole series of shots be?"

"I don't know, let's see," she said. After a minute or so of clicking on the keyboard, she calmly replied, not even looking up, "Eighteen to twenty-five thousand dollars."

The rest of my OCD's metamorphosis was breathtakingly swift. As the word "thousand" escaped her lips, my OCD assumed the full stature of the Triad of Hell, and in doing so, it sucked every ounce of air from my lungs and left my heart feeling as if it had just been ripped right out of my chest.

"Eighteen ... to ... twenty-five ... thousand ... dollars?" I repeated, incredulous.

"Yes," she said, looking at me with pity. "The vaccine is very expensive."

Holy shit.

My OCD, invisible to everyone but me, was now three times my size, looming over me, gnashing its teeth at the billing agent.

What are we going to DO? it snarled, throwing itself around the room, foam flying from its mouth as it screamed expletives at the uncertainty of the situation.

In the ultimate irony, it looked for all the world like my OCD had rabies.

As the billing clerk rolled her computer cart away, I leaned back on my hospital bed and tried to think rationally. It was impossible.

What if insurance doesn't cover this?! my OCD yelled.

The bottom dropped out of my stomach, as if I'd travelled back in time to when I'd almost always agreed with the legitimacy of my OCD's threats.

What if, this time, my OCD was right?

Since learning that my rabies shots were potentially going to cost as much as my Volkswagen Beetle, I'd been diligently working to accept the uncertainty of the situation. I'd determined that there was a small risk my insurance company wouldn't cover it, but I'd tried to use Shoulders Back and accept that I had no control over the situation, managing to mostly keep OCD from stealing yet more of my life.

Until two weeks after the bat collided with my arm, when I received a letter from my insurance company:

```
Our records indicate you recently had
an emergency room claim that was not
covered under your plan.
```

Barely breathing, I walked in a trance into my house, straight to my computer to log into the insurance company's site. I'd checked my claims online once in the past week to see if the rabies shots had shown up yet, and they hadn't, and I'd decided it would be compulsive to look any more.

But now it was not compulsive, because I knew they'd denied my claim, and I wanted to know how much they were saying I owed.

Ten thousand six hundred and thirty dollars.

Just for the first round of shots. My stomach lurched. The huge potential bill my OCD had feared was actually coming true.

A year prior to my encounter with the bat, Jeff and I had packaged concepts from his book *When in Doubt, Make Believe* into a motivational wrapper around ERP, calling them our "Four Keys

Out When Locked in Doubt." These keys motivated us to do the hard work of ERP, and they became a foundation for how we both managed our recoveries.

The first key is a Triple-A attitude of appreciation ("Thank you for this great opportunity to practice doing ERP, OCD!"), authenticity ("I am not my OCD's doubts and fears"), and abundance (the paradigm-shifting belief that the universe is friendly).

The second key focuses on maintaining perspective and remembering the bigger picture, otherwise known as the Greater Good.

The third key is mindfully doing the exposure, acting on our Greater Good and recognizing that we want to move toward, not away, from anxiety.

Finally, the last key is letting go, a task especially challenging for those of us with monsters who throw fits when things don't go their way. *This is terrible!* my monster likes to scream, immediately throwing the "bad" label on any outcome that doesn't meet its criteria for certainty, comfort, and control.

But what might monsters learn from the Chinese farmer parable?

> A Chinese farmer and his son wake up to find their only horse is gone (seemingly bad), then arise the next day to find the horse has returned, bringing a herd of wild horses with it (seemingly good), only to have one of the new horses throw the son off his back the following day (seemingly bad), which then keeps the son from getting conscripted into the army the day after (seemingly good, but hey maybe not!).

The story poignantly illustrates the essence of the fourth key: that we can't judge things as "good" or "bad" until much later, if even then.

Through our work with Beyond the Doubt, Jeff and I try to convey that being mentally healthy is about being psychologically flexible, being able to accept life's changing course, as well as mistakes and disappointments. This acceptance is easier when we're self-compassionate and when we take the attitude that life is a classroom full of new insights for us to discover.

The morning after I received the insurance denial letter, as I spoke with people at the insurance company and hospital who all held sway over whether I'd be giving away more than ten thousand dollars, it dawned on me that this situation was a great opportunity to practice applying the Four Keys. In fact, it was the quintessential example of the fourth key: an experience that I couldn't judge as either "good" or "bad." However, I could allow for bigger plans than my own to unfold, because life is a classroom and I'm here to learn.

Over the coming weeks and months, I shared my bat story with all my friends, taking pleasure in the jaw-dropping, saucer-eyed look I came to anticipate when I quoted how much rabies shots cost, how my insurance company was asking that I pay almost eleven thousand dollars, how at this point my balance was overdue, and how the situation was still completely unresolved.

At dinner one evening in Midtown Atlanta, an area of town filled with hip bars and dimly lit, upscale restaurants, a friend shared that her boyfriend had been overcharged by a few hundred dollars for a doctor's visit, but because he didn't want to deal with the uncertainty of what would happen if he contested it, he'd paid it. "It's really impressive how you're living with so much uncertainty," she said as she sipped her wine.

"Yes, it is," I agreed. "To living with uncertainty and being happy anyway," I said, holding up my wine glass for a toast to how far I had come.

As the weeks and months went on, "I can't judge any of this as 'good' or 'bad,'" and "I'm going to allow for bigger plans than my own to unfold because life is a classroom and I'm here to learn" became my mantra. I added in self-compassion, treating myself as I would treat Sydney if she were struggling, and paired all of this with Shoulders Back.

I used my mantra so much that one day I said to Jeff over the phone, "You know, these statements are really good rules to live by, even if you don't have OCD. But even better if ..."

I paused, stunned by the weight of my own words, the hands on the clock of time stopping just as they had when I'd first heard Reid say that "ERP is the gold-standard treatment for OCD."

Ignoring Jeff as he started to say, "Yes, they definitely—" I blurted out, "Oh my gosh! These are rules. These are new rules. They are my new Rule #1!"

I commemorated my new Rule #1, a replacement for the rule that OCD had used to dominate so much of my life, with a set of bracelets: one in aluminum stamped with "I can't judge this as good or bad," another in copper engraved with "Allow for bigger plans than my own to unfold," and a third in brass etched with "Life is a classroom and I'm here to learn." Finally, a fourth in silver that says "Self-Compassion." I wear them every day, and these principles, paired with Shoulders Back—the embodiment of acting as though what OCD says doesn't matter—became engraved in my consciousness over the coming months.

A few months after my run-in with the bat, I visited the University of Illinois with my senior-year roommate at my sorority, Susan, and two of her children. Before driving from suburban Chicago to Champaign, I shared my bat tale with Susan and her husband, both physicians, and her kids, at dinner. I shared it because at this point, I just thought it was a great story. I'd forgotten what Susan did for a living.

"Are you kidding me?" she said, fork suspended in midair, the clinking of silverware on plates like little percussion riffs, highlighting her words. She stared at me in disbelief. "Of course you had to get rabies shots. That's the protocol. The insurance company has to cover it!"

Then I remembered. Susan was an infectious diseases doctor.

She pledged to write a letter on my behalf to the insurance company explaining that covering rabies shots in this situation was not optional, that failing to cover it would be going directly against both CDC and World Health Organization protocol.

I felt a weight lift from my shoulders.

While we were visiting the University of Illinois, Susan gave me the opportunity to read out loud the chapter I'd written about my life with body dysmorphic disorder when we were in college. As I arrived at the final sentences in the chapter, I was struck by the surrealism of the moment. Here I was, reading about dreams I used to have about the university while sitting in a hotel room that was walking distance from the subject of those dreams: the sorority house that Susan and I had lived in, but that my BDD had never allowed me to call home:

> I know I'm at the University of Illinois. Sometimes I even know I'm in a dream. I also know instinctively, every time, that I'm supposed to go back to my sorority house and live there. But can I find it?
>
> And if I do, will they know me?
>
> Will I know them?
>
> Or will I continue to be lost, lost, lost, entranced by enticing, echoing whispers, and miss the life that's right before me?

Choked up, I was barely able to finish reading. Looking up from the pages, I saw Susan's eyes glistening with tears.

"I never knew, Shala. I never knew."

That's the curse of having OCD. Or BDD. Or depression. Disorders whose inner workings no one can see. Invisible forces of mind that are incredibly powerful—powerful enough to rip sufferers' lives apart.

The day after Thanksgiving, almost six months after the bat ran into my arm, the insurance company sent me an email. They were going to cover the rabies shots, thanks in large part to Susan's letter, but I wasn't getting off scot-free. I owed five thousand dollars, my portion of the claim.

Though I didn't enjoy sending the hospital five thousand dollars, I felt it was the perfect outcome—because it was imperfect. I didn't owe twenty-five thousand dollars. But I didn't owe zero dollars either. I owed something in the middle. The result wasn't the black or white of OCD's world; it was the gray of reality. The gray of living in a world of uncertainty and being happy anyway.

"Shala?" OCD had climbed up on my shoulder and was now tapping on it, trying to get my attention.

"Yes, OCD?" It always barged in at the most inopportune times. "I'm trying to finish writing *Fred*, OCD. You're interrupting me."

"I know, but how can we be sure we're finished? What if we forgot to tell them something? What if we could have told different or better stories? What if we left something out?"

I sighed. Answering questions like these was part of life with a monster. Even now that the monster was relatively well behaved.

"I'm not sure, OCD. Remember, Shoulders Back. We may or may not be finished. But we're going to act as if we're confident that we *are* finished, wanting our anxiety, embracing uncertainty."

I stopped typing and turned to face my OCD, patting it on its soft orange head, giving it my full attention as I continued, "I've accepted that you and I will always be together, and I've also accepted that we'll never be sure about anything. And both are okay. I'll keep helping you with all this, with living in the gray, okay?"

"Okay," my OCD replied.

I smiled as it turned its back on me, slid to the floor, and quietly returned to its knitting.

Afterword

NO MORE!

No more shame-filled silence. No more living in a private, secretive world, too afraid to share, convinced that no one will understand or that you will be shamed by your disclosure. No one deserves this. Not for two decades, not for two years, not for two weeks. SAY IT. Say it out loud. Say it to someone you think you can trust. At first, you won't know if people will understand you or accept you. But speak up anyway. Break the silence. Stumble through the words, again and again if you have to, until you stumble into a hug. Until someone says, "I'm so sorry you're suffering like this." Until someone offers, "Let's find you the help you need."

OCD trained Shala from an early age. By the time she was in fourth grade, it had instilled a primary message that was guaranteed to keep her suffering in her private world: "This isn't normal, so I can't let myself get caught." Then OCD added a manipulative belief based on the false logic of this cunning mental health disorder: "Why would I think about this terrible outcome if it wasn't going to come true?!" Then it delivered a third blow to her sense of safety through a kind of magical thinking: "If you tell anyone—if you break our code of silence—then all of these bad things will happen."

So, 9-year-old Shala took a stand: "It's my job to keep everyone safe." Now OCD had her in its clutches. The playful joys of childhood were replaced by the misery instilled by a dominant abuser. Any inkling of her assertiveness was met by an escalated threat of that inner voice, from *They will die* to *Do you feel this gun at your temple?* She could not trust that these were false threats. Breaking Rule #1 would bring such devastation to her life that she dare not challenge the authority of the imagined gun.

Can you tame OCD? Bet your life on it. That's why Shala wrote this book. She collected experience after experience until she built a skillset that worked. Her top skill was to engage OCD through a specific, healing point of view. And she wants to share her experiences with you. She wants you to become powerful by stepping forward with a new and different attitude. Yours may be different, but hers is, "I want to be anxious and uncertain because I want to beat you, OCD." Notice how she returned to that stance, again and again, story after story throughout the book.

Find the therapeutic perspective that works for you. Experiment with different orientations if necessary, but do find a point of view that you are willing to trust, because that will guide your actions. Over time, Shala adopted a set of principles, strategies and tactics, and she alludes to them throughout the book. You may need to read it again to spot them all. If they intrigue you, try them on, just as you would try on a jacket in the store to see how it fits. But all of those strategies and techniques coalesce here: "I want to be anxious and uncertain."

You can't help but notice that Shala has personified and externalized her OCD. It's certainly an engaging way to animate her text for the reader, but it's so much more than that. If you have OCD, you have a part of you that is being dominated by a mental health disorder. Be sure to make this distinction: There's the disorder (that is NOT you), and then there is you. Now, go one step further. There is the part of you that is being victimized by the disorder, and then there needs to be a separate part of you that takes actions that will help you heal. What does that process look like?

- First, recognize those two distinct parts of you. You've already met the part that has been getting kicked around by OCD. You'll need to bring forward that second, more active part of you that is ready to get stronger, ready to experiment with a new therapeutic strategy, and ready to develop trust in that strategy.

- Now, see OCD as separate from you. Don't waste your time declaring it as "bad" or "wrong," but do see it as a grand manipulator, a clever strategist, and a formidable challenger that is currently dominating you. Pull up that part of you that's ready to get stronger, and then take on the task to be *just as* manipulative, *just as* cunning. That's how you win your life back: by cunningly manipulating the disorder that's currently manipulating you. What's the best kind of manipulation? To do the absolute opposite of what OCD needs to sustain its dominance over your life.

  - OCD wants you to get rid of your scared feelings? Ha! Not a chance! <u>Welcome</u> those scared feelings.
  - OCD wants you to treat all its threatening messages as alarmingly serious warnings? Ha! No way! <u>Welcome</u> the message! But welcome it as an absurd message that needs no response. "Hey, OCD, thank you for scaring me!"
  - Don't bother entertaining OCD's threats or arguing against them or using logic to make yourself feel better or seeking reassurance to comfort you. Don't do any of that in response to OCD's scare tactics.

○ And when you're done welcoming and embracing those absurd threats, then turn your attention back to the task at hand.

Sure, you'll feel anxious when you do all that. You'll absolutely feel doubt and insecurity. And you'll be somewhat distracted when you try to return to your task. That's how you know you're doing a good practice. You will not win over the disorder by going toe-to-toe with OCD in a battle over its frightening logic. You <u>must</u> work paradoxically. *Is Fred in the Refrigerator?* is brilliantly alive with this paradoxical strategy. Use Shala's memoir as your empowering inspiration. Personify OCD as this trespasser into your life, and employ your new, clever strategies to diminish the power of this intruder by moving *toward* uncertainty—not away from it.

To tame OCD requires that you step toward doubt, not around it. You get *past* it by going *through* it. Just hours after first hearing about this therapeutic approach to facing the disorder, Shala grabbed her fledgling trust and experimented with this "through-not-around" idea. She allowed herself to step right up to that PETA exhibit on the National Mall. In that pivotal moment, standing face-to-face with one of her greatest threats, she wasn't just doing exposure practice; she was doing exposure practice *with attitude*. As she stared down those posters, she wasn't telling herself, "I'm supposed to do this exposure in order to get better." She wasn't saying, "I really should do this, even though I don't want to." While there may be some truth to those messages, they don't reflect her new self-directed stance. "I'm supposed to..." and "I really should..." are not messages of empowerment. You won't get stronger by following directions or complying with a therapist's request to perform some exposure exercise. Shala took possession of her work and supported herself with an honest, authentic voice: "I can handle this. I can do this. I WANT to do this."

What did she get for her efforts? Pure terror. A cold chill washed over her body while OCD screamed in her ear. *If you do not stop looking at these posters, you are going to cause some animal to die!* How did she respond to this admonition? She took her determination up a notch. She didn't just push herself toward the threatening event; she confronted the event *with a new point of view.* "THIS. TIME. I. AM. NOT. DOING. A. RITUAL!" She got bigger in the face of fear, and she won that moment.

OCD is a fierce, unconventional opponent in a high-stakes game of 1-on-1, and it will use an entire repertoire of skills—smack talk, cunning moves, fake-outs—all to incite fear and uncertainty. It wants you to feel insecure about something valuable in your life. It wants you to feel worried and confused about the possibility of making a grave mistake or not being able to stop something that feels highly distressing. If you permit OCD to dominate the court—if you succumb to its offensive tactics—it will then grant you a fleeting sense of certainty and relief. If it can get you to elevate the need for certainty above all else, it wins. It is an incredibly manipulative challenger, and if it can keep you from learning its strategy, it can control you. Before long, it has you trained.

The only way to discover that OCD is "all talk and no game" is to see through its tactics and drop your defenses. Shala's petition to you has been loud-and-clear in this book, and it is the correct message: *Certainty is the domain of fools. Please, allow my story to inspire you so that you won't play the fool for as long as I did.*

Shala models a powerful opening strategy: Externalize OCD and personify it. Attribute your threatening thoughts, images or impulses to the disorder. Consider that your urges to escape or to ritualize come from the part of you that falls for the intimidating invocation of the disorder—and recall that you have another voice inside you (that second, more active voice) that is strong enough to withstand the distress of doubt and uncertainty.

At some point you're going to need to talk back to OCD with as powerful a voice as you can muster. But, of course, you can't be all talk. You also have to embrace the daunting task of stepping <u>toward</u> uncertainty. You will need to risk being confused and sometimes lost. And you absolutely have to risk being wrong.

The disorder delivers to you a disturbing perspective and point of view—an erroneous belief that seems so real and so valid that it catches you in its web. Do you want to break free? Then you have to step back and recognize that, no matter how strong that belief is, it is generated by the disorder to keep you tied up, unable to move forward with your life. You have to notice it, see it for what it is, and then voluntarily choose to hold a *new* perspective that pushes you toward the thing you fear most. Crazy, right? But that's what is required: an engaging, paradoxical strategy.

After The Accident, Shala concluded that the world was a dangerous place and that she must always protect herself. For forty years, she made both large and small decisions while seeing the world through that lens. But Shala's outlook was a skewed version of reality. We all lead our lives like this, through our built-in and learned perspectives. We make our decisions through our beliefs— not through some impartial, objective view of the world. The sooner you understand that, the sooner you can begin to challenge the beliefs dictated by the disorder.

After decades of operating as though the world was dangerous, Shala chose to adopt the new belief that the universe is "friendly." Is the universe truly friendly? Who knows. But that stance allows her to change her once pessimistic outlook to an optimistic one. Now she can make decisions *as though* it's safe for her to feel optimistic. *As though*. This is the critical concept, because when facing anything related to your distressing theme—whether it's contamination, or harm, or perfection, or "I've got to get comfortable"—OCD doesn't allow you to know the truth in that moment. You have to *feel* your doubt and yet *take actions as though* everything's okay. It's the only way you will get stronger: to deliberately, voluntarily choose to accept the doubt that the disorder dishes out... and to simultaneously recognize that it is generated by the disorder. It's not the truth. It is simply a faulty perception that you currently believe is valid.

It took Shala forty years before she recognized that she could embrace a new, totally contradictory assumption about her world. The infinitely more difficult task was to then take action based on that assumption. She's done tremendously well, and she is leading a life she loves now. But (keep in mind) she still has to push through her doubt. *Every single day.* Sometimes, when she's tired or stressed or faced with a brand-new form of her ever-morphing obsession, she has to put tremendous effort toward handling her obsessions and her urges. Other times, it's as easy as this: The obsession pops up, she notices it, she shrugs her shoulders, and she brings her attention back to whatever task she was engaged in. That might take as little as three seconds—a skill she has built over time with serious dedication. Shala is imploring you to learn from her long, arduous journey so that you can shorten the time between suffering and freely choosing your life's direction.

Remember, this is an aggressive sport, and OCD is a dominant competitor. You need to get bigger than OCD. You need to own the court and challenge its fear-inducing messages.

- First, get bigger by surrounding yourself by those who support your endeavor. Find friends who are willing to learn about what it takes to get strong enough to take on the disorder. Enlist family members who are ready to stand behind your intention to push through this intensive period of doubt and distress.
- Second, get bigger by recognizing OCD's primary tactic: It needs you to focus on the <u>theme</u> of your obsessions. Yet,

OCD has nothing to do with accidentally running someone over with your car, or mistakenly bringing salmonella home to your children, or burning the house down because you neglected to turn off the stove. It simply takes advantage of those frightening thoughts, images and impulses in order to make you feel scared, avoidant and compulsive. Stop falling for that! No one in their right mind is going to accept the possibility that they just ran someone over or that, if they're not careful, they will become a pedophile. No one can tolerate such threats. And that's how OCD beats you: It makes you think it's about those themes. It's not. It never was, it never is, and it never will be.

- Third, get bigger by welcoming your distress. To tame OCD, you have to be willing to feel anxiously uncertain. But not uncertain about anything. Yes, your spontaneous thoughts, impulses or images will be about your theme, but your job is then to step back from that moment, recognize that this is OCD's handiwork, and then step up to a healthy perspective. What's that perspective? "I need to ignore OCD's invitation to battle over the topic of my obsession. I need to win the real game against OCD. I'm going to tolerate this generic feeling of uncertainty and keep stepping forward. I know I'm going to keep falling into worries about my specific topic. I expect that. But as soon as I notice myself doing it, I'm going to shift over to the real work here, which is to tolerate a general, anxiety-provoking feeling of 'not knowing.' If I keep doing that, I will win back my life."

Stop trying to keep OCD from showing up! That's none of your business. The disturbance that OCD generates within you is unconsciously mediated. Allow it to show up, because it's coming anyway. Instead, focus your attention on *how* you respond to its invitation to worry, to check, to wash, to get rid of, to avoid. And then do the opposite.

When you are ready to address your doubt, realize that OCD has <u>nothing</u> to do with being irresponsible, negligent, sinful or repulsive. The disorder <u>doesn't care</u> what you feel doubtful about; it just needs you to become scared about a state of uncertainty. It will look around until it finds something that is important to you personally, and then it will scare you about that. As long as you will play your assigned role as victim and to do anything necessary to get back to a place of comfort regarding your specific theme, then it wins. Don't let it win. Ignore the theme it picked for you. Don't answer that frightening question that is so significant to you. (*Did I do that? Is everything going to be okay? Has it gone away? Am I sure I wouldn't do that?*) Sit with your <u>generic</u> state of doubt and distress. Rise above the content of your specific worries and welcome this broad and general state of uncertainty and discomfort. Is it easy to do this? No. In fact, it's quite hard. But it's not a complex task, and you can endure it. What you can't tolerate is giving your family salmonella through your negligence or turning into a pedophile or burning the house down. That's why OCD survives as long as it keeps you focused on those undesirable, <u>personal</u> topics. And that's why you need to rise above them.

Shala made a decision to become as aggressive toward OCD as it had been toward her. When she felt the invitation to struggle with an obsessive moment, she threw her shoulders back. "Shoulders Back" was her cue to "...act as if what it was saying didn't matter." She didn't refute the message from the disorder. She didn't argue against the logic of the message. No matter what the disorder said, she treated it as irrelevant noise, and therefore gave it zero response. OCD wants to transact with you. It doesn't care what your response is, as long as you engage with it. If you never accept the invitation, then you don't have to end the transaction. So, feel free to hear the disorder's message, and allow yourself to have a little jolt of distress, a little punch to the gut, when it penetrates your defenses. By doing that, you'll be applying a unique form of the letting go process within mindfulness. Don't refute the message! Don't accept OCD's invitation to transact. If you never pick up the message to start with, then you don't have to work to set it down again. Because you CANNOT win OCD's game. The sooner you comprehend this, the sooner you will be on your path to recovery.

Shala kept repeating this process represented by "Shoulders Back." She repeated it, moment-by-moment, as soon as she recognized OCD's challenge. She won her life back moment-by-moment. You should follow in her footsteps and focus only on winning these moments. Begin accumulating more and more of these moments. Before you know it, you've created a life for yourself.

Reid Wilson, PhD
Chapel Hill, NC

Reid Wilson, PhD, is author of *Stopping the Noise in Your Head: The New Way to Overcome Anxiety and Worry* and the classic self-help book *Don't Panic: Taking Control of Anxiety Attacks*. He is coauthor of *Stop Obsessing!* and *Anxious Kids, Anxious Parents*, as well as *Playing with Anxiety*. He is a Founding Clinical Fellow of the Anxiety and Depression Association of America (ADAA) and Fellow of the Association for Behavioral and Cognitive Therapies. In 2014 ADAA presented him with the highest national award given in his field. He offers self-help resources at www.anxieties.com and www.NoiseInYourHead.com.

Acknowledgements

I'd like to thank the following friends and family whose influence shaped not only this book, but also the course of my life. At the same time, I'll self-compassionately hold my shoulders back and live with the uncertainty that I may have forgotten someone. After all, this book did take almost a decade to write!

Years ago, I shared a first draft with Priscilla Walter, who gently told me what I'd written sounded like a treatment manual and I needed to focus on what readers want: a good story. I hope I've implemented her advice well.

M.J. Pullen read a first draft of *Fred* and gave me spot-on feedback. Beth and Cookie Pickard took the time to share memories of the day of The Accident. Bennett Bibel allowed me to make The Boat one of my writing retreats. Mark Wood gave me great editing advice that I've used throughout my writing process. Jethro "Fro" Felton introduced me to The Editorial Department (TED), and Ross Browne at TED embraced *Fred* from the start, expertly managing the process as I worked with my editor, Julie Miller. Julie's unparalleled attention to detail, enthusiasm for the book, and willingness to repeatedly push me as a writer brought *Fred* to life. Betsy White and Doug Wagner at TED were *Fred's* master proofreaders; you can blame any typos you find on my enthusiastic approach to keeping my OCD in check (see the P.S. below).

Saul Bottcher of IndieBookLauncher.com came up with the subtitle *Taming OCD and Reclaiming My Life*, artfully highlighting what *Fred* is all about. BespokeBookCovers.com created *Fred's* beautiful cover, and Stephanie Anderson at Jera Publishing created the stunning interior layout. I wouldn't have survived the self-publishing process without Kimberly Martin at Jera Publishing, who shared her considerable expertise as we turned a Word document into the book you're holding today.

Jennifer Kahling Czupek, author of *Genuinely Speaking* at www.jenczupek.com and her food blog at www.aperitiffriday. com, graciously allowed me to reprint parts of her blog post "Ring Ching Ching." Master storyteller Karen-Eve Bayne came up with the concept of WDNG radio and also told me about the work of Brené Brown, whose e-course *The Gifts of Imperfection* introduced me to self-compassion, a cornerstone of my recovery.

Jeff Szymanski, PhD, executive director of the International OCD Foundation (IOCDF), gave me the honor of presenting the keynote at the 2013 national conference. The IOCDF has also been incredibly supportive of my advocacy work, giving me the chance to write for its newsletter and blog, to co-run a special-interest group, and to present numerous times at the national conference.

Tam, Nancy, Bob, Dustin, and Jenny have provided unconditional support when my OCD wanted to take part in horseback riding. Debbie has been there for me since we were kids. Linda has lovingly supported me since our time at Disney. Joan Herbig continues to share her wisdom and guidance. There's also my Therapists-with-OCD support group, whose members shall remain nameless but who are always there for me when OCD tries to morph into the Triad of Hell.

Becky Beaton, PhD, offered me an internship doing Exposure and Response Prevention Therapy (ERP), and she continues to be a stalwart advocate in the dissemination of ERP as the appropriate treatment for OCD. Kathleen McKinney Clark, LPC, provided compassionate supervision as I worked toward full licensure. Jennifer Vann, LMFT, gave me a welcoming home for my private practice at Cornerstone Family Services. Ashley Smith, PhD, was an early mentor who has been instrumental in my development as a therapist and one of the most passionate supporters of *Fred*. Joan Davidson, PhD, another early supporter, went above and beyond to help introduce me to the world of publishing. Kimberley Quinlan, LMFT, lent her business acumen to the book's marketing and promotion.

Eric Storch, PhD, Gail Steketee, PhD, and Denis Asselin took time out of their busy schedules to review specific chapters of *Fred* pre-publication. All the people who reviewed advance copies of *Fred* and wrote endorsements were incredibly generous with their time, and I'm honored by their support.

Jonathan Grayson, PhD, gave me the chance not only to touch a dumpster and lick my hand at one of his virtual camping trips, but also to present with him at two IOCDF conferences—highlights of my career. Jon and his work have had an incredible impact on my career as a therapist and my recovery as a person with OCD.

Jonathan Hershfield, MFT, just happened to drive cross-country a few years ago, making a fortuitous stopover in Atlanta. Shortly thereafter, Jon gave me the great honor of writing a book with him, which launched my career as an author, a much better daily meditation practice, and our ongoing delightful collaboration. His positive influence on my work as a therapist, my OCD recovery, and my life in general continues to be invaluable.

Reid Wilson, PhD, uttered the first fateful phrase that changed my life: *we all know that ERP is the gold-standard treatment for OCD*. I started emailing him questions the week after the 2010 IOCDF conference, and he's never been too busy to answer every single one. Over the eight years I've known him, I'm honored that he's had so many important roles in my life: from therapist to teacher, mentor, colleague, and friend. I've told him a thousand times the difference he's made in my life, but I'll say it again here: Reid, by teaching me to turn ERP into a game with "I want this" as my key strategy, you empowered me to turn the tables on my OCD, saving my life.

Jeff Bell uttered the second fateful phrase that forever altered my future: *you can choose to believe the universe is friendly*. He took me under his wing, giving me the opportunity to form Beyond the Doubt. Our daily emails, blogs, workshops, and online course now reach a worldwide audience. Several years ago, I timidly asked whether he'd take a look at *Fred*, and as we drove along Bay Area highways, I read him the first three chapters. His unbridled enthusiasm and willingness to listen to *every single chapter* (twice!) encouraged me to keep writing. Jeff, thank you for your never-ending passion for my story. As I was creating *Fred*, I felt like I was writing it for you. I am blessed every day by the light and insight you've brought into my life.

Corey, I know it wasn't fun to live with someone with untreated OCD all those years, and I'll always be grateful for your patient and loving support as I stumbled through all the twists and turns of recovery.

Mom and Dad, you probably wondered about my not-so-well-hidden struggles for decades, and my OCD and BDD bow their heads in apology for the anguish they caused all of us. Through it all, however, you provided endless love and support, never faltering in your belief that I could figure things out. You patiently modeled, in the way you live your own lives, that I could make lemonade out of lemons, and I'm so lucky to have you as parents.

It takes a village to recover from major mental illness. To everyone in my village: I love you all and will be forever grateful that you helped me turn my life around.

P.S. A special shout out to Nathaniel Van Kirk, PhD, who suggested I purposely plant some mistakes in *Fred*. How could I possibly pass up the opportunity for such a great exposure? Find them if you can!

Resources and References

The resources listed are ordered by the chapter in which they first appear in the book.

Chapter 4
- *Type A Behavior and Your Heart* by Meyer Friedman, M.D., and Ray H. Rosenman, M.D.

Chapter 5
- Excerpt from "Ring Ching Ching" by Jennifer Kahling Czupek http://jenczupek.blogspot.com/2014/04/ring-ching-ching.html

Chapter 7
- *Kissing Doorknobs* by Terry Spencer Hesser.

Chapter 11
- The International OCD Foundation www.iocdf.org
- The IOCDF annual conference https://iocdf.org/programs/conference/

- *Stop Obsessing: How to Overcome Your Obsessions and Compulsions* by Edna B. Foa, Ph.D. and Reid Wilson, Ph.D.
- *OCD Treatment Through Storytelling: A Strategy for Successful Therapy* by Allen H. Weg.

Chapter 12
- Reid Wilson's Weekend Treatment Groups: www.anxieties. com/weekend
- The GOAL Group Manual: https://iocdf.org/wp-content/ uploads/2014/08/OCD_GOAL_Manual.pdf

Chapter 13
- *Freedom from Obsessive-Compulsive Disorder: A Personalized Recovery Program for Living with Uncertainty* by Jonathan Grayson, Ph.D.
- Anxiety and Depression Association of America (ADAA): https://adaa.org/

Chapter 14
- IOCDF Affiliates: https://iocdf.org/about/local-affiliates/
- "Is Fred in the Refrigerator?" at OCD Unveiled! http://www. shalanicely.com/about-shala/2013-iocdf-keynote/
- Brené Brown: https://brenebrown.com/

Chapter 15
- *When in Doubt, Make Belief: An OCD-Inspired Approach to Living with Uncertainty* by Jeff Bell.

Chapter 16
- "Your body language may shape who you are" by Amy Cuddy: https://www.ted.com/talks/ amy_cuddy_your_body_language_shapes_who_you_are

- *Stopping the Noise in Your Head: The New Way to Overcome Anxiety and Worry* by Reid Wilson, Ph.D. www.NoiseInYourHead.com
- "Why Your Critics Aren't the Ones Who Count" by Brené Brown https://www.youtube.com/watch?v=8-JXOnFOXQk

Chapter 17

- *Rewind, Replay, Repeat: A Memoir of Obsessive-Compulsive Disorder* by Jeff Bell.
- Beyond the Doubt: *www.beyondthedoubt.com*
- *Feeling Good About the Way You Look* by Sabine Wilhelm, Ph.D.
- *Cognitive-Behavioral Therapy for Body Dysmorphic Disorder* by Sabine Wilhelm, Katharine Phillips and Gail Steketee.

Chapter 18

- OCD and depression as causes of disability: "Murray, C. J. L., & Lopez A. D. 1996. The Global Burden of Disease. Cambridge, MA: Harvard University Press.
- *Everyday Mindfulness for OCD: Tips, Tricks and Skills for Living Joyfully* by Jon Hershfield, MFT and Shala Nicely, LPC.
- Kristin Neff, Ph.D.: www.self-compassion.org
- *Buddha's Brain: The Practical Neuroscience of Happiness, Love, and Wisdom* by Rick Hanson, Ph.D.
- "The Hidden Power of Swearing at Your OCD: Three ways to use the art and science of cursing to power up your recovery:" https://www.psychologytoday.com/blog/beyond-the-doubt/201711/the-hidden-power-swearing-your-ocd
- Thriving with OCD: Four Keys Out When Locked in Doubt: https://beyondthedoubt.teachable.com/p/thriving-with-ocd/?coupon_code=FRED&preview=logged_out (coupon code FRED)

- KeyWords: Daily Motivation to Thrive with OCD: http://beyondthedoubt.com/keywords-daily-motivation-to-thrive-with-ocd/
- *Slowing Down to the Speed of Life: How to Create a More Peaceful, Simpler Life from the Inside Out* by Richard Carlson and Joseph Bailey.
- Rick Hanson's Spirit Rock Workshop *Opening to Allness* http://dharmaseed.org/teacher/312/, Part 4, the beginning to minute 6:45
- Theodore Roosevelt's "The Man in the Arena" passage from the "Citizen in a Republic" speech: https://en.wikipedia.org/wiki/Citizenship_in_a_Republic

Treatment Provider Databases:
- Tips on Find the Right Therapist: https://iocdf.org/about-ocd/treatment/how-to-find-the-right-therapist/
- The International OCD Foundation: https://iocdf.org/find-help/
- The International OCD Foundation website and database for BDD: https://bdd.iocdf.org/
- The Anxiety and Depression Association of America: https://adaa.org/finding-help
- Association for Behavioral and Cognitive Therapies: http://www.findcbt.org/xFAT/ or http://www.abct.org/Home/

Other Great Resources:
- http://a2aalliance.org/ The Adversity 2 Advocacy Alliance is a nonprofit dedicated to promoting and fostering the power of turning personal challenges into service to others with similar challenges.
- https://www.cbtschool.com/ Providing research-based online courses and resources for OCD and related disorders.

- http://www.ocdchallenge.com/ An online, interactive, behavioral program designed to help people suffering from OCD.
- http://www.peaceofmind.com/ The Peace of Mind Foundation is a non-profit whose mission is to help improve the quality of life of OCD sufferers and caregivers through education, research, support, and advocacy.
- http://www.shalanicely.com/ Other useful resources in the Books and Resources sections and in my Aha! Moments blog.
- http://theocdstories.com/ Real stories that educate and inspire those with OCD.

About the Author

Shala Nicely is an OCD survivor, author, advocate and cognitive behavioral therapist specializing in the treatment of OCD and related disorders in Atlanta. She is the coauthor with Jon Hershfield, MFT, of *Everyday Mindfulness for OCD: Tips, Tricks and Skills for Living Joyfully*. She is cofounder with Jeff Bell of BeyondtheDoubt.com, an initiative dedicated to helping people learn to thrive through uncertainty. Shala is an advocate for The Adversity 2 Advocacy Alliance and blogs for *Psychology Today*, offering an inside perspective on life with OCD.

50248158R00173

Made in the USA
Lexington, KY
26 August 2019